the
virtual
embodied

The Virtual Embodied is intended to inform, provoke and delight. It explores the ideas of embodiment, knowledge, space, virtue and virtuality to address fundamental questions about technology and human presence. It juxtaposes cutting-edge theories, polemics and creative practices to uncover ethical, aesthetic and ecological implications of why, how and in particular where, human actions, observations and insights take place. It problematises the power which we imagine virtual space to have, considers the extent to which it can encompass and enhance human wisdom, and raises topical questions about the myths, desires and false assumptions of 'digital' discourse.

The Virtual Embodied spotlights a number of different ways in which the human being is insinuated within technology. It refuses simply to hold a euphoric view of technology yet equally resists the apocalyptic scorn which surrounds the new. The contributors use a range of interdisciplinary strategies to point to a reworked aesthetic for embodying knowledge and explore such areas as colonialism and the Internet, the virtual unconscious in electronic systems, 'information' and the capitalist society, ecstatic bodies and the rave scene, desire and the 'virtual comfort' zone.

In *The Virtual Embodied* many of the authors, artists, performers and designers apply their interdisciplinary passions to questions of embodied knowledge and virtual space. In doing so this project chooses to acknowledge the limitations of the conventional linear book and uses them creatively to challenge existing genres of multi-media and networked consumerism.

Contributors: Rachel Baker, Lisa M. Blackman, Margot Leigh Butler, Peter Cresswell, Ronald Fraser-Munro, Andy Goffey, Damien Keown, Gustav Metzger, John Monk, Maria Pini, Garth Rennie, Victor Jeleniewski Seidler, Olu Taiwo, Max Velmans, Claudia Wegener, Robert Wells, John Wood.

John Wood is Co-ordinator of the Design Futures MA at Goldsmiths College, University of London before which he was Deputy Head of Fine Art at Goldsmiths. He has created public art works, polemical writings, 'eco-i

the
virtual
embodied

presence/practice/technology

edited by

john wood

london and new york

First published 1998
by Routledge
11 New Fetter Lane, London EC4P 4EE

Simultaneously published in the USA and Canada
by Routledge
29 West 35th Street, New York, NY 10001

Typeset in Rotis by Keystroke, Jacaranda Lodge, Wolverhampton
Printed and bound in Great Britain by Biddles Ltd, Guildford and King's Lynn

British Library Cataloguing in Publication Data
A catalogue record for this book is available from the British Library

Library of Congress Cataloguing in Publication Data
The virtual embodied : presence/practice/technology / edited by John
  Wood.
      p. cm.
  Includes bibliographical references and index.
  1. Philosophy. 2. Virtual reality. 3. Body, Human (Philosophy)
  I. Wood, John
  B29.V55 1998
  128–dc21   97–38905

ISBN 0–415–16025–1 (hbk)
ISBN 0–415–16026–X (pbk)

contents

list of figures   vii

list of contributors   ix

shuffle   margot leigh butler   xii–xiv

preface: curvatures in space–time–truth   1
        john wood

part one   **embodied knowledge and virtual space**

one   **embodied knowledge and virtual space**   15
        gender, nature and history
        victor jeleniewski seidler

two   **the digital unconscious**   30
        john monk

three   **physical, psychological and virtual realities**   45
        max velmans

part two   **nature and virtue**

four   **nature = x**   63
        notes on spinozist ethics
        andy goffey

five   **embodying virtue**   76
        a buddhist perspective on virtual reality
        damien keown

six   redesigning the present   88
             john wood

part three   embodying truth

seven   hubble telescope   105
             the artist in the eye of the storm
             gustav metzger

eight   a more convivial perspective system for artists   109
             peter cresswell

nine   ancient oaks   122
             a one-act play
             garth rennie and ronald fraser-munro

ten   culture, technology and subjectivity   132
             an 'ethical' analysis
             lisa m. blackman

part four   when becoming meets becoming

eleven   the dream garden   149
             notes on a virtual idyll
             robert wells

twelve   the 'return–beat'   157
             'curved perceptions' in music and dance
             olu taiwo

thirteen   'peak practices'   168
             the production and regulation of ecstatic bodies
             maria pini

part five   between saying and showing

fourteen   [saɪt]   181
             claudia wegener

fifteen   + and ÷   196
             margot leigh butler

sixteen   PDF™   206
             the digital hostess
             rachel baker

seventeen   messages from sir arthur and the rev. bill   213
             ronald fraser-munro

index   217

figures

3.1	typical beliefs about physical, psychological and virtual realities	46
3.2	a dualist model of perception	47
3.3	a reductionist model of perception	48
3.4	a reflexive model of perception	48
3.5	a painting by peter cresswell using radial perspective	53
3.6	a virtual model of perception	56
3.7	relationships between individual selves and virtual realities	58
8.1	two views of the famous *ambassadors* painting by holbein	112
8.2–8.6	diagrams showing how radial perspective is constructed	117
8.7–8.8	two images of a regular solid constructed with radial perspective	119
8.9	the wheatstone stereoscopic viewer	119
12.1	the 'linear-beat' time graph	158
12.2	the 'return-beat' time graph	159
12.3	comparisons between the two modes	160
12.4	preparations for the clapping experiment	160
12.5	relaxation exercise	161
12.6	flow chart for the clapping experiment	161

contributors

RACHEL BAKER obtained a degree in Interactive Arts before completing an MA in Design Futures at Goldsmiths College, University of London. She is now an artist and researcher developing Net-based art projects, often in collaboration with Irational (www.irational.org), Backspace (www.backspace.org) and Moscow WWWarts.

LISA M. BLACKMAN lectures in the Department of Media and Communications at Goldsmiths College, University of London. Her PhD was an exploration of the use of history to understand the discursive constitution of contemporary psychological objects, specifically looking at the phenomenon of hearing voices. She has published mainly in critical psychology journals.

MARGOT LEIGH BUTLER is an artist, cultural activist and theorist. Her recent PhD research at Goldsmiths College, University of London, focused upon contemporary artists' collective projects in relation to politics, subjectivity and epistemology. She has belonged to several artists' collectives and has taught cultural theory, history and practice in London and Vancouver.

PETER CRESSWELL is a painter with a long-established interest in drawing methods. He was Head of Fine Art at Goldsmiths College, University of London, before becoming Dean of Arts. During this period he directed two major research initiatives, an investigation into the innovative work of the Pan-Cultural Project, and the creation of a holography workshop.

RONALD FRASER-MUNRO is a writer, multi-media artist and performer whose publications include *Le Shovelle Diplomatique* and *K3 Kinder Kunst Korporation*. His many personae include Sir Arthur Stuffed-Shirt and Cyberschwartze, with whom he has performed at venues including the Royal Court and the ICA in London, and at numerous national, international and intergalactic venues.

ANDY GOFFEY taught, until recently, at the Université de Paris IX, Dauphine. He recently completed his PhD thesis 'A Logic of Multiplicities' on the philosophy of Gilles Deleuze. He is currently conducting research into the political and philosophical implications of the concept of programmes.

DAMIEN KEOWN is Senior Lecturer in the Department of Historical and Cultural Studies at Goldsmiths College, University of London. He is editor of the award-winning 'Journal of Buddhist Ethics', a Web-based publication available at http://www.gold.ac.uk/jbe/jbe.html. He is currently conducting research into contemporary moral issues in Buddhism at Cambridge University.

GUSTAV METZGER is an artist and activist who introduced the concept 'auto-destructive art' in 1959. He became a founder member of the Committee of 100. More comprehensive biographical details can be found in K. Stiles and P. Selz, *Theories and Documents of Contemporary Art* (Berkeley, University of California Press, 1996) and in the book *Gustav Metzger; Auto-Destructive Art: Damaged Nature*, published by workfortheeyetodo, London, 1996.

JOHN MONK is Professor of Electronics at the Open University. He is a chartered engineer who specialises in control systems, digital systems and networks. He is interested in broadening engineering education and is therefore a student of the philosophy, history and sociology of technology (and the saxophone).

MARIA PINI is currently completing a PhD on femininity and club cultures at Goldsmiths College, University of London. Recent publications include 'Cyborgs, nomads and the raving feminine' in H. Thomas (ed.) *Dance in the City* (1997), and 'Women and the early British rave scene' in A. McRobbie (ed.) *Back to Reality? Social Experience and Cultural Studies* (1997).

GARTH RENNIE has recently completed a PhD examining the politics of academic authority in Psychology. He carried out this work in the Department of Media and Communications at Goldsmiths College, University of London.

VICTOR JELENIEWSKI SEIDLER is Professor of Social Theory at Goldsmiths College, University of London. He has written widely in moral theory and sexual politics. Recent books include *The Moral Limits of Modernity* (1991), *Unreasonable Men* (1993) and *Recovering the Self* (1994).

OLU TAIWO is a dancer, actor and percussionist. After obtaining a degree in Fine Art, he completed his MA in Dance Studies at the Laban Centre, London. He was a founder member of the Imule Theatre Company and he has performed at festivals in Bath, Edinburgh, Cardiff and Glastonbury. He currently lectures at King Alfred College of Higher Education in Winchester.

MAX VELMANS is Reader in Psychology at Goldsmiths College, University of London. His extensive publications on consciousness include 'Is human information processing conscious?' *Behavioural and Brain Sciences* (1991), 'A reflexive science of consciousness', in *Ciba Foundation Symposium*, 174 (1993), and *The Science of Consciousness* (1996).

CLAUDIA WEGENER is an artist completing PhD research on 'The Monumental' in the Department of Visual Arts at Goldsmiths College, University of London. She has organised a conference under the title 'Redefining Art' (together with Mark Ryder) and is a member of the artists' group known as Foreign Investment.

ROBERT WELLS is a painter and landscape architect currently engaged in a major environmental project about lake ecology and a historical landscape of restoration of Battersea Park. He studied Fine Art and Landscape Architecture, and has recently completed his MA in Design Futures at Goldsmiths College, University of London.

JOHN WOOD (j.wood@gold.ac.uk) recorded and performed widely with the cult band 'Deaf School'. He has created public art works, electronic toys, software systems and 'eco-inventions'. He was Deputy Head of Fine Art at Goldsmiths College, University of London before writing several design courses including the Design Futures MA programme which he now co-ordinates (http://futures.gold.ac.uk).

preface

curvatures in space-time-truth

john wood

This collaborative[1] work grew out of the meetings and discussions that followed the 'Embodied Knowledge and Virtual Space' conference at Goldsmiths College, University of London in June 1995, and which drew together a rich diversity of ideas, theories, ideologies and embodied practices. Like the conference, it is intended to be enjoyed. Much of its inspiration has come from a common concern for issues surrounding information technology and 'Nature', and in sharing our related passions, we have come to see our project in terms of a meaningful continuity and interplay between ethical, aesthetic and ascetic concerns when addressing questions of human presence. What is 'human nature' in a technocentric era of globalised capital and consumerism? How, for example, can we reimagine, or reinvent, the collective self in a commodified world where data is valorised as information, where information is confused with knowledge, and where knowledge is oversold as wisdom? In addressing these questions we use the metaphor of 'embodiment' to explore the ways in which we notice the world, acquire knowledge, make informed decisions, and act out our perceived roles in society.

presence and practice

However, in referring to embodiment we must be cautious. The idea of privileging bodily presence in the static sense would be problematic if it were to reinforce the infamous mind and body dualism that has dogged the Western mindset for several centuries. This would be contrary to our intentions. Arguably, the word 'body' is more than a concrete noun, and when we speak of 'embodying' information we try to emphasise action and practice. We do so to acknowledge that the individual mind is not merely the internal workings of a small blob of matter known as the 'brain' but to suggest that it is – in scientific terms – part of the general continuum of space–time.

We may understand the acquisition of knowledge or, more subjectively, 'wisdom', as an insight into what we are, in our 'becoming', as human beings. In this sense we could also think of individual embodiment as an aspect of our general predicament in the changing present, and we have been mindful of this when creating the book. Aristotle's rules of rhetoric included the important stage in which the speaker must memorise his (written) arguments to attain a performative fluency. In our meetings over the last two or three years we have tried to encourage this Aristotelian text-into-speech embodiment and then to focus our attention upon the imagined book itself. In embodying each other's concerns, we have enjoyed going a bit beyond the usual protocol of an academic book and hope that it registers our (be)coming together at a formal level.

the disembodying tradition of the book

Before the first monks developed the technique of reading-in-silence, the practice of reading aloud from the written word had ensured some continuity with oral traditions. In the European medieval scriptoria, however, the need to copy books by hand tended to exaggerate the 'unsituated' aspects of writing. That the arrival of serial, alphabetical writing tended to fix and to differentiate social roles is well known. The Book became fetishised as an icon of power and the Christian Church introduced a sense of bodily denial, or disavowal, of the (writer's own) body. This self-questioning phenomenon led to Descartes' self-denying, egocentric scepticism that continues to haunt the academic research tradition.

In today's consumerist culture of book sales and information technology we can still discern the intellectual traditions of solitude and bodily restraint that were established in medieval book culture, and which informed prevailing attitudes of austerity, discipline and detachment in the universities of Europe. These led to the metaphor of scholastic 'rigour',[2] a term of approval still applied in the modern research context, despite the emergence of networked information systems that work at the speed of light, and which speak of 'fluency', immediacy and (ex)change rather than 'stillness' and 'fixity'. Furthermore, most academics still favour methods of writing that mask any directly personal feeling or knowledge. They ask students to write in a generalised and unsituated way and to refrain from indexical or contingent assertions and arguments. For similar reasons, they would be unlikely to praise the 'bench manual' as a model for academic writing. Students are seldom asked to write 'with', to write 'for', or to write 'to' specific 'writer-readers'. The effects have been manifold. The myth that writing is somehow a direct, linear transcription of facts or truths survives as a tacit conspiracy that renders us amnesiac about the situated and creative practice of writing. Because monastic conventions have demanded that the book must be totalising, comprehensive and self-denying, conventional academic wisdom tends to remain sentential, using oratorical stances, narrative sequences and the logic of deduction and induction.[3]

tacit knowledge

Whilst some of these constraints may now be loosening, new technological and market-influenced trends have begun to automate and to deskill the task of writing and reading. Since the secularisation of the Book, and since the increasing decentralisation and automation of mechanical printing, we have learned to depend upon 'smart' technologies such as computer-assisted word-processing. Even now, there are surprisingly few indications of a move away from the monastic model of the one-person work-station (or 'book-station'), despite many years of developing virtual conferencing systems and large-screen technologies. It seems more likely that portable devices will be increasingly miniaturised and networked so that individual workers can become ever more productive – or, at least, *active* – while they travel or perform other duties simultaneously.

We can argue that, so far, all of these developments have moved us progressively further away from the social, situated and embodied skills of 'presence' that are so crucially important in oral cultures. For many creative practitioners in the traditions of studio and stage it is here, at the level of embodiment itself, that we are likely to confront the rational limits of the intellectual tradition. The task of learning to ride a bicycle is often used to illustrate the gulf between text-oriented disciplines of theory and the practice-oriented disciplines that we find, for example, in the plastic arts. We all know that bookish knowledge alone cannot teach us how to ride a bike. Similarly, once we have learned to ride it, we cannot 'say' *what* we have learned, even though we may be able to say things *about* it. This example is not too distant from more intellectual pursuits, such as reading and writing, in which we unconsciously scan alphabetical characters with our eyes and make writing gestures with our hands.

To summarise this in a more pedantic way, in making a book we have been concerned with gathering 'technologies–truths' of the 'mind–body–presence' in 'space–time'. Unfortunately, although some of our perceptions may be provocative, many must remain implicit. Some of these must be 'shown' rather than explicated in the serial logic of text; and, despite our desire to use only plain and simple terminology, some of the key terms we have come to share are inevitably complex or problematic in their horizon of meaning.

nature and human nature

The word 'Nature' is a case in point. A glance at this word in the dictionary will show how we ascribe at least three different meanings for it, and this provides a helpful caveat for today's increasingly egocentric playground in which advertisers routinely make claims for their product's 'naturalness', and where, as pampered consumers, we are urged to follow our individual 'human natures'. In his chapter on 'The Dream Garden', Robert Wells shows how today's commercial interests tend to repackage, and oversimplify 'Nature' as a kind of 'virtual Eden', bringing the Disneyesque world of interactive entertainment closer to that of domestic DIY gardening. In an increasingly artefactual world, it is not surprising that the romance of technology has inclined us to technologise the role of nature. Whereas, in the past three hundred years or so, we have dreamed of redesigning nature, some of us are realising that we should redesign *human* nature, or realign *ourselves*, as a way to reduce the relentless damage to ecosystems and species of life. Such an ambitious project would require a deeper understanding of the terms by which we recognise the 'authentic' and 'illusory', the 'real' and the 'harmful'.

the virtual

In the early 1990s the buzzword 'virtuality' became as complex and interesting as the word 'Nature'. It is commonly used to describe anything that is the case, although not in the fullest sense. Arguably, in a highly materialistic era, it gets its exotic appeal from the depth and ambiguity of its associations. Today, it is applied in many different senses, as we may note from chapters by Max Velmans and Damien Keown. Earliest usage signified the 'morally virtuous' and described things that were effective or potent in some way. In these originary forms we find only positive qualities. The Latin root word *virtus*, for example, could hardly be more beneficent, in that it combined the semantic idea of 'truth' with the ethical idea of 'worth'. It is intriguing, therefore, to find that the word 'virtual' has lately become so equivocal that it now foreshadows its own opposite case. When we hear of a product described as being 'virtually safe' we know we should not trust it. Why, then, has this word become so capricious?

One possible factor is the unfortunate influence, or popular misreading, of Platonic idealism. Plato proposed that appearances, or 'perceptibles', are merely an imperfect and changeable outer shell on a deeper and inaccessible reality of pure forms, and it is difficult to ignore this account when we try to understand what happens to us when we 'surf' the Net or experience the space–time of virtual reality systems. When talking about mimetic art, Plato invited us to imagine a portrait painting that was so 'realistic' that viewers might mistake it for the actual person depicted. Much later, Kant turned the proposition on its head by asking what would happen if human beings were physically incapable of misinterpreting or reinterpreting how things 'really are'. He offered a characteristically ethical answer: 'if appearances are things-in-themselves, then freedom cannot be saved . . . '

In Plato's scenario, what seemed at first to be self-evidently 'true' is subsequently unmasked as artful deception. In offering this thought, he raised an ethical question about illusion. Here we can discern an asymmetrical relationship of power between the creator of the illusion and the person who is tricked. Crucial to both propositions is the question of 'situated reality', rather than an eternally 'true' (i.e. Platonically 'virtual') reality. Here, Kant agrees with Plato's belief in a clear demarcation between form and material presence, i.e. between the 'real' and the 'actual'. In this dualistic proposition, Plato openly sided with the 'real' – i.e. the timeless but imperceptible form of something – in preference to what he saw as its untrustworthy presence as the 'actual' or, in other words, its world-weary manifestation. He believed that divine powers alone were responsible for creating the originary Forms which craftsmen subsequently copied, albeit imperfectly, as actual beds, tables, cups and plates. Not until the Enlightenment did philosophers such as Locke come to reinterpret the notion of 'Idea' (originally a Greek word for Form) as an originary initiative of the individual mind.

It is possible that this crucial shift in perspective has helped to diminish our regard for the environment. By believing reality to be 'out there' and ideas to be 'in here', we distance ourselves from nature, philosophically and spiritually, and this continues to invite dangerous consequences in environmentalist terms. The ubiquitous metaphor of 'navigation' used in human–computer interface design provides a good illustration of this conflict. When we 'navigate' around data in a software application we understand this in two contradictory ways. Our Cartesian vision of landscape is both external to us, like a map that is both autonomous and arbitrary, whilst our individual presence is an undeniable part of the virtual 'datascape' itself. This is an old conflict. In making a strong association between (external) Form and the Good, Plato not only helped to give the 'virtual' its latent sense of the 'virtuous', but he also paved the way for our modern penchant for 'objects' as commodities. Equally important, in reinforcing the spectre of 'reality' as an assortment of autonomous 'bits' (i.e. 'things-in-themselves'),[4] Kant used Plato's notion of form to inspire an intellectual cornerstone for post-Enlightenment science and technology.

Here, the book will be seen to interweave the threads of several critical traditions that identify destructive aspects of the Baconian and Cartesian mindset. Behind these many critical discourses – from Kropotkin to Naess; Heidegger to Deleuze; Fourier to Nancy; Merchant to Haraway – we can still glimpse the spectre of idealism which underpins our politics of identity and which can be said to inform prejudices in the medical and scientific establishments. Here, the strongly dualistic mindset of Western culture encourages the polarisation of conditions such as 'truth' and 'illusion', 'self' and 'society', 'normality' and 'health', and informs a range of beliefs that colour the way we regard learning difficulties and the capabilities and forms of individual bodies.

Maria Pini's chapter explores the tendency for some social sciences research to make dualistic distinctions between, for example, 'freedom' and 'constraint', 'utopia' and 'dystopia' when it analyses 'rave' dance cultures. Margot Leigh Butler uses an ingenious approach to get readers to 'de-dualise' certain oppositions by actively 'hinging', or moving between them, as in one case, saying them literally 'in the same breath'. Damien Keown's chapter is useful, here, in that it includes a historical outline of Western dualism, and Andy Goffey's contribution is especially helpful in identifying a possible basis for a genuinely monistic view.

This is a difficult undertaking. At first glance, the Kantian model of cognition seems to integrate the human subject with her world by declaring the imagination to be essential to perception and knowledge. This sounds reasonable to the Western mind, yet Kant's idea of 'imagination' is essentially dualistic, being described as a powerful agent 'for creating . . . a second nature out of the materials supplied to it by the first nature'.[5] When we close our eyes we assume that the visible world is still 'out there', otherwise every time we turn off the light and walk towards the bed we would not need to avoid falling over the 'real' objects which we know to be there.

Simple and persuasive scenarios such as this are part of a web of assumptions that sustain Western dualism.[6] Despite their inconsistencies they are hard to exorcise. In dealing with this problem, some chapters attempt a weak form of monism by continuing to invoke these 'oppositional' worlds and then seeking to integrate them. In subscribing to the Kantian discourse of the 'thing-in-itself', Max Velmans argues that we share the same world as all other 'things-in-themselves'. What is proposed here is that we can subscribe to dualities such as the phenomenal versus the noumenal, the epistemological versus the ontological, provided we remind ourselves that they infiltrate each other's boundaries in subtle ways.

ethics, aesthetics and ascetics

As we have suggested, the idea that because deeds are embodied they are therefore bound by pragmatic limits raises crucial ethical issues about the limits of action afforded to each individual mind–body, and about the modes of representation which permit us to monitor and prescribe these actions. Gregory Bateson[7] once commented that the board game 'Monopoly' was inherently anti-ecological because it demonstrates a logic of play that would be impossible, and therefore potentially dangerous, in the actual world. The 'zero-sum' rules of the game ensure that a single individual will eventually win all of the real estate properties on the board, even though such an outcome is unsustainable, either economically or ecologically.

Bateson's ethical position seems to conflict with that of Jaron Lanier, the imputed inventor of virtual reality. Lanier's anthropocentric vision of a kind of 'virtual playground' offered plausible, yet sometimes 'physically' impossible scenarios that defy the forces that normally harm us in what we refer to as the 'real' world. As such it asserts the rhetoric of technologically delivered freedom above 'natural' constraints such as gravity or hunger. One of the many concerns in Victor Seidler's chapter deals with the way some individuals – usually males – use the power of technology to bolster, or to disown, aspects of their persona. Ours is a dangerous era of stridently assertive human rights – i.e. consumer rights – in which the perceived importance of individual gratification increasingly seems to outweigh that of the long-term collective good. This book calls for latitude and open-mindedness for how we perceive and represent events so that we can confront ethical concerns at their more intricate 'micro-levels'.

In investigating how technologies of virtual space might help to emancipate the human psyche, Lisa Blackman's chapter looks beyond what we assume to be the pristine sanctity of 'the virtual' and invokes ideas of 'filth', 'transgression' and 'self-mutilation'. In the above examples we are reminded of the inescapable interplay between the ethical, the ascetic and the aesthetic. Where we attempt to reshape modes of representation, we are immediately confronted by matters of taste; and where we make aesthetic judgements about formal matters, we must eventually deal with the ethical and ascetic implications of our decisions.

Aristotle noted that actions are usually symptomatic of a larger set of prevailing relations and conditions that we come to identify in aesthetic terms. We may assume that at the neural level, ethical beliefs migrate to adjacent regions to inform or to modify aesthetic sensibilities. This may happen when an immediate distaste of something new becomes normalised as a pleasure, and is most likely when we believe it to be associated with beneficial consequences. Unsweetened tea is unpleasant when we first convince ourselves to give up white sugar. After a few weeks, however, it becomes palatable. Eventually we are surprised to find that an unexpected sip of sweetened tea makes us recoil in disgust. Similarly, we may notice an adaptive shift from the (optically) 'virtual' to the 'real' when we learn to normalise what is visually unfamiliar. The famous Claude Lorraine Glass was a portable, dark-tinted convex mirror which was used mainly in the eighteenth century. It enabled coach passengers to appreciate hitherto unattractive aspects of 'Nature' because it made the English landscape, for example, resemble the fashionable French landscape paintings of Claude Lorraine. Just as virtual images from the

Claude Lorraine Glass offer intrinsic features, or 'affordances' when used in a given context, so humans are locally bound by what is always presently possible, rather than what is impossible.

the curvature of space–time–truth

How should we understand these developments? Why is it that the old maxim of 'bearing false witness' seems inadequate for unmasking the rhetorical excesses of the modern advertising industry? In today's fragmented and Machiavellian world, where information is purveyed as an ideal, or virtual, commodity, the ethical value of 'straightness' in truth – i.e. virtue – may have come to seem patronising, anachronistic, or just plain boring.[8] Here, the relationship between the beneficial and the harmful, the true and the false, the real and the virtual may, increasingly, seem curved rather than straight. Why is this surprising? We speculate that bonds of human agreement in pre-historic times would once have been more straightforward if they derived from transactional economies in which participants established more or less symmetrical, 180° affiliations with society, and with one another.

The Western concept of truth is based on this metaphor of one-to-one 'straightness'. In the past we have tended to textualise fundamental moral and epistemological principles in generalised, unequivocal terms. Truth has been inscribed as the opposite of falsehood, and 'right' has been formalised as diametrically opposed to 'wrong'. Etymologically speaking, the metaphor of straightness stands for uprightness and steadfastness and underpins modern words such as 'rights', 'right' and 'rectitude'. For the same reason, admonitions of the 'Thou shalt not' category may appeal to some of us for their directness, yet may fail to enlighten specific problems at a 'micro-ethical' level. Today, decisions about what medication should be given to a dying patient, for instance, are increasingly acknowledged to be matters requiring partial and situated judgements rather than a following of universal edicts and axioms. Twentieth-century discourses surrounding relativity and quantum mechanics have also challenged the ontology of straightness, and have made curvature the leitmotif for a more plausible mode of correspondence between events and their descriptions.

There are several explanations for this. Sometimes the act of making rational judgements becomes difficult where the scale of events is either too large or too small for non-statistical judgements to be useful. Statistical methods have increasingly tended to replace categorical truths with a curved profile of probabilities. Another reason is the increasing popular awareness that the very act of framing a question may unavoidably influence the answer. Heisenberg's 'Uncertainty Principle' of 1927, and Gödel's 'Incompleteness Theorem' of 1931 may have come to inform our unconscious apprehensions surrounding economic and cultural change and, in so doing, helped to loosen our romantic adherence to clear notions of authenticity, or unreconstructed modes of sincerity. By inviting modes of irony, cynicism and nihilism, post-modern culture seems to curve the correspondence between experience and representation, bringing together worlds which once seemed incommensurate. They may also problematise certain links with the agreed-remembered past by rendering them anachronistic or unfashionable.

the idea of rigour in four dimensions

A troubling aspect of Plato's laws of form is their ranking of 'matter' above 'movement', and 'form' above 'matter', and we are still trapped in the Platonic[9] dualism of Newtonian science when we casually detach time from space in everyday conversation. Ironically, it took Einstein's allegedly anti-intuitive 'thought experiments' to bring them together again for the esoteric few. Encumbered by this profound division, the rest of us are still catching up. Our antiquated legal grammar, for example, struggles to reframe notions of 'theft', 'export' and 'authorship' in the age of data crime. In this Alice in Wonderland world, the delineation between hard cash and information, between giver and taker, between reader and author, become increasingly mercurial. Digital 'properties' may be 'stolen' without the 'owner' noticing, and it may even be legal to 'hide' saleable software data by encryption, or to divide it into unrecognisable fragments and reassemble it across different geo-temporal borders under a different name.

Similarly, from the way in which Euclidean solids are drawn and modelled inside a digital computer, we can still find anachronisms of Platonic thought. Modern computers create moving representations of three-dimensional forms by modifying Platonic solids and modelling each volumetric form in a static position before adding a surface 'skin'. This memory-hungry process is then repeated many times a second to simulate movement, rather like the changing frames of a movie film. There are technological, ideological and political implications here. For one thing, this slow and wasteful process makes few concessions to the way we actually 'see' things. The geometry used to map a three-dimensional scene or subject onto, for example, a flat 'image' derives from the famous paradigm of monocular 'viewing' which so strongly epitomises the uncompromising and intrusive qualities of Baconian science.

Gustav Metzger in Chapter 7 reminds us that a similar rhetoric of power–knowledge can be found where NASA makes implicit claims for the Hubble telescope's ability to 'see', using rational techniques that are closer to how we count than to how we 'picture'. Another artist, Peter Cresswell, offers in Chapter 8 a more congenial, or 'well-tempered', version of the linear perspective drawing system that is associated with this tradition. Likewise, Olu Taiwo, a musician and dancer, shows us in Chapter 12 that, just as observation is integrated with consciousness itself, in the varying 'width' of its temporal focus, so the making and listening to simple rhythms can change the quality of our shared presence. All three chapters raise deep questions about the role and significance of peripheral perception in the way we apprehend and embody information. Other chapters, notably by Garth Rennie, Claudia Wegener, Margot Leigh Butler, Rachel Baker and Ronald Fraser-Munro use satire, pastiche or poetic forms to make self-conscious demonstrations of the curvature, or circularity, of truth claims, and the limits of what can be said in a given form. As we have shown, each form has an aesthetic presence which is contingent upon our situated predisposition towards it; which calls for, and is then called by, its repertoire of ethical possibilities. Just as we may, conceivably, criticise a heavily moralistic artwork for its unsatisfying appearance, so we may be shocked by the failure of a more exciting art form to be in accord with its ethical implications.

embodied knowledge

As we have noted, you may be able to 're-enact' the experience of drawing, dancing, listening or acting, but you cannot 'think' it in the verbal sense which informs writing. Most of us are still steeped in these fixed, linear values of the textual book and in the truths which they claim. When we see Euclidean geometrical figures we invariably see them as static shapes; and we forget that the original drawings once emanated from a Greek individual called Euclid and are therefore simplified traces of (his) embodied, and therefore autographic, actions in space–time. Moreover, in emphasising curvature as a general truth of some of these practices in dance and in drawing, we may remind ourselves that we do not achieve it by 'bending' straight lines, but by embodying our imagined presence within a journey that is mindful of other dynamic events.

As Einstein showed, an understanding of curvature as a profound metaphysical truth becomes apparent to us when we take up an embodied role which acknowledges other bodies moving in relation to us. In the light of the popular dualistic image of Einstein as a 'mind' detached from the 'material' (real) world, it is important to remember what this means in experiential terms. In what he called 'the happiest thought of my life', he coupled a proprioceptive insight to a 'thought-experiment', to rationalise an already embodied but previously *unthought* under-standing that if he were to go into a state of 'free fall' he would not experience the weight of his own body. This led him to conclude that, for a falling observer, the trajectory path of a cannon ball would appear as a straight line. From this he deduced that space–time itself is curved, and that it is this intrinsic curvature which manifests itself as gravity.

Professor Stephen Hawking's work raises more specific questions about the notion of human presence and about the situated, actual embodiment of knowledge. Using his famous artificial voice system, Hawking can keep a 'live' audience of thousands enthralled, and make them laugh spontaneously. He is quoted as saying that he is the 'luckiest man in the world'. Here, it is interesting to look at the provenance of his discovery that black holes in space are not totally 'black' because they emit a faint, residual (i.e. 'grey') level of radiation in the form of 'virtual particles'. Professor Hawking was able to show that so-called black holes are subject to the same laws of physics as any other body in the heavens. It is difficult not to notice the poignancy of the 'not-completely-black-hole' as a metaphorical 'figure', in that it reminds us of the bodily predicament of its inventor.

space and absence

As we have suggested, although Plato acknowledged the lived space of 'becoming', his ideas tended to emphasise a more disembodied account of mimesis and repetition. Again, this illustrates a confusion between presence and absence which derives from his theory of pure forms. And it follows that we are likely to accommodate the 'pure form' principle as a denial of difference.

Extending this logic, when we see one cup and saucer on the factory production line, in essence, we have seen all of them. Similarly, when we erase and retype an alphabetical character on a

computer screen, it looks so precisely similar to its replacement character that it deceives us into thinking that we are resurrecting the very same letter that we just erased. Baudrillard and others have made much of the potent simulacrising properties in digital and other technology; associating it with a kind of disembodying, or de-materialising alienation.

Leibniz's 'identicality of indiscernibles' declares a principle of 'sameness' for entities of the same class, or of identical attributes. Leibniz's theory is a useful starting point for looking at design in the age of digital information technology as it can be seen to underpin Shannon's modernist hypothesis of 'Information Theory',[10] which continues to inspire the arbitrary quantification and commodification of human discourse. As such, whilst it conveniently adopts the dualistic distinction between information and matter, it also appears to disembody, to desituate, and to homogenise all signification.[11] Yet even if we disapprove of the philosophy behind digital engineering, we cannot deny that it enables computers to conduct faultless 'searches' for matches between identical words and other serial strings. In other words, computers use the (artefactual) identicality of alphabetical forms to 'read' meanings on our behalf.

Heidegger refers to the task of the language translator and suggests that, although it may be part of a painstaking and sympathetic support for an author's intentions, the final translated text may nevertheless remain 'unthought' by the translator. Likewise, we can speculate that for the monks who copied books in the medieval scriptoria, the practice of slavish duplication would also have rendered the contents of their texts as 'unthought'. Digital technology has exacerbated this situation by upholding the illusion that 'a rose is a rose is a rose'. It has done so with the claim that representational veracity is sharpest when a signifier can be uniquely quantified, and thereby replicated, away from the human mind–body.

the virtual, embodied

A problem with the commodification of information and the advent of electronic libraries is that when we 'download' an exciting document we may imagine that by owning it we are also, in anticipation, virtually embodying it. The same may have always been true, more or less, of avid collectors of paper books but the dislocating and disembodying effects of the virtual book are more profound when we can conduct instant 'global' search by keyword, and where automatic 'intelligent agents' can screen out information deemed unappealing to our consumerised predelictions.

John Monk's chapter shows that the individual unconscious is becoming increasingly amalgamated into networked data systems which hold representations of our beliefs, identities and credit ratings. His argument challenges traditional dualist ideas of space and time in the sense that we have been accustomed to an increasingly untenable idea of the 'mind' as a local computer, trapped within the spatio-temporal confines of the 'body'. Today, it is difficult to deny that we are insinuated within technology and that technology is insinuated within us. Phenomenologically speaking, we have long been experts in managing 'out of body' experiences when, for example, we telephone a loved one on the other side of the world. In this sense, the crisis for post-Enlightenment dualism is not that the 'mind' may be found to be inextricably part of the 'material' world, but that in the redrawing of boundaries between private and public we may challenge cherished notions of egoistic autonomy.

a more situated ethics

As Damien Keown's chapter points out, Western 'rights' ethics derives from received assumptions concerning individual virtue, power and entitlement. Lately, via the fashion-conscious public sphere of consumerism, it has even tended to sink below the register of individual ethical *actions* and into a shallower register where individuals merely need to be 'seen to stand for' good causes to be deemed ethical. Increasingly, within consumerist capitalism, this asymmetrical equation encounters considerable difficulty in balancing individual rights with collective responsibilities. More importantly, it has ignored the balance between human and other sentient forms of life, and between humanity and nature as a whole.

In facing what happens when we create surrogates for human presence, we are also brought face to face with what we are, as human beings. Here, it is clear that in designing software robots for exploring the Internet, we must exceed Platonic limitations of designed forms because the dynamic attributes of play and interplay are more important than their assumed properties of shape and materiality. Within vast distributed systems, decisions are increasingly being taken by local algorithms and subroutines, and we may remind ourselves that there will be a variety of simultaneous results with emergent properties with local and aggregate consequences. Arguably, each level of decision making has its own (micro) ethical and (micro) aesthetic properties which may change from moment to moment, as they drift in and out of human consciousness. Every time we delegate such decisions to automatic systems we risk losing touch with our own presence. Can we shield our (shared) presence from the alienating forces of such technology, when it has already begun to redefine our received notions of the 'here and now'?

The choice between an immediate face-to-face encounter and a virtual one is no longer a simple matter. As I suggest in my own chapter, we must reinvent the present in order to reinvoke the convivial. This does not mean moving from a crude, consumerist hedonism to a forgetful, or epicureanist, 'now-time'. We must invent a present that is governed by a watchful empathy for our ancestors and for our unborn children. As Benjamin noted: 'every image of the past that is not recognized by the present as one of its own concerns threatens to disappear irretrievably.'[12]

notes

1. I would like to express my indebtedness to all of the book's contributors. Whilst it will inevitably seem unfair not to thank all of them by name, the trust and support of Sarah Kember and Rebecca Barden were vital in getting the project started. The direct assistance of Andy Goffey during final stages of editing, and the insight, enthusiasm and moral support of Garth Rennie, Claudia Wegener, Margot Butler, Olu Taiwo, Gustav Metzger, Peter Cresswell and Lisa Blackman, were also especially helpful in enabling this book to see the light of day. Thanks also to Katherine Hodkinson and Chris Cudmore.

2. I have argued that the metaphor of rigour became problematic since Einstein's claim that substances can never travel faster than the speed of light. Cf. Wood, J., 'The idea of academic "rigour" in 4-D space; Dynamics of the IDEAbase "situated knowledge system"', presented at the '4D Dynamics' conference: De Montfort University, 20–21 September 1995.

3. Peirce's category of abduction would be a worthwhile addition to this list. See other proposals in Wood, J., 'Situated criticism and the experiential present', *Design Issues Journal*, guest editor Prof. Nigel Whitely, June 1997.

4. *Ding-an-sich.*

5. Warnock, M., *Imagination*, London, Faber & Faber, 1976.

6. Cf. Wood, J., 'Design after Dualism', paper given at the 'International Product Design in Education' conference, Brunel University, July 1997.

7. Bateson, G., *Steps to an Ecology of Mind*, London, Paladin, 1973.

8. This was evident in the disappointment expressed by members of the public during the UK Labour Party's final advertising campaign before the 1997 election that made unvarnished claims such as 'Labour will Cut Tax' in headline style, and without images.

9. Or, at least his Parmenidean metaphysics of a solid universe.

10. This influential idea of 'information' was developed by C.E. Shannon and W. Weaver (*The Mathematical Theory of Communications*, Urbana, University of Illinois Press, 1963) to help in the development of communication technologies. It is useful to engineers because, instead of facing complex multidimensional issues of human signification and intention, it regards information as a serial flow of signs expressible as numbers. This is easier to understand if we imagine human conversation as a flow of electrical data along the lines (or 'channels') between telephones (a close system). When quantified, engineers can draw statistical conclusions about the most effective way to transmit and receive these finite units. Perhaps it should have been named 'data theory', because it ignores the hermeneutic aspects of how readers and listeners contribute to the formulation of meaning, and it distinguishes between 'information' from 'noise' as though the attribution of meaning were isolated from the site of discourse.

11. This notion is especially painful when we remember that ubiquitous information systems are becoming increasingly integrated with financial currencies (i.e. 'virtual money'). Perry Barlow used the image of 'wine without bottles' to describe how technology treats information; and we could extend this metaphor to the idea of 'liquid gold' to conform to current paradigms of banking. This notion should, however, remind us that this reputedly 'pure' substance can be removed from the teeth of living victims, carried across national borders into bank vaults, and transmuted into technologies of annihilation.

12. Osborne, P., 'Small scale victories, large scale defeats', in P. Osborne and A. Benjamin (eds) *Walter Benjamin's Philosophy; Destruction and Experience*, London and New York, Routledge, 1994, p. 89 quoting from W. Benjamin, *Illuminations*, trans. H. Zohn, London, Fontana, 1992, p. 257.

part one

embodied knowledge and virtual space

chapter 1

embodied knowledge and virtual space

gender, nature and history

victor jeleniewski seidler

modernity, knowledge and nature

Within an Enlightenment vision of modernity there is an assumption that knowledge is independent, objective and impartial, for the Enlightenment was largely cast within the terms of the scientific revolutions of the seventeenth century. This marked a profound shift[1] from an organic towards a mechanistic conception of nature. With the 'death of nature' we witness the reduction of nature to matter which is largely to be explained through the discovery of scientific laws. Progress is identified with the control and domination of an external nature just as it is in relation to inner natures. Just as outer nature is there to be controlled, since it is governed through external laws, so our inner natures also have to be controlled if we are to exist as rational selves. This was crucial to Descartes, who prepared the secular terms for the mind–body dualism which has also characterised modernity.

As mind is to be radically separated from body, so reason is to be separated from nature. The mind is conceived as existing separately from the world that it is endeavouring to explain. For Descartes it is as rational selves that we face an 'external world'. It is mind which is identified with reason, and consciousness which defines the new Cartesian vision of what it means to be 'human'. We still find echoes of the idea that to be human is to be a rational animal, that it is an independent and autonomous faculty of mind/reason which is categorically separated from an 'animal nature'. So it is that knowledge is deemed to be crucially disembodied and universal. This prepares the ground for a radical structuralist distinction between culture and nature, and the assumption that identities as rational selves are crucially articulated within the terms of culture alone. Where traditionally it was an independent faculty of reason which defined an existence as a rational self, it is language which is deemed to be independent and autonomous, and which supposedly provides us with experience.

This may help us to recognise just how unsettling is the question of whose knowledge is to be embodied. The notion that knowledge has to be 'situated' and 'embodied' is part of a crucial feminist challenge to the terms of an Enlightenment vision of modernity. It is also part of the challenge of the later Wittgenstein's philosophy, which sought to question the autonomy and independence of language. He recognises, as does Freud, a crucial tension between language and experience. It is part of the attraction of Freud's work for Wittgenstein and it is what places each of them in a critical relationship to modernity. Wittgenstein articulates this in the introduction to the *Philosophical Investigations*[2] as a way of explaining how his writings are likely to be misunderstood. In this he anticipates misreadings of a philosophy of language; misreadings which too often enshrine the very autonomy of language which his work seeks to question.

There is a resonance between Wittgenstein's questioning of a Cartesian inheritance with crucial aspects of feminism and ecology. In different ways they help to question the disdain for nature, the body and sexuality that has been deeply rooted within the dominant Christian traditions in the West. They help to unsettle too firm a distinction between nature and culture, and in different ways they open up questions about the ways we can be part of both nature and culture. As I have tried to think this in *Unreasonable Men: Masculinity and Social Theory*,[3] it helps to name a particular relationship between a dominant white, heterosexual masculinity and a vision of modernity that insists upon a categorical split/dislocation between reason and nature.

A dominant white heterosexual masculinity can alone take its reason for granted. This becomes a way of affirming male superiority, for it is women, Jews, people of colour who are deemed in diverse ways to be closer to nature. For Kant it is men alone who can establish a secure inner relationship with reason and so who can be independent and self-sufficient. This means that women supposedly need men in a way that men do not need women, for it is only through accepting the subordination of marriage that women can secure the guidance of reason. So women are trapped traditionally into accepting subordination as a means to their freedom and autonomy. This is because women are more closely identified with their bodies and sexualities. It falls as a responsibility for men that they need to control their partners within heterosexual relationships, for women's sexuality is deemed to be a threat to male reason.

It is crucial here that a dominant, white, heterosexual masculinity is framed within a Cartesian tradition and its separation between mind and body. This means that within modernity the self is already gendered and racialised as a rational self. It is the dominant white, heterosexual male self that is identified with mind/consciousness and so with a reason that is disembodied. This independent faculty of reason is taken to be the source of impartial and universal knowledge. Men are encouraged to 'rise above' their 'animal natures' and so, implicitly, to disdain their bodies and sexualities. As Susan Griffin has it in *Pornography and Silence*,[4] a dominant masculinity learns to project a relationship to the body, sexuality and nature that it is obliged to deny. It is women who are made to carry those aspects of the self that are denied. Men learn to identify with culture alone, for to acknowledge emotions and feelings is a sign of weakness and so a threat to male identities. So it is that men remain estranged from themselves in crucial respects.

In the light of this disenchantment, nature can no longer serve as a source of meanings and values, and human beings no longer reflect upon what would be an appropriate relationship with nature. Rather, these issues are suppressed as nature is presented as something that needs to be dominated and controlled. This means that there can be no communication between people and nature, for nature supposedly has no voice of its own. Animals and trees are no longer the bearers of intrinsic value. Rather, within an Enlightenment vision of modernity it is human beings who are, alone, the source of meanings and values which they impose upon a disenchanted nature. This is part of the arrogance of modernity which defines values in terms of exchange values on the market. The trees supposedly only have 'value' as timber that can be sold as a commodity on the international market. It is crucial that human beings do not regard themselves as 'part of' nature but that they exist categorically separate from it. At some level nature is the enemy against which we prove ourselves as human beings. This is crucially a masculinist vision, though often it is not named as such.

embodying knowledge

For Descartes it is crucial that as rational selves we have an inner relationship to reason, mind and consciousness and an external relationship with our bodies. Put crudely, bodies are not part of 'who we are' as rational selves, but are part of a disenchanted nature. So it is that the body exists as an 'object' of medical knowledge and our experience of our bodies is automatically discounted as subjective and anecdotal. As children we learn to be silent in front of the doctor and so we learn to devalue the knowledge that we have of ourselves. If we learn to value the knowledge of our minds, we learn to disdain whatever knowledge emerges from our bodies. If this is set within the terms of dominant masculinity, it also sets the terms in which women are obliged to evaluate their experience. For women can never take their rationality for granted and it remains something they have continually to prove. Within modernity this means that their status as human beings is always in question. As feminism learnt to recognise it, women exist as second-class citizens.

As Kant develops an ethical tradition, there is a radical split between on the one hand thoughts that are linked to the mind, consciousness and reason and, on the other, emotions and feelings that are placed in the body. So it is that Kant's inclinations are deemed to be forms of determination and a lack of freedom. They are constructed as externally determining our behaviour, so taking us away from the path of pure reason. Within the West we inherit the Christian identification of purity with spirituality. The idea is that pure love is a love that is not tainted with sexuality, which is linked to the body and identified with the sins of the flesh. This shows more clearly how knowledge comes to be 'disembodied' within an Enlightenment vision of modernity. Within Kant's terms we have to learn to 'rise above' our animal natures so that we can learn to live in the light of reason alone. With Kant's identification of reason with morality, it is only if we act against our inclinations that we can be sure that we act in relation to the moral law.

So it is that the body and emotional life are silenced as we learn to aspire to live as rational selves. We learn to control our emotions and suppress our impulses, especially as men who have learnt to identify a dominant masculinity with independence and self-sufficiency. Rather we can feel threatened by the revelations of our natures for they can bring into question the idealised images we have of ourselves. We learn to discount experience as a source of knowledge within structuralist traditions that assume that it is through language alone that experiences are articulated and subjectivities defined. This is part of a deeply rooted disdain for the body and sexuality, as Freud investigates it in *Civilisation and Its Discontents*.[5] He insists that the repression of sexuality is not a personal and individual issue, but is structured within the historical experience of modernity. Often we learn to relate to bodies instrumentally, treating them as possessions that are at our disposal. This is particularly relevant for men who learn to train their bodies and who can feel trapped into constantly testing their male identities against the limits of the body. If they get sick or their body lets them down in some way, they feel entitled to punish it.

Learning to listen to our bodies involves beginning to develop quite a different relationship with self. It involves recognising the body as a source of knowledge and recognising ways that memories are carried, not only in the mind but also in the cells of our bodies. Rather than treating the body as separated off, as part of a disdained nature, we learn to bring the mind and body into relation with each other. This was a process which Reich begun in his early relationship with Freud. He recognises ways that we tighten the body against feeling, and the ways that muscles hold emotions in particular ways. He began to explore how, for instance, 'being uptight' not only reflects an attitude of mind, but also reveals a certain way of holding the body. But this involves going beyond post-structuralist theories which can help to recognise the body as a space upon which cultural meanings are drawn. As Freud recognised, it also involves redefining liberal conceptions of freedom which suggest that we can split from our emotional histories to find freedom and autonomy in the present. Rather, we have to learn to face the emotional realities of the past, if we are to find more freedom in the present.

Embodying knowledge involves more than recognising the body as a means of expression, or thinking that we can shape or pierce our bodies in ways that can express our freedom and autonomy. Postmodern theories tempt us into thinking that we can constantly remake identities in the present, and that we can leave the past behind. Sometimes they suggest that there has been such a radical disjunction with the past that we are forced to create identities out of whatever is culturally available in the present. To suggest otherwise is to slip back into visions of authenticity that imply that traditions exist in some protected spaces of their own. Freud, however, makes us think otherwise, for we can only escape the influences of the past if we are ready to acknowledge them in the present. We might wish to split from painful emotional histories as well as from cultural histories full of pain and suffering, but the repressed will return to haunt us. A time will come when we will have to face what we have chosen to split from. At some level this involves coming to terms with ourselves in a way that postmodern theories suggest we can evade.

If we are to establish a deeper contact with ourselves, then we have to recognise what we have chosen to suppress. Freud has a particular grasp of how this is to be carried through as a process of transference. Alternative forms of psychotherapy offer different paths suggesting diverse ways in which the present is tied in with the past. Often they put less stress upon a process of regression and are more concerned with the ways in which conflicts in the present return us to unresolved issues in the past. But there is a shared sense that we cannot split from the past but have to be ready to acknowledge emotions and feelings as they emerge. There is also a sense that we cannot control our lives through the control of our experience, even if a Weberian tradition seems to promise this. This is part of a dominant masculine dream which suggests that men can control their lives through being able to control the meanings they assign to their experiences. But Freud knew otherwise. He recognises tensions and contradictions between the different levels of experience and the terms in which we choose to make sense of it.

Freud recognises the unreality of experience when it is shaped in relation to denial. He acknowledges the consequences of denial for the level of contact which we can establish with aspects of ourselves. If we find it hard, as men, to recognise fear because this threatens male identities, then we suppress these unacceptable emotions and we wish them out of existence. But Freud recognises that what is suppressed finds a place in unconscious life. It has consequences for the ways we can be with ourselves and the ways we can relate to others. If we have suppressed fear to the extent that we cannot recognise it for what it is, this makes us less sensitive than we could be. Sometimes we will project fear onto others, unable to acknowledge it in ourselves. We might identify ourselves as protectors to others deemed to be 'weaker' than ourselves. It might take years before we can begin to acknowledge our own fear for what it is. At some level this involves undoing some of the control we have asserted over our own experience. It can also be part of a process of reframing masculinities as we recognise that fear does not have to compromise male identity. It does not make us less of a man, but gives us access to resonate with what others are going through, as we can recognise more of our own experience.

This becomes part of a process through which men, for instance, can learn to embody their knowledge of themselves. But this involves questioning an Enlightenment vision of modernity that insists that a dominant masculinity has to learn to control its experience. Rather than treating the body as if it were property at our disposal, separate from a sense of self, as part of a disenchanted nature, we have to learn to listen to what our bodies are trying to say to us. This is a challenging notion and often it is only through illness that people grasp what this might involve. Testing yourself against the limits of your body as a way of affirming your masculinity makes you insensitive to your relationship with your body. This reinforces the Cartesian notion which treats the body as part of matter, so impersonalising the relationship and setting it in instrumental terms. It is a matter of the body being obedient to the commands of the mind, and being punished if it fails to do so. There can be no communication which transgresses these boundaries, for the body is taken to be part of an inner nature. So it is that men and women in different ways learn to leave the body behind, at some level still linked to the 'sins of the flesh'. We learn to 'rise above' our animal natures so that we can identify with a pure reason which generates disembodied knowledge. Taking knowledge to be 'real' if it is objective and universal, there is a fear of the subjective and the personal. We feel uneasy with emotions and feelings as sources of knowledge. This helps us to grasp ways that feminism and ecology served as challenges to modernity, but also to grasp ways we often think about technology.

virtual space

The Enlightenment vision of modernity is often unwittingly reproduced in our thinking about virtual space, even in its postmodern forms. Often there is an aspiration to leave bodies behind. This is part of leaving behind the supposedly fixed and situated identities of gender, 'race', ethnicity and sexualities to enter a free space of the imagination in which we can supposedly choose 'who' to be and 'how' to be. This is part of a postmodern dream that echoes, in significant ways, the Kantian shift from a realm of necessity to a realm of freedom. This also helped to shape Marx's dreams of emancipation. It is linked, somewhat paradoxically, to the dominant Christian notion which treats the body as if it were a prison for the soul. In some utopian visions around the new technologies we find a different means of release.

There is a dream that through these new computerised technologies we can leave behind the hierarchies and 'unfreedoms' of gendered and racialised identities. A regime of 'fixed' identities is implicitly linked to patriarchy and this is contrasted with the 'feminine' space of the Net, where identities can supposedly be fluid and temporary. This becomes the space of freedom and autonomy where people can at last choose the identities they want to live from moment to moment. As Kant promises, people can escape from their emotional and cultural histories into an ethical space. These aspirations can at last be realised within the space offered by the Net. We do not have to 'work though' traumatic experiences in the past, as Freud has it, to find greater freedom in relation to ourselves. Nor do we have to come to terms with class, cultural, racial and ethnic histories, for these supposedly remain unknown in the communications we are free to set up on the Net. We are free to present ourselves as we would want to be. This is the end of history, or so we are often encouraged to think.

But in crucial respects these visions remain tied up with the dreams of modernity. The idea that differences are signs of determination – a lack of freedom that can be transcended – was also Kant's dream of how as free and equal autonomous selves we can 'rise above' our empirical selves to meet within the intelligible realm. This is another vision of the dominant Christian notion that became so crucial in the anti-Semitic discourses of the West that readily castigated 'carnal' Israel. As Daniel Boyarin has shown in *Carnal Israel*,[6] it was the Jews that were to be identified with the sinful/sexual body. They were unable to 'rise above' their animal natures for they refused the distinction between the material and the spiritual. As Levinas has pointed out in different ways in *Difficult Freedom*,[7] this is what makes Judaism so crucial if we are to understand the limits of modernity. If we are to rediscover traditions that recognise that knowledge has to be embodied if it is to be 'real', then we have to engage with traditions of Jewish philosophy. The disdain for the body runs deep within Western culture, and the wish to escape from it is given new forms within visions of cyberspace. It was a crucial dream of modernity that as rational selves we could communicate as disembodied/rational minds alone. As I have argued, it is also linked to a dominant, white, Christian, heterosexual masculinity which establishes its superiority through a disdain for the body and emotional life, so often identified with the feminine.

So it is that men often inherit a fear of the emotional and the intimate, and seek refuge in abstracted and disembodied conceptions of knowledge. The independence of reason allows men to legislate what is good for others, without really having to communicate with women and children. A middle-class father can feel secure that he is providing his son with the best possible education by sending him away to boarding school. For the son to protest is to open him to further rejection, for 'no son of mine winges' and this only goes to prove that 'you need the training' that the school will provide. This vision of reason becomes a male possession and a source of masculine superiority that can so easily be taken for granted. The school will 'make a man of him'. This marks the way the boy thinks and feels about himself, for often he is desperate for the approval of his father. He will not allow the father to see his tears. He will hold them back for himself as the tight 'upper lip' takes form.

Often boys who have been sent away to boarding school grow into men who have difficulties with intimacy and contact. They learn to fear their own emotions as signs of weakness, and so as threats to male identity. They learn to control their bodies and to silence their emotions. They only allow those emotions, like anger, which they might rationally be able to defend in advance. What is more, anger is not deemed to be a threat to male identity so that feelings of vulnerability or sadness are often transformed, before we become aware of them, into an anger or violence that can affirm a threatened male identity. So it is that men are often fearful of the revelations of their natures. They often do not want to know what they are feeling, for this might bring into question the images they have of themselves. So it becomes important to control others to whom they are close, and who might identify emotions that men do not want to acknowledge. This is part of men's control of women and it helps to explain why it becomes so important for men to discount women's ways of knowing . It is a dominant masculinity which can alone take its reason for granted and it is women who are deemed to be 'irrational' and 'unreasonable'.

The long-distance telephone call exemplifies an earlier form of virtual reality. This allows us to enter a virtual space in which we can 'be with' someone we are dear to. The question within a heterosexual relationship 'Do you love me?' is more often asked by a woman, possibly out of a need for reassurance, and is often responded to, not at a like level, but with the response 'of course I do'. This can be heard also as a rejection of the request, a sense that it should not have been asked. It can trigger its own disappointments. But this communication is not to leave the body out of account as we enter a virtual space, as anyone who has attempted to sustain a long-distance relationship will recognise. We can feel the pain of yearning in our bodies and we can feel the tension of miscommunication. We can feel grateful for the contact but also frustrated at the gulf in between.

There can be similar forms of miscommunication on the Net and it can be helpful to compare different experiences of virtual reality. Often it seems, in contrast to the theoretical utopian visions, people on the Net want to discover your 'true' identity. It also seems that many more men pretend to be women. In part this can be a sign of freedom of exploration and imagination. But we might be able to value whatever new freedoms the Net might offer without falling back into reproducing the dreams of modernity that would treat gender, 'race' and sexuality as somehow incidental and contingent in relation to identities. In thinking that we have entered a realm that can transcend traditional identities, we can end up by producing visions of homogeneity.

There might well be a place for transcendence, but we have to think carefully about its relation to identities. Cornell West in his insightful dialogues with bell hooks talks about James Baldwin as a 'race-transcending prophet'; as

> someone who never forgets about the significance of race but refuses to be confined to race . . . He never understood black people solely as victims. But, at the same time, he recognised that part of our plight was to be continually victimised by racism even as we struggle against it.[8]

This is to break with an easy liberalism that so easily returns within postmodern discussions that focus upon the opportunities for people to create themselves. We have to remember Marx's insight into the ways that people make themselves, but not in circumstances of their own choosing. This helps us to escape from an easy contrast between freedom and determinism that seems to return within a postmodern guise. It can be important to recognise the responsibility that people have for themselves, as well as the responsibility we have for others. This is central to Levinas, who recognises the crisis in liberal political theory when the rights afforded by the Weimar State as a proof of citizenship, and so as a guarantee of a status as human beings, could so easily be taken back by the State. This left Jews as 'subhuman' within Nazi discourse[s].

In the wake of the Holocaust it becomes difficult to trust politics and this becomes crucial to Levinas's return to the ethical, and his insistence that the ethical relationship to the Other takes precedence over the epistemological. This is the strength of Jerusalem and the Jewish (in contrast to Athens and the Greek) tradition in philosophy. For Levinas, the relation we have with others is primarily a moral relation, even if we do not recognise the responsibilities that we carry for them. This is something he wants to remind us of. Rather than fleeing from our responsibility for 'the other', or subsuming others under generalised categories, we have to recognise others in their singularity, in our face-to-face relationship with them.

Bauman[9] also reminds us that the Holocaust was not a momentary aberration within the Western vision of historical progress. He shows the ways that the Holocaust was tied up with Western conceptions of bureaucratic rationality. Rather than a moment of madness, what was disturbing in Nazi Germany was the way in which the extermination of Jews was carefully planned as they were first isolated from their everyday involvement in social life. There was a careful process of institutionalisation whereby Jews were to be excluded from schools and workplaces in which they had been familiar for generations. First they were marginalised and then excluded as they became regarded collectively as 'subhuman'. The extermination process was to come later, after it had been already invoked against the mentally ill and people with learning difficulties.

There is a warning here about the ease with which we can treat others as 'less than human' within modernity. Though we talk about treating others with respect, we easily end up relating to others instrumentally. It is with an awareness of how technologies worked to reduce people to numbers, that we also have to think carefully about the use of recent technologies for the spread of fascist propaganda. There are disturbing signs of the ways the Net is being used to organise new 'right' groups across the world. It is easy for a liberal conscience to argue that technology is neutral and that it is available for people to use for good or for evil. But this is to avoid questions about the form of new technologies and the ways in which they sustain new forms of instrumental relationships.

We have already hinted at the relationship between a dominant masculinity and a particular form of instrumental rationality. There is some evidence that boys and girls relate to computer technologies in different ways. Not only do computers give young boys a sense of control but they are also becoming the means through which boys establish and sustain their relationships with one another. Boys can also sometimes feel more comfortable and at ease within virtual space than they can within the newly troubled waters of gender relations. There is considerable uncertainty for what it means to be a boy in the face of feminism when the traditional macho notions of masculinity seem to be in crisis. Often, boys feel uneasy in their sexual relations with girls: they are unsure of what girls now expect of them and unsure what they want from the relationships for themselves. It does not help to theorise the Net as a 'feminine' space in which boys and girls are free to create new identities for themselves.

re-inventing nature

If we are to come to terms with the ways in which the new computer technologies are transforming inherited visions of nature, history and the 'common good', we have to recognise the ways they are transforming young people's lives and relationships. But this involves recognising how gendered subjectivities are also being transformed, as well as the terms in which young men and women learn to relate to themselves, their bodies, sexualities and emotional lives. This means questioning the dreams of modernity, which we re-presented within postmodern terms, when we think of the Net as a site of freedom, as if we can somehow leave differences behind as we enter a new 'sacred space' of fluid identities.

But the Net can be a space in which people can reach out beyond their own culture and circle of acquaintances to gather new information and insight that is unavailable to them in their everyday lives. It can help diverse people to confront problems and issues which their taken-for-granted cultural frameworks do not help them recognise. At some level this can be to accept histories while respecting the contradictions in lived experience which this leaves people to 'work through'. This can be part of finding new freedoms while at the same time acknowledging the tensions which, for example, young Asian women can feel when torn between, on the one hand their loyalties to families and traditional cultures and, on the other, the freedom offered by their Western schooling. Like other young people they want to go out at night but do not want to shame their families. These conflicts cannot be wished away. They might be in the process of creating new hybrid identities, but we should not underestimate the pain and suffering that is involved when young people can experience themselves, literally, being torn apart. Nor is it helpful to think of these conflicts in terms of the freedom offered by the West as set against the limitations of traditional Asian cultures. This is already to think of the situation in terms of a framework provided by modernity. But it is a strength of postmodernist writings that it can sometimes recognise that it is not a matter of there being everything to gain in assimilating to Western liberal values and nothing to lose. The issues are more complex and they do not concern loyalty to family and tradition alone. They also concern challenges to Western conceptions of freedom and autonomy and the importance of sustaining a resistance which allows for the validation of ethnic and spiritual identities.

If we are involved in a process of reinventing relationships with nature, this should include relationships with our inner natures. This questions the Kantian distinction between reason and nature which defines nature as somehow given and beyond history and culture. Freedom supposedly lies in reason while determination and lack of freedom lie in nature. This articulates the disdain for nature that we have already identified as deeply embedded within a dominant Western Christian tradition of sin and salvation. We have to escape from the influence of our 'animal nature' if we are to find freedom and autonomy. Levinas draws upon a Jewish tradition that does not separate reason from nature in this Kantian way; a tradition that recognises the transformation of inner natures, not through the external intervention of reason alone, but through a respect for emotions and feelings as sources of knowledge.

If we seek embodied knowledge then we must have the courage to listen to our bodies and to attend to the contradictions in our emotional lives, rather than feel that we can leave them behind because our emotions somehow do not fit with how they are rationally supposed to be. If we are to acknowledge tensions between how we feel and the ways we are supposed to think, then we are opening out contradictions between language and experience. This is the ground that Wittgenstein and Freud open up in different ways. But it can also be a tension, as the example of the young Asian woman shows, between the ways women feel and what traditional cultures expect of them. This is something that Freud was sometimes personally insensitive to, regarding religious practices as forms of superstition. He objected to his wife lighting the Sabbath candles.

Postmodern theories sometimes talk about reinventing nature, as if nature were there as part of culture. Nature no longer exists as a reminder of a natural world with which we have lost connection; consequently we are now in a different relationship with ourselves. Rather, there is a continuation with the modernist notion that progress lies in the control and domination of nature. But BSE reminds us of the dangers of crossing boundaries between different species, and of feeding meat products to animals that were vegetarian. A scientistic culture had no respect for the boundaries that separated different species and we find this played out in genetic engineering in relation to foods. Ecology makes us question that transgression of these natural boundaries and can give us a new respect for the natural world. It can help us to think about what an appropriate relationship to this world would be. This calls for a different vision of science in its relationship with nature.

If there is to be communication with nature, as we recognise nature as a source of meanings and values, so there also has to be a different relationship with our bodies. Computers can help us imagine different forms of communication and can paradoxically make us more aware of the part that intuition and sensitivity play in our lives. Rather than simply be focused upon our analytical capacities, we may learn to respect the supposedly 'feminine' qualities of intuition and sensitivity. An opening to different forms of communication opens up the boundaries between different bodies. For some postmodern theorists this serves to undo the distinction between 'humans' and 'machines', especially as spare-part surgery uses machines such as heart pace-makers. But this can move in different directions. It can reproduce the body as a machine or it can question the instrumental relationship which modernity has established with the body, when it seeks to explain it in mechanistic terms.

As we question the distinction between thoughts and emotions, so we begin to be able to validate emotions and feelings as sources of knowledge. This can help us appreciate non-physical forms of communication. But we can also recognise how emotions such as depression can work energetically on the body to produce illness. Psychotherapy might, in some cases, link the depression to repressed anger but as this is turned inwards against the self, it can have diverse somatic effects. This serves to undo traditional ways of thinking of psychosomatic illnesses, as if they were a loose category of illnesses that we cannot yet explain in physical terms. The discussion of ME is a good example, where the doctors were reticent to recognise it as 'real', which meant that it was 'just' psychological.

If an appreciation of virtual realities can help us to recognise the possibilities of different forms of communication, so it can also question the distinction between the physical and the non-physical. This is part of a shift away from Newtonian conceptions that helped organise the seventeenth century scientific revolutions. This has also involved exploring connections between the new physics, which questions linear conceptions of time and space. Notions of relativity have opened the ways for exploring links with Eastern traditions of thought and so have refigured the relation between a 'superior' Western science and a 'backward' religious tradition in the East. This helps open up a different vision of progress which is not connected with the control and domination of nature, but which seeks a different relationship with it, which more readily recognises human beings as part of nature.

inner and outer realities

Within modernity, people as rational selves learn to look outside and beyond themselves for the truth. The modernist notion, given currency by the TV programme *The X Files*, that 'the truth is out there' serves to undermine people's relationships with their inner selves. Rather, people learn automatically to distrust the indications of their bodies, thinking that it reflects a lack of self-control. As we learn to challenge the rational self which underpins notions of modernity, we also learn to question the fragmented self which has characterised much postmodern theory. For we recognise how the rational self was even then not a unified notion, but was already set within the terms of a dominant masculinity which was divided against the self. It was built upon a sense of inner rejection as men and women learnt to police their desires in different ways.

As we challenge the humanistic vision of the rational self, so central to a Cartesian vision of modernity, we learn to think of relationships with bodies in different terms. It involves an attunement with our bodies that has to be created through learning how to respect our emotions and feelings as integral aspects of self. In this way we begin to develop a deeper contact with displaced aspects of self. This is a process that takes time, and it might mean time away from the screen so that when we are communicating we are doing so with greater awareness. To recall the body and emotional life is not to be entrenched in a form of Enlightenment humanism. It is more complex, for within modernity freedom has gone hand in hand with disembodiment. The Net may help us to explore and open up more embodied conceptions of freedom, for if we are also concerned to re-vision notions of the 'common good', it will be through an acceptance and respect for differences.

However, we also have to be careful about characterising the kind of freedoms which the Net offers. Within a culture that still finds it difficult to accept emotions and feelings as sources of knowledge, we can find ourselves unskilled in how we work with our inner emotional lives. Often it is easier to project upon others and to feel that the solution to our problems is somehow waiting 'out there' to be discovered. Within the context of psychotherapy we can 'work through' some of our projections, understanding more about where they come from. This is to ground some of our fantasies. Being called upon to verbalise what we are feeling with others can move us along in a process of development. But these face-to-face meetings, as Levinas has it, are not available on the Net. We communicate at one remove and even if we take time and space to learn from information we receive that might be blocked within our own communities, we can feel locked into our projections.

The self-arranged sex murder of Sharon Lopatka has shocked the local community of Pikesville, Maryland, where she grew up as one of the five children of Abraham Denburg, cantor of the local synagogue for thirty years. The large Orthodox Jewish community has reacted to the death with stunned and embarrassed silence. She was outwardly at least a respectable and happily married member of the community. One of the few people who knew her who was prepared to comment is quoted as saying, 'I won't believe this could be her. She was conservative and careful.' The community has found it almost impossible to come to terms with the fact that Sharon Lopatka, 35, had used computer bulletin boards to advertise for a man to turn her fantasies of being sexually tortured and murdered into reality.

After several refusals Lokpatka eventually made contact with Robert Glass, 45, a computer programmer in North Carolina. During their e-mail contact, Glass described in detail how he planned to abuse and kill her. When she eventually went to meet him she left a note for her husband: 'If my body is never retrieved, don't worry. Know that I'm at peace.' A few days later Sharon – who had once worked as a clerk for the FBI and was very familiar with the Net – was found strangled and buried in a shallow grave a few feet from Glass's mobile home. Glass is now in jail awaiting trial for murder and claims her death was an accident during 'rough sex'.

Was her death an isolated tragedy or a possible turning point in a debate about controls for the emerging Internet culture? In the United States the case has been used to show the dangers of the Internet and to argue for strict new controls, such as holding service providers responsible for conversations on-line. Sherry Turkle[10] argues it would be a terrible mistake, and reminds us that:

> By itself, the Net is neither good nor bad. It is nothing. It will be what people make of it ... We should actively be making it the most positive experience that we can, such as bringing people together in their local communities.

She draws parallels with the first years of video when there were moral panics because it created a mass market for pornographic films. As far as she is concerned, 'We are all globally experiencing growing pains trying to understand that the Internet is not a broadcast medium, but a speech medium and needs to be protected.' She argues that 'Computers are the new location for our fantasies.'[11]

But we have to be careful about how we think of fantasies and the ways they can be brought in relation with reality. Some of our fantasies take a different shape when they are brought into contact with people in our everyday lives. In some ways they are tested against reality and we recognise, for instance, that the fantasy we have about the ways someone feels for us, does not exist in reality. There is a way of appreciating fantasies whilst also recognising the space they play in our lives. There might be specific risks in the ways fantasies are played out on the Internet. As Turkle imagines it:

> The Internet allows people to express, learn and play out aspects of themselves on-line. When that happens, there is a kind of 'play space' – a consequence-free zone which enables people to learn to know themselves in different ways.[12]

The Net can certainly be used in this way and it might create a space that is not otherwise available to people, though as a virtual space it does not allow the movement that takes place when we share our fantasies with people face to face, say in a therapeutic group. This can help us recognise that fantasies are not shameful and that we can begin to question a dominant culture that defines them as shameful and which leaves us feeling bad and worthless because of them. The very privacy of the Net, which can be a release, can also bind us into structures of shame and can intensify fantasies which never have to be brought into contact with the reality of everyday life. Sexual life can be a realm in which we play out different fantasies and feel the trust and understanding to do so. This can be difficult within restrictive sexual cultures which might block the possibilities for such exploration, making the Net a more exclusive space. This might be particularly difficult for people who have difficulty drawing a distinction between reality and fantasy. Though Baudrillard might argue that such a distinction lacks any sense within a postmodern culture, he fails to appreciate the psychic pain and suffering involved.

Sherry Turkle recognises that the case of Sharon Lopatka is horrifying 'but it has to do with someone who knew that she was acting in the real world. The Internet is a powerful medium for communication and these very disturbed people use it to communicate with each other about their personal pathologies.' But this does not really help us understand the power of these new technologies in the shaping of subjectivities and the refiguring of distinctions between inner and outer realities. They play a part within larger cultures which can leave us tragically illiterate in relation to inner emotional life and so more ready to project unacknowledged desires into a virtual space. Turkle seems convinced that Lopatka knew what she was doing and would have found other ways of satisfying her desires if the Internet had not been there. The technology is deemed to be neutral and it seems to play no role in bringing particular desires into existence. As Turkle describes it, 'They found partners willing to gratify very dark things within themselves. If this had happened on the telephone, the case would have been equally sad, equally depressing, equally shocking.' What is more, she reports that 'Other members of Lopatka's discussion group tried to help her. They said: "Hey, wait, these are supposed to be fantasies", and she basically said: "Leave me alone. I know what I'm doing".' This presents the case as being about someone who clearly knew what she was after and was determined to use the Net to get it. It puts aside the more troubling thoughts that you might be drawn into something you might otherwise regret, through the kind of relationship that you can develop on the Net.

Whilst it is important to protect the kind of explorations of freedom that can develop on the Net, it might be that we have to question notions of the neutrality of technology if we are also to be aware of some of the dangers it carries. It is not just an alternative means of communication but it refigures subjectivities and identities in potentially more radical ways, especially with children who grow up with the Net. She argues that computers are 'the new location for our fantasies, both erotic and intellectual. We are using life on computer screens to become comfortable with new ways of thinking about evolution, relationships, sexuality, politics and identity.'[13]

Within a culture that is dominated by disembodied forms of knowledge, it becomes tempting to escape into mental fantasies. It becomes easy to lose ourselves, as minds become overcharged and we literally come to live in our heads. Hence virtual space becomes as much a refuge, into which we withdraw, as a space of freedom and exploration. Young boys can hide in virtual reality, which becomes a medium in which they are assured control. They might find it much harder to take risks in their everyday lives and relationships. In a time when gender relations have become a site of conflict and when boys can no longer assume the superiority their fathers took for granted within a patriarchal culture, it becomes tempting to live in denial. So it is that the Net affords opportunities, but it also has risks. However, for many young boys it is less risky than finding their way without the traditional gender maps to rely upon.

The possibilities of embodied knowledge call for a different relationship with virtual space. Rather than a space in which people can hide, it also becomes a space in which people can learn about themselves. But it is important to recognise that virtual space is not a space outside history, any more than it is a space for personal exploration outside or beyond nature, history and culture. As Foucault would have reminded us, it is not an innocent space beyond the reaches of power. It might well be a space that we can escape to, or even to lose ourselves in, but men brought up to aspire to the terms of a dominant masculinity are all too familiar with these possibilities. It is a different challenge to live with more reality in our lives and more emotional truth and honesty within our relationships. Often we are too familiar with denial, which is built into a modernity that promises men control over their experience though controlling the meanings we assign to it.

But if we are to be aware of the tensions and contradictions between the quality of experience and the discourses within which we make sense of our everyday lives, then we have to be wary of computers becoming yet another 'toy for the boys'. We need to be able to recognise the 'reality' of the sexist, pornographic, racist and anti-Semitic images that it carries and the consequences these have. This is not an innocent virtual reality within which anything goes, but it is also an organising ground for the new right. This makes it important to think carefully about the ethics of new technologies, rather than assume their neutrality. These are 'real' and unsettling questions which we are left with. It becomes crucial to explore the moral cultures in which people come to these new technologies.

As we learn to appreciate the significance of embodied knowledge, which is part of the challenge of feminisms and ecologies towards an Enlightenment vision of modernity and its disembodied conceptions of knowledge, we recognise how we might only have the faintest glimmerings of what this could mean. Growing up to identify with the mental life of the mind alone, we are often estranged from bodies and from emotions and feelings as sources of knowledge. This is part of a process of growth and development as we reach a deeper connection with ourselves. Virtual space can help in this process but it carries its own risks and dangers.

Freedom entails responsibilities, not only for ourselves, but also, as Levinas constantly reminds us, for others. As we allow ourselves, as women and men, in different ways to connect to sensitivity and intuition without feeling threatened and uneasy, so we can learn to become more aware of the sufferings and indignities which others are made to endure. So it is that an engagement with new technologies can help in the refiguring of traditional forms of philosophy and social theory which have been largely blind to the possibilities of embodied knowledge.

notes

1. See Merchant, C., *The Death of Nature; Women, Ecology, and the Scientific Revolution*, London, Wildwood House, 1980.

2. Wittgenstein, L., *Philosophical Investigations*, Oxford, Basil Blackwell, 1953.

3. Seidler, V., *Unreasonable Men: Masculinity and Social Theory*, London, Routledge, 1994.

4. Griffin, S., *Pornography and Silence*, London, Women's Press, 1981.

5. Freud, S., *Civilization and Its Discontents*, trans. Riviere, J., London, Hogarth Press, revised edition, 1963.

6. Boyarin, D., *Carnal Israel: Reading Sex in Talmudic Culture*, Berkeley, California UP, 1993.

7. Levinas, E., *Difficult Freedom: Essays in Judaism*, London, Athlone Press, 1990.

8. West, C., *Prophesy Deliverance!: an Afro-American Revolutionary Christianity*, Philadelphia, Westminster Press, 1982.

9. Bauman, Z., *Modernity and the Holocaust*, Cambridge, Cambridge University Press, 1989.

10. Turkle, S., *Life On The Screen: Identity in the Age of the Internet*, London, Weidenfeld & Nicolson, 1996.

11. From an interview with David Winner: 'Deadly Messenger', *The Jewish Chronicle*, 20 December 1996, p. 22.

12. Turkle, S., *Life on the Screen: Identity in the Age of the Internet*, London, Weidenfeld & Nicolson, 1996, p. 22.

13. Ibid.

chapter 2

the digital unconscious

john monk

individualism

Realms of solidarity, the objects of social theories, have proved to be chimera and individualisation has taken a grip. Technology makes its contribution by distorting the social context. Long-distance communication and travel are not new, but their increasing convenience, prevalence and personalisation have snatched the time of individuals and induced change in people's social locations that impels them to construct individualised, dynamic, non-local networks. Industrialised, formalised mass education provides 'credentials leading to individualized career opportunities', but in an atmosphere of competition and with standardised qualifications people are forced to 'advertize their individuality' and to undermine solidarity with their peers.[1] People, therefore, seek sovereignty over their presentation as individuals and attempt to stay in command of their biographies which are kept by various agencies and treated as private property.

A blossoming commercial doctrine promises 'Success in the Info Age' by using technology 'to individualise and personalise services and products'.[2] This creed transforms biographies, indispensable to the individual and essential for the operation of corporations and bureaucracies, into assets that are hoarded, protected, concealed, exploited and manipulated. One company 'offered a list of 250,000 Internet addresses' which were 'gathered from newsgroups, chat groups and Web sites' without people realising 'that their addresses were being captured, compiled and sold'.[3] Since 'demographic data translates into real dollars', the virtuous offer compensation to people for their personal 'information with give-aways, sweepstakes, discounts and other benefits'.[4]

Desire for individual identities fosters the development of individualised goods. The products of individualisation include timepieces, once the centrepieces of communities, now transformed into fashion accessories. In the orbit of the Internet, one company, having 'anticipated the value of personalized and permanent e-mail addresses', offers 'quality names' including the domain names 'sweetness.com' and 'bubblegum.net'.[5] Posited technologies are 'automatically personalized' and devices inscribed with personal preferences become 'a reflection of who we are',[6] so 'firefly . . . your own free personal software agent' learns 'about what you love and what you hate',[7] and the 'Info Agent' incorporates 'a representation for . . . the kind of relations the user has, his interests, his past history . . . etc.'[8] Personal collections of information technology transform our view and simultaneously project an identity, much like spectacles. Accordingly, through communication technology 'each person's preferences become coordinated and accessible to devices and services to define an individual's "personal world"'.

relationships

Social theories treat people as members of amorphous classes that conceal personal relationships and equalise individual feelings. Alternatively an obsessive focus on the individual reduces relationships to goal-directed, utilitarian, ephemeral transactions. To avoid this bleak portrayal of fragmented relationships, I prefer to describe relationships as enduring yet dynamic, intangible collections of beliefs held by a number of people who all maintain their own unique cluster of beliefs about the relationship which their experiences transform or affirm. Activities amongst the partners, their attempts to provide experiences for one another, provide the binding force between their separated clusters of beliefs that constitute the relationship.

Experiences of those in a relationship cannot be identical or synchronised, thus the sets of beliefs that frame a relationship are never equal nor in harmony. Consequently, someone may predict confidently the experiences that somebody else generates, while others feel insecure because of their inadequate forecasts; their incapacity may shock or surprise them and cause them to adjust their perceptions and modify their beliefs.

An *individual* is a relationship composed of the different identities which participants in the relationship retain. An individual is, inevitably, an asymmetric relationship, since some-*body* will believe that their cluster of beliefs about an individual is about them-self, while other people will believe that the individual is some-*body* else. Actions, through the experiences they precipitate and the beliefs they affect, change identities and transform the patchworks of beliefs that form individuals. The traces of people's actions litter our world and are treated as mosaics of biographical fragments. Identities colour the stories we tell about people in monologues or while collectively chattering, gossiping, arguing and debating so that, as Lacan notes, we identify ourselves in language.[9]

The conviction that some beliefs are allied is a feeling, and the identities that convictions bond are private and personal. Identities remain incomparable, thus agreements about identity simply demonstrate that extant narratives and biographies currently do not stimulate objections. Every new experience is a trigger for a realignment which shifts and distorts identities. The inevitable contradictions and inconsistencies provoke debate so the maintenance of any identity, including our own, promotes a discourse, which can be tranquil, but can also be offensive and, occasionally, violent.

ceremonies

Secure relationships are a source of power. They allow us to control and constrain what others do. Where a relationship proves to be insecure, that is, where a confident prediction about someone's actions proves to be untrustworthy, there is a loss of power that can be bewildering, frustrating and possibly traumatic. To insure against personal losses of power we engage in ceremonies that formalise and secure changes. Ceremonies often demand witnesses, involve memorable rituals, or generate enduring and unique inscriptions; ceremonies employ conspicuous symbolic artefacts, times and locations; ceremonies can be theatrical and require rehearsal. These characteristics induce experiences that reinforce or refresh beliefs which mould a relationship. A ceremony, then, is a technology for imprinting a relationship on the webs of beliefs of a number of people.

Identity, which emerges from narrative, is impregnated with a film of quotations since a story or text, as Barthes remarks, 'is a tissue of quotations'.[10] The repetition implied by quotation is a feature of the ceremonial. There are name-giving ceremonies, password-issuing ceremonies, the elaborate ceremonies of academic awards, job interviews, medical consultations, immigration procedures, legal proceedings and commonplace rituals, like buying food, gossiping or going to work – all contributing to the fabrication of individuals.

Austin[11] explained that we say things, not necessarily to describe states of affairs but also to participate. He notes that when 'I say before the registrar "I do", I am not reporting a marriage: I am indulging in it.' Saying 'I bet' establishes a contract or when an authority announces 'I declare war' then the war exists. Austin designates utterances of this kind as 'performatives'. Barthes treats all writing as performative – an enunciation which 'has no other content ... than the act by which it is uttered'.[12] And in the world of software a 'KQML message is called a performative ... The message is intended to perform some action by virtue of being sent.'[13]

Austin explored the conditions required for a performative to be effective: it must be part of an accepted procedure; the participants must adopt appropriate roles; and the procedure must be executed correctly, completely and with sincerity. Effectively, Austin described ceremonies and indicated that ceremonies alter relationships. Furthermore, what people utter, what they inscribe, or what their software discloses can activate a change in relationships. Bureaucracies, for example, are characterised by their austere and primarily linguistic ceremonies, such as form-filling and committee meetings, which transform individuals, and the mischievous pleasure of the rumour-monger is to declare that certain individuals are charlatans, rakes, liars or cheats.

Ceremonies grounded in language thus provide a means for non-violent, collective action; they ritualise behaviour, adjust expectations and modify authorities. Experiences of a text or a narrative alter or strengthen beliefs. Thus the production of texts and narratives, utterances and inscriptions is a part of the technology for transforming relationships and acting on individuals.

identifiers

Biographies simultaneously resonate with identities and augment beliefs about identified individuals. Ceremonies exploit cryptic biographies, identifiers, as keys that lock performatives to particular individuals. Special ceremonies refine distinguished biographies; they fabricate biographical events and issue biographical artefacts like medals, affidavits, birth certificates or credit cards. Ceremonies, for example, engrave names into biographies through endless repetitions. Practices in formal education, for instance, continually rehearse people's reactions to their ascribed names.

Names are tiny fragments of biographies and, alone, are seldom unequivocal identifiers. Many names imply gender or ethnic connections, and nicknames carry connotations, so isolated names unintentionally correlate with stereotypes; for instance, 'most regular businessmen don't want to deal with someone named "Agent Steal".'[14] Secure identities are built. For example, Alice may engage in networked discussions anonymously but 'under a continuous identity'. She may 'sign her messages as "Andrea"', then by 'participating in discussions under a consistent . . . "nym"' Alice 'can establish Andrea as a digital persona'[15] secured by a growing biographical collection of messages.

A bundle of beliefs about an individual is more than a list of attributes; it also includes beliefs about occasions and situations kindled by events or evoked by biographies. For example, some-*body* can be identified as an owner and not as a thief when people recall a host of details about the ceremony surrounding a purchase. 'Wanted' posters are biographical; they can address an anonymous identity using a portrait, and a villainous biographical account.

signatures

The destruction or exploitation of the authority embedded in a secure relationship provides incentives to infect identities. Saboteurs fabricate delusive fictional biographies which induce experiences that correlate with individuals. For example, someone obtained credit and committed traffic offences in the name of a childhood friend. Police realised the identities were confused but 'now police computers think they are the same person!'.[16] For a spell you could forge a biography by fraudulently entering 'a child molester into the database'; there was no verification since 'responsibility for accuracy' rested 'entirely with the persons posting the information'.[17] Biographies are also plundered for their identifying power; for instance, when a crime ring placed 'an enticing job offer in a large newspaper', and then used the 'applicant's detailed résumés' to fill out 'credit card application forms'.[18]

Because of the potential loss of power and security, many of our actions attempt to prevent the infection, loss or obfuscation of identity, and maintaining an identity becomes a contest 'in a world which is doing its best, night and day, to make you everybody else'.[19] Counter measures make forgeries of biographies difficult, for example, by making identifiers hard to reproduce or camouflage. Signatures are identifiers secured by evidence of idiosyncratic skills. The signatures that vestiges of actions carry help onlookers to correlate their experiences with an identity; such as in 'the days of telegraphy when operators would identify each other by recognising "the fist of the sender"'.[20] Like the secret knock on the door that offers reassurance about identity, the revelation of a secret, an idiosyncratic recollection, can provide authentication.[21] Digital signatures, for example, are texts encoded using a secret key which has a unique and public counterpart. Receipt of encoded texts that can be deciphered with the complementary public key offers evidence that a holder of the secret key endorsed the originals.[22]

The secret key, like a signet for making wax seals, leaves an impression that connects a document with a key holder. Swipe cards are a contemporary form of signet. Passing a card through a reader creates an electronic signature that seals a transaction, and PINs are simply memorised numerals but, with a keyboard, can be converted into an electronic signature. Thus 'the average business person may use more than a dozen computer passwords – personal identification numbers (PINs) for automated teller machines, licences, and telephone calling, membership, and credit cards'.[23] These collections of signets present distinctive biographies recounting agreements with, for instance, banks.

Displays of unique apparel act as signatures, like the 'ring of peculiar workmanship upon a finger' which offered the opportunity to 'discover the identity of her whom Rokoff was persecuting'.[24] Appearances are chronicles of people's experiences and their grooming text about their self-identities. Where appearances are signatures, cameras exploit the body as a signet, and experiences of portraits correlate with identities and augment biographies. Thus, on 'receiving a print they at once recognised their son' partly through idiographic detail since 'as proof of identity, he had reproduced the bullet wound in his left temple'.[25] On occasions a textual image is acceptable: 'your appearance . . . I have never seen you before. But that is not necessary – you conform perfectly to the printed description of you with which the kingdom is flooded'.[26]

When the response of a machine to part of some-body is treated as a signature, body parts become signets, for example where a 'machine measured finger length and was installed in a time-keeping system'.[27] But an author points out that 'one could fool the device by . . . creating a fake hand'.[28] Another machine exploits 'unique patterns of veins buried just beneath the skin's surface' though there is the gruesome probability that desperate people 'won't be adverse to cutting off a person's hand and taking it to the cashpoint'.[29] A text is easily altered, and photographs and videos can be doctored. Anybody can attempt to disguise their appearance by donning 'the wigs and other bits of theatrical make-up which hide the identity'[30] or by mimicking 'the archetypal global superstar' who 'harnessed plastic surgery to erase traces of his original age, gender and ethnicity'.[31] Signatures, like names, do not offer absolute proof of identity.

technology

Biographies are constructed from accumulations of recorded data derived from, for example, transactions with supermarket chains that 'are collecting millions of pounds a year from selling data'.[32] Financial organisations keep accounts of income and purchases, and governments and employers retain personal records. Internet directory services,[33] contact agencies, electronic conference systems, and advertising agencies all seek personal data. On the World Wide Web people voluntarily publish autobiographical pages; writers are advised to include 'a photo, something about their family, hometown, occupation, hobbies, etc.'[34] and to embrace 'more subtle forms of content that demonstrate your interests and outlook on life'; and some pages offer the ultimate hypertextual biography – where almost 'every link . . . is to a person, place or thing that has had an impact on my life'. An expanding toolbox of query languages, crawlers and search engines helps find biographical material that matches elaborate keys which pass for signatures. One company professes to have 'the most powerful on-line system available for developing background information on individuals' which 'instantly searches over 600 nationwide, regional, and local databases',[35] while another 'taps into the Usenet global electronic bulletin board network' and forms 'user profiles of people who post messages'[36] and the Los Angeles public library offers a 'household profile search'.[37]

Sensors can collect biographical data covertly. Struggles for power provide motives for observation using technologies that bolster asymmetries in relationships. For example, a woman's employer, motivated by 'jealousy and rejection', stole her password and monitored her voice mail.[38] Infinity transmitters, installed in phones, monitor 'conversations in the area';[39] systems detect and decode telephone codes 'such as voice mail numbers';[40] there are 'hidden cameras in the clothes of researchers who roam the high street posing as ordinary consumers';[41] and on the Internet 'a small piece of software' can record data accesses and forward them to a third party.[42] More intimately, medical technology reveals to others our hidden internal bodily processes; for example a portable locator can monitor 'vital signs such as pulse rate and blood pressure'[43] and when 'someone wants to enter a high security area, Scentinel . . . obtains an odour profile and compares this with the profile in its memory'.[44]

With personal items such as mobile phones, an account of a handset's use implicates whoever provided biographical data when registering for the service. Cellular phones offer a way of locating some-body;[45] service operators automatically record details of calls, note the user's behaviour to help detect thieves[46] and thus accumulate biographical records. In a version of the indelible brand, a 'transmitter is attached to an offender's ankle or wrist and sends periodic RF signals'[47] which identify the individual who is ankleted. Criminals can be tracked by systems that record 'every place the offender went – and the time he or she was there', and it is conceivable that the whereabouts of their tag 'could then be cross-indexed against known crime scenes and times'.[48] 'Similar systems are already being used to keep track of children in daycare centres, and babies in hospitals'.[49] In commercial organisations, too, people are tagged: 'Everyone working at Makuhari wears a smart badge which gives them access into and around the building'.[50]

Vehicle registers are rich seams of biographical data. A vehicle owner's name is linked with a time and a location after the vehicle's 'licence plate is scanned and compared with the numbers held in a database',[51] or after the vehicle passes through a toll payment system that lists 'a driver's name, address, and the precise dates and times and places where tolls were charged'.[52] Internet Web servers can record a cookie 'right on the customer's machine'.[53] Cookies permit 'a remote service to compile a 'list of your travels' to their site. If during a transaction you offer 'personal information . . . this "clicktrail" can be associated with you'.[54] If people operating different sites co-operate, then 'cookies . . . could easily be used to track a user's movements'.[55] Thus phones, vehicles and networked computers tag their owners, act as signets, and help build biographical profiles.

effigies

Electronic biographies develop in response to events, but they can be altered in advance of events to create a fiction that is performative. Mutable biographies are effigies that govern rather than record events and so administer and pre-empt changes in individuals.

At a college, students swipe a card through a reader to unlock doors. The access system acquires students' electronic signatures, equates signatures with access privileges and operates locks automatically.[56] Modifications of a biography on a database would automatically alter constraints on a cardholder's movements. Each biography is therefore a digital effigy manipulated by those with access to the database. For companies, databases link privileges with effigies of 'valued customers whom they want to retain'. For example, 'airlines use records stored on their database to upgrade frequent customers to first class in preference to occasional travellers'.[57] When Web browsers fetch certain hypertext pages, hidden references are made to an 'Internet Profiles Database' which retrieves and updates biographical 'information about the user'[58] that directs the selection of the advertisements that the user experiences.

Manipulated, reproduced and transmitted, effigies propagate changes in identities. Computing, networking, writing, printing, photocopying and publishing become instruments for impelling alterations in relationships. They are performative technologies that relay actions and sensations and extend the reach of participants in a relationship; these technologies can save time (in the rush to form more relationships) and can portray some-body in their absence. For instance, the 'Softbot eliminates a person's need to "drive" the information superhighway . . . allows a user to specify what to accomplish, while it handles the decisions of how and where to accomplish it.'[59] Clients cannot be sure about the fidelity of their delegated actions, or their mediated experiences, and cannot be certain that relationships are growing as they would wish since 'we can easily imagine malicious and deceitful agents, trying to rip off honest ones'.[60] To sustain their client's trust, agents reinforce their credentials by conveying signed biographical artefacts that authenticate reports of events and performative actions. Agents trade in biographies and, according to their programme, change them when they '"meet" and interact, performing transactions on behalf of individual users while the users are disconnected'.[61] Such operations on effigies provide means to run bureaucracies, to abuse individuals and to commit fraud. But to be effective, the authenticity of the effigy has to be sustained.

Mechanisms for assuring compliance vary. A proposed traffic system that monitors speeds, distances and road conditions, and incorporates the traffic rules may 'enforce correct behaviour by various means, such as fines, licence or speed limitation'.[62] In some health systems, doctors become the agents of 'smart software programs' since 'a doctor will follow the computer's advice or find another health plan to work for',[63] and a tagged offender could be the subject of actions determined remotely and relayed through a microprocessor to 'trigger the release of a measured amount of tranquilizer or a sexually dampening chemical' or, more drastically, to apply 'the option to "shut down" an offender'.[64] Thus the body provides a connection with the pleasures and pains that secure the authenticity of effigies.

Bureaucrats, like cyberlovers, are acquainted with identities created by effigies, where, following the precedent of the novel,[65] the mundane liveliness of electronic presentations entices them to believe that they deal with people rather than text. The illusion creates a subtle shift in language use, so a service provider claims[66] that a directory service 'lets you search for People' though, of course, what you can search for is a database record. We are instructed: 'Database Now On-line!!! Looking for someone? Find them here',[67] though what you find is text. And even after their last gasp we find 'a significant portion of the 800,000–900,000 people who die each year must be on a database',[68] though it is unlikely that it is their corpse that will be found. In the confusion 'a convincing on-line meta-personality on the Net' which 'really IS you' is re-presented as 'an isotope of you. Or a photocopy of you'. So the fantasy is that 'with computers, we photocopy our very *being*'.[69] As the materialist metaphor tilts towards the literal, so individuals become indistinct from globally distributed computing resources accessible to owners, tax collectors, merchants, traders, processors and fabricators. Databases and hypertexts become repositories for people, and because 'the "author function" is tied to the legal and institutional systems',[70] institutions that maintain effigies govern individuals.

People are treated as facsimiles of insentient artefacts and not as autonomous and feeling individuals; the fragility of this distinction is exploited by oppressors and administrators. For example, where captives 'had to stand naked in line and undergo a detailed examination by the camp physician. Then, each was given a tag and a number'. These were events 'calculated to strip away one's identity and to reduce the individual to an item within an impersonal system'.[71]

the unconscious

In the above example, performatives become blended into characteristic biographies which address the individuals represented. The performatives are enacted when the authorities deliver the biographies into an actual situation. These performatives infect people's beliefs and, once differences are reconciled or suppressed, people begin to recount, and act in accordance with, reconstituted biographies that induce agreement with the authority. Discrepancies between biographies, for instance the differences between an autobiography and other published biographies, are symptoms of latent asymmetries amongst the identities held by different people. To attempt to explain these disparities we invent an unconscious that resides in the unobservable territory that distinguishes a self-identity from an individual.

Unconscious asymmetry emerges when people have different outlooks on an individual as, for example, when spectators, but not Verman, saw that he was 'wholly unconscious that the lids of his right eye were swollen shut and that his attire, not too finical before the struggle, now entitled him to unquestioned rank as a sansculotte'.[72] Misread actions create unconscious differences, for example when 'I saw him make a sudden motion with his head, which I mistook for a token of recognition and good morning. In reality, he was attempting to warn me to throw my ashes over the lee side. Unconscious of my blunder, I . . . flung the ashes over the side to windward'.[73]

Biographical events do not always figure in an autobiography because they are forgotten or overlooked; for example, when 'unconsciously she sipped coffee from the china cup, ate fried evaporated potatoes, and spread marmalade on her biscuit'.[74] Distractions blunt awareness and hide events so that 'two persons were walking rapidly, as if unconscious of the trying ascent – unconscious through preoccupation'.[75] And people become oblivious to conspicuous behaviour when, for example, '[s]he lay unconscious of the wild little cries she uttered at the last'.[76] We neglect embellishments to our actions, and disregard slips that others heed. We take for granted our own routines like the character who habitually 'rouged a bit, smoked a bit, and wore abbreviated frocks; but she did these things unconsciously'.[77] Well-rehearsed skills become reflexes, and some acts draw attention but are absent-mindedly executed, for instance when '[u]nconsciously clapping the vinegar-cruet to one side of her nose, she ruminated for an instant'.[78] People are often unaware of their catalytic effects on others, they sometimes lack empathy or lack experience, like the man who 'is unconscious and ignorant as to the sources of true happiness, and won't submit himself to cold mutton and three clean shirts a week'.[79]

Emotions drive asymmetric changes in identity like the unseen gesture when 'he felt very bitter towards Mabel, and scowled fiercely at Allan Thorpe . . . though, as it was dark, the artist was happily unconscious of it'.[80] Thus episodes that we fail to notice can affect our identity as seen by others, or our self-identity can be affected by events ignored by everyone else. The consequential, enduring asymmetries in identity can be attributed to the unconscious.

electronic records

Electronic technologies maintain effigies, of which we are dimly aware. Changes made to databases and hypertexts affect how our electronic biographies and our bodily selves are treated and can stimulate beliefs that are discordant with our self-identity. Nourished by ignorance of a recorded persona that others observe, copy, distribute, manipulate and invent, the aggregate disparity in beliefs might be said to be caused by the digital unconscious.

Concealed records affect people when the secret is discovered. For instance, a woman was shaken when she found e-mail messages showing that her husband, 'was . . . having a cybersex affair with a Canadian woman'.[81] A couple may have been quite unconscious of biographical record of them 'having sex in a doorway' in a '"voyeuristic" compilation of films' obtained from 'closed circuit TV . . . in stores and high streets' and showing 'unwitting and possibly unwilling members of the public'.[82] Credit cardholders were unconscious of their exposure when certain Web sites had improperly installed software intended to assist in purchases which revealed credit card numbers to Web browsers.[83] Anyone could use the unveiled numbers, as signets, to add biographical events to the cardholders' accounts.

Mysterious events hold clues to the unconscious record, for example, gas consumers, unconscious of the gas corporation's concealed digital effigies, were puzzled to receive 'bills for £10 million, while others who paid their gas bills regularly were threatened with disconnection'.[84] Disclosure of once hidden, authoritative biographic statements can transform ignorance into offence. In one computer system, users 'have a personal identification number and speak a password'. The technology is not infallible although 'the error rate for false acceptances and rejection is less than 2 per cent'. The system controls 'access to office computers and networks'.[85] Rejection implies that an authorised person's signature does not match their record, instead they resemble unconsciously the stereotyped effigy of an interloper. On one occasion 'a public health worker took a laptop and disks with confidential lists of people with AIDS and HIV . . . to a gay bar to check out the HIV status of potential dates and offered to look up names of people his friends were interested in dating'.[86] The prey were, presumably, unconscious that their confidential biography was affecting people's behaviour towards them.

A company with the slogan 'Software Quality Assurance for the Real World' was criticised for alleged errors on its Web pages. The critic concludes that having a page 'filled with typos gives the impression that you may be sloppy in other things too'.[87] Such inferences, prognoses and speculations often embellish biographies. For example, 'statisticians turned to neural networks to fill in gaps in their data, where interviewees had failed to answer particular questions'.[88] The subjects of interpolated effigies become unconscious hostages to esoteric inferences of capricious authorities exploiting inconstant theories surrounding, for instance, physiological, genetic or financial data.

An effigy, like a text, is subject to varying interpretations. When a student changed schools, he was barred from classes. His two schools used different conventions and interpreted his disciplinary record differently. The new school assumed wrongly that he had been caught with drugs.[89] The boy, unconscious of the presumed misdeed, was undoubtedly shocked.

Lottery tickets are signets of gamblers and lottery draws create effigies of winners and losers. When 'a software error caused the wrong lottery numbers' to be broadcast, disappointed people 'threw out their tickets thinking they lost' while others celebrated prematurely. Apparently 'two of the six numbers were altered in the transmission process',[90] and this caused gamblers to adopt unconsciously a self-identity incompatible with the cloistered authoritative effigies. Thus technologies unaided construct disturbing biographical fictions. For instance, a man withdrew money and on 'the same day, someone used a stolen card'. The 'clock in the video camera filming bank customers indicated' that the man 'withdrew his money at the same time as the fraud occurred'. The video image was broadcast. The man went to the police where he was 'interrogated for 45 minutes', however it was proved that 'the video-camera clock . . . was out by about one hour'. The recording technology had constructed an effigy which transformed him unconsciously into a suspect. He was released.[91] Sometimes sources of discrepancies are never uncovered. A police officer 'found his account . . . empty', he was unconscious of making any withdrawals and complained. He was told that 'he must be mistaken or lying'. He persisted, was reported, tried, convicted and jailed, although the trial exposed 'the somewhat ramshackle nature' of the financial institution's security procedures.[92] After an appeal, the man was acquitted on the grounds that 'the defence must have access to test and see whether there is anything making the computers fallible' and this access had been denied.[93] The man, unconscious of any fraudulent activity, eventually had his legal biography restored so it no longer violated his self-identity.

conclusion

The digital unconscious is disembodied, distributed, collectively constructed and substantive. It creates a concealed persona and triggers unanticipated, inexplicable, occasionally distressing actions. When the anguish becomes unbearable, a search for hidden records can expose the digital unconscious and provide explanations for events. The search needs not a psychotherapist, but a computer specialist. This analysis offers not a cure but an understanding; it can transform, as Freud wrote, 'hysterical misery into common unhappiness'.[94]

A rapacious designer could set out to create information technology that increases anxiety, and undermines power. It is something that many designers may wish to avoid, but perhaps it is unavoidable. The balance of power sustained by our relationships is a mutual exploitation of our anxieties, and technology is a means to adjust that balance.

We invent the unconscious when explanations of someone's behaviour cannot be squared with our circumstances. The unconscious lurks in latent dissimilarities between a self-identity and other clusters of beliefs about some-body formed, increasingly, from experiences of fabricated biographies captured in a global electronic net. When these cryptic electronic effigies are fancied to be the authentic sources of reputations, self-identity is undermined, and the manipulation of effigies becomes an authoritarian means to normalise behaviour through technology. 'Who I am' becomes governed by enigmatic digital records, and the scope for individual responsibility or wisdom is destroyed.

But effigies are not beliefs and the effectiveness of their performative action depends upon the authority they carry. Responsibility means uncovering the authorities that propagate performatives and judging whether to accept or reject their command. Where performatives are propagated unconsciously through diffuse networks of unwitting agents, the unconscious influences must first be actively sought, then critically analysed and accepted or rejected.

notes

1. Beck, U., *Risk Society*, London, Sage, 1992, p. 94.

2. Lewis, Ted G., 'Living in real time', SpinDoctor 1995–1996. http://www.spindoczine.com.

3. Markwart, Rich, 'Email addresses for sale by direct marketing agency', *Computer Privacy Digest*, 7(32), 1995.

4. http://icode.ipro.com/, Internet Profiles Corporation, Redwood City, Ca., 31 October 1996.

5. http://www.iName.com/, iName, New York, 1996.

6. http//:www.navio.com/, Navio Communications Inc., Sunnyvale, 1996.

7. http//:www.ffly.com/, Firefly Network, Inc., 1996.

8. D'Aloisi, D., and Giannini, V., *The Info Agent: an Interface for Supporting Users in Intelligent Retrieval*, Fondazione Ugo Bordoni, Rome, 7 November 1995.

9. Lacan, J., *The Function and Field of Speech and Language*, London, Tavistock, 1977, p. 86.

10. Barthes, R., 'The death of the author' in *Image, Music, Text*, ed. and trans. Heath, S., Glasgow, Fontana, 1977, p. 142.

11. Austin, J.L., *How to Do Things with Words*, Oxford, Clarendon, 1962.

12. Barthes, op. cit., pp. 145–146.

13. 'Software design document for KQML Revision 3.0', Unisys Corporation, Paoli, March 1995.

14. Murray, E., Futplex: 'Re: Nym use in the real world', cypherpunks archive, 27 January 1996.

15. Froomkin, A.M., 'Anonymity and its enmities', 1995 J. ONLINE L. art. 4.

16. *Boston Globe*, 7 March, 1994.

17. 'Child molester's hall of shame query', http://www.greatworld.com. Now removed.

18. agitprop@shrine.cyber.ad.jp, 'Re: postal privacy', *Computer Privacy Digest* 9(018), 1996.

19. eecummings, 'Learning' in *Complete Poems 1904–1962*, ed. Firmage, G.J., New York, Liveright Publishing Corporation.

20. Miller, B., 'Vital signs of identity', *IEEE Spectrum*, 31(2) 1994, pp. 22–30.

21. CCITT X.509, 'The directory – authentication framework', Melbourne 1988. Section 9.1.1.

22. http://digitalid.verisign.com/id_faqs.html/, Verisign. Inc., Version 2, 21 May 1996.

23. Miller, op. cit.

24. Burroughs, Edgar Rice, *The Return of Tarzan*, New York, Ballantine Books, [1913] 1990, p. 16.

25. Conan Doyle, Arthur, *The Vital Message*, New York, George H. Doran Co., 1919, p. 160.

26. Burroughs, Edgar Rice, *The Mad King*, New York, Grosset & Dunlap, 1914, p. 30.

27. Miller, op. cit.

28. Sidlauskas, D., 'HAND: Give me five', *IEEE Spectrum*, 31(2), 1994, p. 24.

29. 'Vein pattern checking: anti-fraud or anti-freedom?', *The Mouse Monitor*, May, 1996, Scope International.

30. Baroness Orczy, *The Scarlet Pimpernel* on http://www.cs.cmu.edu/People/rgs/scarp-I.html.

31. Rawsthorn, A., 'Out of tune with the times', *FT*, 25 June 1996, p. 17.

32. Oram, R., 'Smoke slowly clears on bar-code battlefield', *FT*, 16 December 1996 p. 14.

33. http://www.whowhere.com/, 1997.

34. I have deliberately omitted references to personal pages.

35. http://www.cdb.com/public/moreinfo/, CDB Infotek, Santa Ana, California, 1996.

36. Garfinkel, S.L., *The Boston Globe*, 13 October 1995.

37. http://www.colapublib.org//fyi//catalog/personal/people.html, County of Los Angeles Public Library, 1997.

38. 'Employer abuse of private voicemail', *Computer Privacy Digest*, ed. Prof. Levine 7(050), 1995.

39. Shannon, M.L., *The Phone Book: Who Is Listening*, San Francisco, Lysias Press, 1995.

40. http://www.t8000.com/eci/brief.htm, Cellular surveillance system 8000, Electronic Countermeasures Inc., Calgary, 1996.

41. Matthews, V., 'Eyes on buyers', *FT*, 23 March 1995, p. 14.

42. http://www.ipro.com/icount.html, Internet Profiles Corporation, Redwood City, Ca., 28 February 1997.

43. Hoshen, J., Sennott, J., and Winkler, M., 'Keeping tabs on criminals', *IEEE Spectrum* 32(2), 1995, pp. 26–32.

44. Cookson, C., 'A brave new olfactory world', *FT*, 8 June 1995, p. 22.

45. Cane, A., 'Let your fingers cut the walking', *FT*, 10 January 1997, p. 9.

46. Cane, A., 'Thieves on the line', *FT*, 23 March 1995, p. 16.

47. Hoshen *et al.*, op. cit.

48. Winkler, M., 'Walking prisons: the developing technology of electronic controls', *The Futurist*, 27(3), 1993, pp. 34–36.

49. Cookson, C., 'On the right track', *FT*, 4 July 1995, p. 16.

50. Cole, G., 'Smart buildings look Sharp', *FT*, 2 November 1995.

51. Ibid.

52. Agre, P., 'Welcome to TNO 2(4)', *The Network Observer*, 2(4) 1995.

53. http://www.jasmin.com, Jasmin Consulting Corporation, 1996.

54. Hedlund, M., 'Re: Knowing Where you Browse?', *Computer Privacy Digest*, 7(26), 1995.

55. Shields, M., 'Re: Knowing Where you Browse?', *Computer Privacy Digest*, 7(26), 1995.

56. 'Security works – smart campus', *Security Management*, American Society for Industrial Security, September 1995.

57. Houlder, V., 'Database Mining', *FT*, 28 November 1995, p. 16.

58. http://www.doubleclick.net, DoubleClick, Inc., 1996.

59. Hermans, B., *Intelligent Software Agents on the Internet*, Tilburg University, The Netherlands, 9 July 1996.

60. Chavez, A., and Maes, P., *Kasbah: An Agent Marketplace for Buying and Selling Goods*, Cambridge, Mass., MIT media lab.

61. http://www.genmagic.com/, General Magic Inc., Sunnyville, Ca. For an extended discussion see White, J.E., *Telescript Technology: The Foundation for the Electronic Marketplace*. White paper, General Magic Inc., 1994.

62. Panel discussion at the Fifth Conference on 'Computers, Freedom, and Privacy', in Burlingame, California in March 1995. Edited transcript in 'Thinking about privacy in Intelligent Transportation Systems', *The Network Observer*, 2(4), 1995.

63. *Wall Street Journal*, 18 December 1995, p. B1.

64. Winkler, op. cit.

65. Ong, W.J., *Orality and Literacy*, London, Methuen, 1982, pp. 152–153.

66. http://www.whowhere.com/.

67. 'Child molester's hall of shame query', http://www.greatworld.com/public/query.htm.

68. Lloyd, C., quoted in Summers, D., 'Direct mail groups want daily death list to update database', *FT*, 10 May 1995, p. 1.

69. Coupland, D., *Microserfs*, London, Flamingo, 1995, p. 327 .

70. Foucault, M., 'What is an author?', in *Language, Counter Memory, Practice*, trans. Bouchard, D.F. and Simon, S., Ithaca, Cornell, 1977, p. 131.

71. Coombs, N., *The Black Experience in America*, New York, Twayne, 1972, ch. 3.

72. Tarkington, N.B., *Penrod*, New York, Doubleday, Page & Company, 1915, pp. 217–218.

73. London, J., *The Sea-Wolf*, in *Selections 1982, Novels and Stories*, New York, Vikings, 1982, pp. 517.

74. Ibid., p. 724.

75. Hardy, T., *Tess of the d'Urbervilles*, ed. Elledge, S., New York, W.W. Norton, 1979, p. 328.

76. Lawrence, D.H., *Lady Chatterley's Lover*, ed. Squires, M., Cambridge, Cambridge University Press, 1979, p. 133.

77. Osborne, W.H., 'After death–what?', *Munsey's Magazine*, New York, 1916, vol. 59, p. 428.

78. Melville, H., *Moby Dick, or, The Whale*, ed. Mansfield, L.S. and Vincent, H.P., New York, Hendricks House, 1952, p. 82.

79. Trollope, A., *The Eustace Diamonds*, ed. McCormack, W.J., Oxford, Oxford University Press, 1982, p. 224.

80. Alger, H.J., 'A fancy of hers', *Munsey's Magazine*, 6, 1892, pp. 697–744.

81. 'Man beats wife after she pulls plug on cybersex', Reuters World Report, Little Rock, 31 October 1996.

82. 'Ban sought on "doorway sex" security videos', *Guardian*, 27 November 1995, p. 4.

83. *Wall Street Journal*, 8 November 1996, p. B6.

84. Corzine, R., 'Customers feel the heat', *FT*, 11/12 January 1997, p. 6.

85. Cole, G., 'Giving voice to security', *FT*, 19 September 1995, p. 14.

86. *Palo Alto Daily News*, quoted by Fickeisen, D.H., 'Health info database misused', *Risks-Forum Digest* 18 (53) 1996.

87. Batterson, D.W., 'Software testing lab's Web site', *Computer Underground Digest* 7(69), 1995.

88. Houlder, op. cit.

89. 'Teen "convicted" by computer', *San Jose Mercury News*, 7 March 1996.

90. *The Washington Post*, 13 September 1996. Reported by Scott Lucero, 'Maryland lottery computer glitch', *Risks Forum Digest* 18(46), 1996.

91. 'Man seeks to clear his name after police error', *Vancouver Sun*, 18 October 1995.

92. Ward, M., 'Court case casts doubt on cashpoint credibility', *Computing*, 3 March 1994.

93. Anderson, R., 'John Munden is acquitted at last!', *Risks-Forum Digest* 18 (25), 1996.

94. Studies on hysteria written with Josef Bruer in 1893 in Freud, S., *The Standard Edition of the Complete Psychological Works of Sigmund Freud*, ed. James Strachey. 24 vols, London, Hogarth Press, 1953–74, Vol. 2, p. 308.

.

chapter 3

physical, psychological and virtual realities

max velmans

introduction

In our predominantly materialist culture we take it for granted that the physical world is *real*. But in what sense are experiences, thoughts and feelings real? And what about virtual realities? Are they physical, psychological, or somewhere in between?

In the present chapter I examine:

1.   the ways physical, psychological and virtual realities differ

2.   the ways in which physical, psychological and virtual realities are the same

3.   the ways in which physical, psychological and virtual realities might relate to some 'grounding reality' or 'thing-itself'.

I also tell a story about the possible consequences of living too long in a convincing, virtual reality.

typical beliefs about physical, psychological and virtual realities

In our everyday intuitions it is common to think about physical, psychological and virtual realities in the ways summarised in Figure 3.1.

physical reality   psychological reality

extended in space – in the world   nonextended in space – in the mind
exists independently of the observer   existence depends on the observer
has tangible properties, e.g. mass and solidity   is relatively intangible and insubstantial

virtual reality

appears to have extension in space, but has no actual extension
appears to be in the world, but is actually in the mind
existence depends on the interaction of the observer with VR equipment
can appear to have tangible properties (with suitable equipment) but does not have such
properties

3.1 typical beliefs about physical, psychological and virtual realities

Following Descartes' classical body/mind split into *res extensa* (stuff that extends in space) and *res cogitans* (thinking stuff), it is common to think of the physical world as having both extension and location in space. By contrast, psychological realities do not have spatial dimensions, and their location is only metaphorically 'in the mind'. In everyday life (and in classical physics) we take it for granted that the physical world continues to exist whether or not we observe it, but psychological realities are only real *for a given observer* – pains, thoughts and other experiences do not exist *in themselves*. These intuitions are confirmed by the fact that physical realities have tangible, substantial properties such as mass, solidity and weight. Psychological properties are, by comparison, intangible and insubstantial.

Virtual realities, however, appear to form a third, distinct category. With appropriate headsets, feedback from bodily movements and visual displays they may give the *appearance* of being virtual worlds extended in physical space, but they have no *actual* 3D physical extension. One may appear to move around such virtual worlds, but these apparent changes in self-location do not correspond to actual changes in location. Such virtual worlds are 'physical' in so far as their existence depends on the information provided by appropriate physical equipment, but unless this information is translated into an observer's experience, no independent 'virtual reality' exists. In principle, virtual objects can be given what appear to be physical properties, for example, the observer may wear a gauntlet which is programmed to resist closing around a visually perceived, virtual object, making the latter feel 'solid'. In truth, however, there is nothing solid there.

what is taken for granted

These intuitions about physical, psychological and virtual realities are grounded in widespread assumptions about how minds relate to bodies, and about how perception works. For example in the 'dualist model' shown in Figure 3.2, light reflected from an external object (a

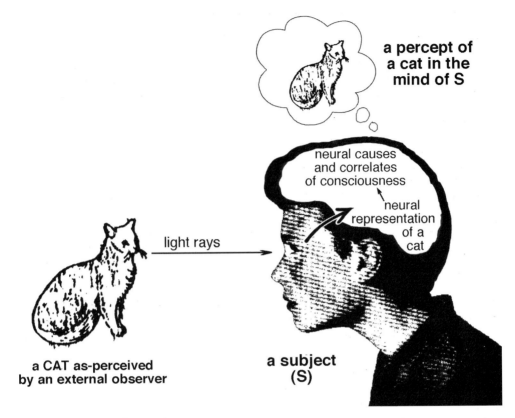

**a percept of
a cat in the
mind of S**

neural causes
and correlates
of consciousness

neural
representation
of a
cat

light rays

**a CAT as-perceived
by an external observer**

**a subject
(S)**

3.2 a dualist model of perception

cat) innervates the visual system of a subject to produce representations of the cat in the brain. Under appropriate conditions, neural causes and correlates of a conscious experience are formed, accompanied by a percept of a cat 'in the mind' of the subject. The external cat (in the world) and the subject's visual system and brain are 'physical', although they are all clearly separate 'bits' of the physical world. The percept of a cat is even further separated from the external cat, being 'in the subject's mind' (without location and extension in space).

The 'reductionist model' shown in Figure 3.3 is very similar. As before, the external cat reflects light rays which innervate the visual system. As before, neural representations of the cat are formed, along with the neural causes and correlates of consciousness. However, reductionists try to demonstrate that the resulting experience (the percept of a cat) is nothing more than a state or function of the subject's brain.

In their effects on our everyday intuitions about physical, psychological and virtual realities, the differences between dualist and reductionist models are not as important as *what they share*. Both models take it for granted that the cat as-perceived in the world *is quite separate* from the percept of a cat. Their dispute is largely about whether the percept of a cat is 'in the mind' or 'in the brain'.

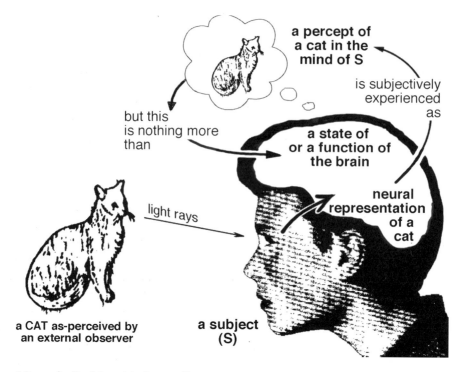

3.3 a reductionist model of perception

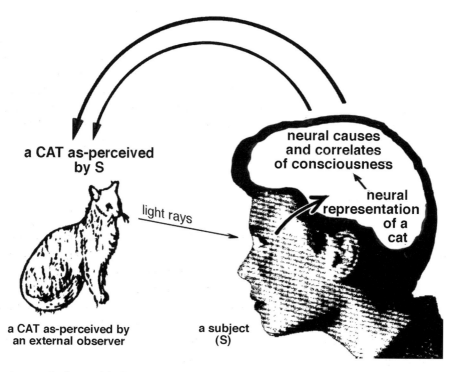

3.4 a reflexive model of perception

fitting virtual reality into a model of perception

Note that virtual realities do not fit easily into such models of the world as-perceived. Dualists and reductionists assume that experiences either have no location or extension, or are located and extended in the brain. However, in VR one *appears* to interact with a virtual world outside one's body although there is no *actual* (corresponding) world there. That is, the VR world appears to have 3D location and extension outside one's body in spite of the fact that it is entirely a phenomenal experience. The VR does not *seem* to be without location or extension, or to be 'in the brain'.

To accommodate virtual reality one needs a model of perception that more accurately portrays the *phenomenology* of what is experienced. Such a 'reflexive model' of perception[1] is shown in Figure 3.4.

In most respects, there is no difference between the dualist, reductionist and reflexive models. All the models assume there to be an initiating stimulus (in this case, a physical cat), reflected light, innervation of the visual system, and the formation of neural representations along with neural causes and correlates of conscious experience in the subject's brain. The models differ only in the way they characterise the resulting experience. In the dualist model, the subject's experience of a cat is *separate from the physical universe, without location or extension in space*. In the reductionist model, the subject's experience of a cat is nothing more than a state or function of the brain. In the reflexive model, the subject's experience of a cat is just the *cat as-perceived out in space*. That is, an entity in space, once it engages the visual system, is experienced as an entity in space. That is why the entire process is 'reflexive'.

Only the last claim conforms to our actual experience. Note too, that while we focus on the cat, a cat in the world is *all* we experience. The neural causes and correlates of what we experience are in the brain – but, subjectively, we have no *additional* 'experience of a cat' in the mind or brain. Nor can such an experience be found in the brain if it is inspected from the outside, by an external observer. That is, the 'experience of a cat' (in the mind or brain) portrayed in dualist and reductionist models is a theoretical fiction. Applying 'Occam's Razor', the reflexive model gets rid of it, giving a description of what is going on that reflects actual phenomenology.[2]

how can experiences be located and extended in space?

Like other models of perception, the reflexive model takes it for granted that the neural causes and correlates of experience are in the brain. Given this, *how* could the resulting experiences be anywhere else? This is an important question. But it is important to distinguish descriptions of *what* happens from investigations of *how* it happens. Before investigating a phenomenon it is necessary to notice it and *name* it. The reflexive model describes what happens. Perceptual processing in the brain can result in experiences that have a subjective location and extension beyond the brain. In Velmans[3] I have called this phenomenon 'perceptual projection'. How spatial encodings and other encodings in the brain are translated into such spatial phenomenology are matters for scientific research.

the evidence for perceptual projection

There is extensive evidence for perceptual projection in all sense modalities (in truth, very little of what we experience gives the appearance of being located in the brain). I have reviewed this in Velmans,[4] so in what follows I will give just a few examples of the ways in which neural activity (in the brain) can result in spatially located, extended experiences.

projected pain

Suppose you stab your finger with a pin. You will experience pain. The damage to the skin is 'physical'. By contrast, philosophers of mind universally agree that the pain that results is an 'experience'. In this situation, the physical damage is located in the finger. But where is the pain? Is the pain 'in the mind', or 'nowhere' as dualists claim? Is it literally 'in the brain' as reductionists claim? Or is it in the finger as the reflexive model claims (in the region of damage to the skin)? If you have any doubts about this, why not try it for yourself?

Note that within a dualist or reductionist world view it does not make sense to describe an *experience* as being 'in the finger'. Conversely, if the pain really *is* in the finger, there must be something wrong with the way dualists and reductionists describe experience. There are, of course, neural fibres which convey pain signals to the brain located in the finger – so even if one accepts that the pain is in the finger, perhaps one could still regard these neural fibres as an extension of the brain. However, if the arm itself is severed from the shoulder one *can still* experience pain in a now non-existent 'phantom limb' or 'phantom hand', along with sweating, itching and so on.[5] The brain combines information arriving from the stump with information in memory to produce a hallucinatory arm and hand extended in space – a clear case of 'perceptual projection'.

projected tactile sensations

Given the deep split between mind and body implicit in dualism, it is crucial to note that the ability of the brain to project pain applies equally to properties more often thought of as 'physical' than 'mental'. 'Hardness' and 'solidity', for example, are usually thought of as physical properties. Nevertheless, the hardness and solidity we *experience* results from the way mechanical deformations of the skin are interpreted by the brain and projected (reflexively) to the location of the stimulated sense organs. Significantly, such perceptual projection to the body surface is applied even to tactile sensations produced by direct stimulation of the brain. Penfield and Rassmussen[6] for example, found that micro-electrode stimulation of the somatosensory cortex produces feelings of numbness and tingling which are subjectively located in different regions of the body, not in the brain – another clear case of 'perceptual projection'.

projected auditory sensations

Our cultural splitting of 'physical' from 'mental' events is also customary in the area of audition. Within dualist and reductionist theory, sounds are usually thought of as physical events out in space, which must be distinguished from experiences *of* sound 'in the mind' or 'in the brain'. However, the auditory sensors do not detect sounds as such. Rather, they pick up patterns of pressure variation in the air, which produce vibrations at the eardrums, whose intensity, frequency and phase relationships are neurally encoded by hair-cells in the inner ear, and conveyed via the auditory nerve to the brain. But there is no 'experience of sound' in the brain. The experienced sound which results from such stimulation is projected by the brain to the judged location of the acoustic stimulus, resulting in a sound as-perceived out in space.

Manipulations of sound localisation, furthermore, provide a particularly clear example of how perceptual projection can operate in different ways to produce an experience that can be subjectively located *either* 'in the head' *or* 'out in space' (thereby undermining this conventional way of distinguishing what is 'physical' from what is 'experience'). That is, subjective location and extension can change although, in other respects, the experienced sounds are the same (they have the same 'qualia' or experienced characteristics). For example, a symphony orchestra played through stereo speakers appears to be distributed in the space outside one's body. But if the same music is played through stereo headphones, the instruments appear to be distributed around the space inside one's head.

Note how difficult it is to maintain any phenomenal distinction between sounds as-perceived and percepts *of* sound in this last situation. While the orchestral music is subjectively located inside one's head, it seems absurd to claim that there is some additional perception *of* the music 'inside one's mind or brain'. There are neural causes and correlates of this auditory experience, but phenomenologically, the music as-perceived (inside one's head) and the perception *of* music are one and the same! Equally, if one switches back from headphones to stereo speakers, it seems absurd to propose that an additional conscious percept *of* music appears at the precise moment that the music as-perceived switches from being in the head to being out in the world. Nor does it seem plausible to argue that the music as-perceived is *transformed* from being an 'experience' to being something 'physical' as it moves from being in the head to being part of the world as-perceived outside one's body, for apart from its changed location, it undergoes no other change in its 'qualia'.

Studies of 'inside the head locatedness' suggest a far simpler explanation. Laws[7] for example, investigated the acoustic differences between white noise presented through headphones (perceived to be inside the head) and white noise presented through a speaker at a distance of 3 metres (perceived to be out in the world) using probe microphones positioned at the entrance to the auditory canal. This revealed spectral differences (produced largely by the pinnae of the ear) between the white noise presented through the speaker and white noise presented through the headphones. Ingeniously, Laws then constructed an electrical 'equalising' circuit to simulate these spectral differences and inserted this into the headphone circuit. With the headphones 'unequalised', white noise appears to be inside the head irrespective of loudness. With the headphones 'equalised', the white noise not only appears outside the head but actually recedes as the loudness is decreased (a finding that is of potential use in VR design).

Again, it can hardly be claimed that the insertion of an 'equalising' circuit suffices to convert an 'experience' to something 'physical'. Rather, the experiment establishes that spectral distortions produced by the pinnae (or their absence) inform the brain whether or not the source of sound lies beyond the pinnae.[8] The experiential model of the source produced by the brain, i.e. the sound as-perceived, is correspondingly located in the head or beyond the pinnae. Although for different purposes we may refer to the sound being 'physical' or an 'experience' (see note 2), the 'qualia' of the sound, other than its experienced location, do not change. As the Reflexive Model maintains, in terms of phenomenology, a sound as-perceived and a percept *of* a sound are one and the same.

perceptual projection in vision

As we are visually dominant creatures, the contrast between physical, psychological and virtual realities in the visual modality is of particular interest – for it is in this modality, more than any other, that the apparent separation of the external world as-perceived from what is 'in the mind' seems most clear. For example, visually perceived objects extended in the three-dimensional space around our bodies seem to have very different qualities to visual images of those objects. If visual images exemplify the 'contents of consciousness', then how could objects as-seen do likewise?

The reflexive model does not seek to minimise these differences in how objects and images are experienced, for in all probability, they represent discontinuities that from the point of view of human interaction with the world, are as important as they are real. Nevertheless, the fact that phenomenal objects are *experienced to be different* from images does not alter the fact that both phenomenal objects and images are *experienced* - that they are equally, in a sense, dependent on perceptual processing in the brain.

Now the dependence of visual imagery on cerebral processing is widely accepted - it is consonant, after all, with the conventional assumption that images are 'in the mind'. By contrast, the very spatial separation of objects as-perceived from brains as-perceived makes their interdependence more difficult to imagine. Nevertheless, the evidence for cerebral involvement in the 'construction' of objects as-seen, including their seen location in three-dimensional space, is compelling. It is well known, for example, that as an object recedes, its perceived size decreases far less than its optical projection on the retina would suggest (the phenomenon of 'size constancy'). That is, perceived size varies not only with the projected retinal image but also with judged distance - and the judged distance of an object is itself influenced by interpretative cerebral processes operating on retinal size, binocular disparity, ocular convergence, textural gradients, the interposition of other objects, motion parallax and so on.

Indeed, three-dimensional phenomenal space can itself be shown to be, at least in part, a 'construct' of the brain. Common examples of such constructive processes are the experiences of three-dimensionality produced by visual cues suitably arranged on a two-dimensional surface, as in stereoscopes, stereoscopic pictures (which develop into three-dimensional scenes if one looks *through* them rather than *at* them), and holograms. For centuries, artists have

3.5 a painting by peter cresswell using radial perspective

achieved similar effects by the use of aerial perspective, linear perspective, gradients of size and texture, and so on. (See Peter Cresswell's Chapter 8 for a survey of some of these methods.) As Shepard[9] points out, the perception of depth produced in paintings is normally muted by the counteracting information provided by binocular disparity, and by the two-dimensional surround which tells us that we are in fact looking at a two-dimensional surface. However, try inspecting Figure 3.5, a painting by Peter Cresswell, through a rolled-up tube of paper, so as to hide the picture edge. In spite of the use of monocular vision, a strong three-dimensional effect should result!

images and hallucinations

The notion that the world as-seen is in its own way as much a construct of the brain as are visual images, is supported by evidence of functional similarities between visual perception and visual imagery. Indeed, there are grounds for believing that the processes that produce visual percepts and visual images are, to some extent, the same.

Under conditions of poor illumination, for example, it can be very difficult to decide whether what one sees in space is an object, a visual image or an hallucination. Perky[10] found, for example, that objects faintly projected on to a screen were often judged by subjects to be the result of their own imagination, while Kulpe[11] found that dimly lit, fluctuating stimuli were elaborated by subjects into hallucinations which they, nevertheless, judged to be 'real'. Even where subjects are in no doubt that they are imaging or hallucinating, they may report that what they see is located out in space (as opposed to 'inside the head'). This is particularly clear with eidetic imagers who typically report their visual images to be projected on to surfaces in front of their eyes, and which seem to them to be quite distinct from visual memories which they report as being 'inside their head'. When they describe such images, furthermore, they describe *what they see* as opposed to *what they have seen.*[12]

Such abilities, when they occur, are usually found in children. However, Spanos, Ham and Barber report that 1 to 2 per cent of adults appear to have the ability to hallucinate an object in a room when asked to do so without the object being present.[13] Very occasionally, the hallucination is so powerful that it is taken to be more 'real' than that which actually exists. Brugger, for example, reports a clinical case history of a young man of 17 suffering from epilepsy caused by a lesion in his left temporal lobe.[14] He was being treated with anti-convulsant drugs to control the condition and was scheduled for surgery when he experienced an 'heautoscopic' episode (a visual hallucination of his body combined with an out-of-body experience) which was disturbing in the extreme:

> The heautoscopic episode, which is of special interest to the topic of this report, occurred shortly before admission. The patient stopped his phenytoin medication, drank several glasses of beer, stayed in bed the whole of the next day, and in the evening he was found mumbling and confused below an almost completely destroyed large bush just under the window of his room on the third floor. At the local hospital, thoracic and pelvic contusions were noted . . .

The patient gave the following account of the episode: on the respective morning he got up with a dizzy feeling. Turning around, he found himself still lying in bed. He became angry about 'this guy who I knew was myself and who would not get up and thus risked being late for work'. He tried to wake the body in bed first by shouting at it; then by trying to shake it and then repeatedly jumping on his alter ego in the bed. The lying body showed no reaction. Only then did the patient begin to be puzzled about his double existence and become more and more scared by the fact that he could no longer tell which of the two he really was. Several times his body awareness switched from the one standing upright to the one still lying in bed; when in the lying in bed mode he felt quite awake but completely paralysed and scared by the figure of himself bending over and beating him. His only intention was to become one person again and, looking out of the window (from where he could still see his body lying in bed), he suddenly decided to jump out 'in order to stop the intolerable feeling of being divided in two'. At the same time, he hoped that 'this really desperate action would frighten the one in bed and thus urge him to merge with me again'. The next thing he remembers is waking up in pain in the hospital.[15]

In short, this patient mistakenly judged the hallucinated body on the bed to be his real one and tried to get rid of his real body (which he judged to be the hallucination) in order to become unified again – a powerful example of the constructed nature of embodied experience.

how virtual realities fit into the reflexive model

As noted above, virtual realities do not fit easily into either a dualist or reductionist vision of the world. But in the reflexive model they are easy to explain. Under normal circumstances, information detected by the sense organs on the surface of, or within, our bodies is subject to perceptual processing to produce a representation of our external and inner worlds. Within subjective experience this takes the form of a world as-perceived, much of which appears to be extended and located in space. Entities located in the external world (such as cats) are usually experienced to be in the external world, events on the body surface (such as skin damage) are usually experienced to be on the body surface (e.g. in the form of pains), and events originating in the mind or brain (such as thoughts) are loosely experienced to be in the mind or brain. In each case the result of the observer–observed interaction is 'reflexive'.

These biologically determined constructions normally represent the energies and events surrounding and within our bodies well enough to support successful, adaptive interaction with the world. However, misrepresentation is also possible. Hallucinations such as phantom limbs or heautoscopic experiences are cases where 'inner' information is mistakenly projected on to the external world. In the manner shown in Figure 3.6, virtual reality systems artificially engage the same normal, constructive processes (including perceptual projection) to produce experienced, artificial worlds. In so far as the information input from VR systems is similar to the 3D information supplied by the normal world, they will be experienced as facsimiles of the normal world located and extended in 3D space.

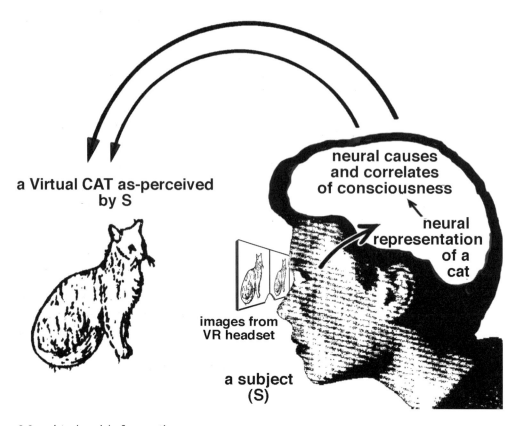

3.6 a virtual model of perception

physical, psychological and virtual realities

Within the reflexive model the physical world *as-experienced* is *part of* the contents of consciousness. The contents of consciousness are not in some separate place or space 'in the mind' or 'in the brain'. That is, no phenomenal distinction can be drawn between what we normally think of as the 'physical world' and the 'world as-experienced'. With our eyes open the 'physical world' *is* what we experience. This provides a completely different view of the mind/body relationship.[16] Suffice it to say that once experienced physical reality is included within this extended view of psychological reality it no longer makes sense to split experienced physical reality from psychological reality (in the ways shown in Figure 3.1). Some aspects of psychological reality (such as thoughts) have no clear phenomenological extension or location in space and appear to be relatively insubstantial. However, much of psychological reality (the experienced external world) does seem to have spatial location and extension and is experienced to have substantial properties such as hardness and weight. The *way* such properties are experienced depends on the perceptual systems of the observer, as well as on the properties of the observed. The phenomenal world constructed by the mind or brain from information detected by the sense organs is, at once, psychological *and* physical.

Note, however, that this *experienced* 'physical world' may be very different from the world described by Physics, for example, in terms of Relativity Theory or in terms of Quantum Mechanics. That is, the *experienced* 'physical world' is just one, biologically determined, representation of energies and events surrounding and within our bodies which Physics, Chemistry, Biology, Psychology and other sciences might represent in very different ways. Within the reflexive model these are alternative representations of some underlying reality or 'thing-itself'. The relative utility of these representations can only be judged *in terms of the purposes for which they are to be used.*

Virtual realities are artificial worlds as-experienced. Like the everyday world that we take to be 'real', they are phenomenal models constructed by the mind or brain, in this case of the information fed to the sense organs by VR equipment. This dependence on VR equipment loosens the constraints of the natural world. Some VR systems might nevertheless provide a facsimile of the natural world; examples include flight simulators, and systems that provide training for surgeons in a virtual operating theatre. Other VR systems produce experienced worlds that are entirely fantastic or fanciful.

The human ability to represent actual states of affairs along with the ability to image or dream hypothetical or imaginary worlds is as old as human history; much intellectual endeavour, now as then, is devoted to the need to distinguish the one from the other. VR systems extend the domain of our imagination, blurring the boundaries between what is imaginary and what is real. Their impact on human life will depend on how convincing they become.

peering into the crystal ball

It is notoriously difficult to predict how far new technologies will develop or what their social impact will be. However, let us suppose that VR worlds eventually become so convincing that they are no longer clearly distinguishable from actual worlds (this blurring of imagination into reality already exists, for some, in vivid dreams). This would *relativise* what we normally take to be 'reality': that is, the everyday 'physical world' as-perceived would be seen as one (biologically given) construction out of many possible constructions. For some this might be threatening. In the development of Western thought, human ethnocentricity has already been shaken by the revelations that the Earth is not the centre of the Universe (Copernicus); that man is not the sole focus of creation (Darwin); and that the conscious ego might in some respects be driven by a dynamic unconscious self (Freud).[17] The *relativisation of experienced reality* might remove the last prop of our ethnocentric assumptions, adding impetus to the historic search for a firmer, more universal ground.

The ability to engage in unlimited, seemingly real, imaginary worlds might also present real dangers to those who are immersed in them – the most obvious one being a loss in the ability to distinguish what is imaginary from what is real. That is, 'VR junkies' may begin to lose contact with the actual world in which they are embodied, and lose interest in the deepening exploration of its nature, or of their own nature.

Engaging in a world of surrogate relationships in cyberspace has similar potential and dangers.

On the one hand one might practise engaging in relationships without the risks attending actual relationships. On the other hand one might engage in virtual relationships as a way of avoiding actual relationships, again losing the possibility of a deepening exploration of their nature.

janet's dream

I do not usually tell personal stories in theoretical papers. However, two days after being invited to give this paper to the Embodied Knowledge and Virtual Space Conference, an event occurred which bears directly on its theme. I have decided to tell it as it was.

I had not mentioned anything about the conference to my partner Janet. But that night (about four in the morning) I was suddenly woken by a shout. Janet was sitting up in bed, clearly disoriented. She had been dreaming about being enclosed in a bubble. I asked her what the bubble meant. After some thought she said it had something to do with virtual reality. Given that I had not mentioned VR to her, this seemed odd – so we switched on the light and talked about her dream.

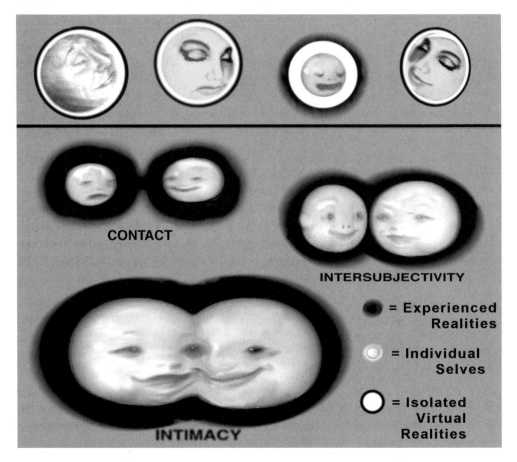

3.7 relationships between individual selves and virtual realities

In the dream there were many people enclosed in bubbles. These bubbles were virtual worlds existing entirely 'in people's minds'. In their own way these were absorbing and beguiling. While people remained in these separate, virtual worlds they might engage in virtual relationships, but there was no genuine contact between them. They remained in their own individual bubbles. In 'real' life people were also in bubbles. But for these people, a genuine engagement with embodied being and an openness to life made their bubbles semi-permeable. Here there was the possibility of genuine exploration with others. Being semi-permeable, these bubbles allowed for contact, intersubjectivity and, sometimes, for genuine intimacy (see Figure 3.7).

To begin with, people had a choice about whether or not to enter into virtual reality or to engage in embodied life. But, gradually, people began to separate into two distinct streams. As the virtual worlds became more convincing, those who chose to spend most of their time in them began to seal themselves off from embodied life, and to lose the ability to distinguish the virtual from the real. Eventually, they became lost in endless games. By contrast, people who chose to explore the potential of embodied being and to remain exposed to the 'realities' of life gradually expanded their experience to become more deeply grounded in their own nature.

In her dream, Janet found herself in a 'virtual bubble' in the wrong stream. With a shout she burst out of the bubble to join the other stream. Make of it what you will.

references

Blauert, J., *Spatial Hearing: the Psychophysics of Human Sound Localization*, Cambridge, Mass., MIT Press, 1983.

Brugger, P., 'Heautoscopy, epilepsy, and suicide', *Journal of Neurology, Neurosurgery, and Psychiatry*, 57, 1994, pp. 838–839.

Haber, R.N., 'Twenty years of haunting eidetic imagery: where's the ghost?', *Behavioral and Brain Sciences*, 2, 1979, pp. 583–619.

Kulpe, O., 'Über die Objectivirung und Subjectivirung von Sinneseindruken', *Philosophische Studien*, 19, 1902, pp. 508–536.

Laws, P., 'On the problem of distance hearing and the localization of auditory events inside the head', Dissertation, Technische Hochschule, Aachen. Cited in Blauert, J., *Spatial Hearing: the Psychophysics of Human Sound Localization*, Cambridge, Mass., MIT Press, [1972], 1983.

Penfield, W. and Rassmussen,T.B., *The Cerebral Cortex of Man*, Princeton, NJ, Princeton University Press, 1950.

Perky, C.W., 'An experimental study of imagination', *American Journal of Psychology*, 21, 1910, pp. 422–452.

Shepard, R.N., 'Ecological constraints on internal representation: Resonant kinematics of perceiving, imagining, thinking, and dreaming', third James J. Gibson Memorial Lecture given at Cornell University, 2 October 1983.

Sherman, R.A., *Phantom Pain*, New York, Plenum Publishing Corporation, 1996.

Spanos, N.P., Ham, M.H. and Barber, T.X., 'Suggested ("hypnotic") visual hallucinations: experimental and phenomenological data', *Journal of Abnormal Psychology*, 81, 1973, pp. 96–106.

Tarnas, R., *The Passion of the Western Mind*, New York, Ballantyne Books, 1993.

Velmans, M., 'Consciousness, brain, and the physical world', *Philosophical Psychology*, 3,1990, pp. 77–99.

Velmans, M., 'A reflexive science of consciousness', in *Experimental and Theoretical Studies of Consciousness*, CIBA Foundation Symposium 174, Chichester, Wiley, 1993, pp. 81–99.

Velmans, M., 'What and where are conscious experiences?', in Velmans, M. (ed.), *The Science of Consciousness: Psychological, Neuropsychological and Clinical Reviews*, London, Routledge, 1996.

notes

1. Velmans, 1990, 1993, 1996.

2. In the reflexive model the 'cat as-experienced' is *phenomenologically identical* to one's 'experience *of* the cat'. However, these referring expressions are somewhat different in meaning. All experiences result from an interaction of observed events and energies with the perceptual apparatus of an observer. These different expressions direct our attention to *either* the observed *or* to the observer. When we refer to the 'cat' or to the 'cat as-experienced', we are usually more interested in the nature of the observed. When we refer to an 'experience *of* the cat' we are usually more interested in the involvement of the observer. This does not alter the fact that *only one experience* results from this observer–observed interaction – a phenomenal cat out in the world.

3. Velmans, 1990.

4. Velmans, 1990.

5. Sherman, 1996.

6. Penfield and Rassmussen, 1950.

7. Laws, 1972.

8. See Blauert, 1983, for a review.

9. Shepard, 1983.

10. Perky, 1910.

11. Kulpe, 1902.

12. Haber, 1979.

13. Spanos, Ham and Barber, 1973.

14. Brugger, 1994.

15. Ibid., pp. 838–839.

16. Discussed in more depth in Velmans 1990, 1993, 1996.

17. Cf. Tarnas, 1993, p. 422.

part two

nature and virtue

chapter 4

nature = x

notes on spinozist ethics

andy goffey

The Western tradition of philosophy is finding itself increasingly challenged by the complexities of the current epoch. The tranquil certainties of a solid foundation for all possible knowledge are being shaken by the proliferation of vastly different, competing and mutually exclusive paradigms of knowledge. The increasingly sophisticated means by which these knowledges are disseminated in culture, and the absence of any clear idea of the ends to which they may be put, beyond their employment in view of the axioms of capital accumulation and/or state control, also confront long-cherished beliefs about the origin and value of science. Since its inception in Ancient Greece, philosophy has demonstrated a persistent desire to find a solid foundation for all kinds of knowledge, that is to say, to find the principles which make knowledges true, and by extension, necessary. However, in the recent modern or postmodern periods it has been argued that the 'arbitrating' role of philosophy, its ability to judge the truth claims of different domains of knowledge, is no longer tenable. Philosophy cannot offer the foundation it seeks. The 'postmodern' era is marked by the end of the master narratives, the end of the stories the West has told itself about the progressive march of enlightenment towards the absolute truth and to a rational mastery over the unknown forces of nature. According to the French philosopher, Jean-François Lyotard, in place of these grand stories we have an irreducible series of little stories which compete to make their truth heard as truth. The suspension of the Kantian tribunal of pure reason yields a veritable Babel for which even the metaphor of the text is probably too consistent and homogeneous.

We need not ask whether an infinite plurality or multiplicity of language games or stories actually exists, because the very idea of such infinite disparities simply presents us with a limit situation, the merit of which is to force us to think the limit of the thinkable. It is, however, pertinent to ask what the ethical implications of such an idea are, for it is evident that infinite complexity imposes an extreme tension on any attempt to make things 'hold together'. In this sense the decline of a single standard by which to measure the truth can easily lead to the return of a situation which resembles the famous Hobbesian description of the war of all against all, touchstone of modern political theories of 'possessive individualism':[1] if dissensus is the norm then only the intervention of some outside force can produce order.

Juxtaposed to such a description of the current situation of knowledge, the work of the Dutch philosopher Spinoza might appear anachronistic, if not irrelevant. His infamous book *The Ethics*, with its ambitious ontological construction of nature as an absolutely infinite substance and its correlative appeal to the deductive procedures of geometry, seems the very antithesis of the nuanced concern with the proliferating fractal diversity of heterogeneous language games. His philosophy of immanence, with its correlative refusal to establish an ontological priority for the human subject or for the mind over the body, is the paradigm of a monism which has often been regarded as precluding the consideration of any kind of plurality at all. And yet for numerous reasons the Spinozist optic on nature is back on the philosophical agenda.

It was mentioned above that one of the key features of philosophical discourse lies in its attempt at finding the first principles of knowledge. The principles which such an endeavour uncovers account for the necessity of something's being true. It follows from the discovery of such principles that one can also deduce what is the best way to act in any situation. In other words the ethical is traditionally founded on first principles.[2] The ascetic position which is usually ascribed to philosophers often results from the founding of knowledge in a principle which privileges mind over body or, indeed, certain human attributes over others. For a long time, 'God' has been the name of this principle: the two attributes which Descartes attributes to God being infinite understanding and infinite will. It is thus possible to argue that in philosophy an ethical discourse is confused with a theological problem of morality, a problem which results in the nihilistic denigration of what does exist in favour of an ideal realm that does not. There are, of course, other names for a first principle, other 'signifiers'. 'Science' is one, 'The Subject' another, and the formal similarity between them makes us ask if the ethical is understood today in the same way as it was in periods when the belief in philosophy or science as providing principles was still in ascendance. In the human sciences the overall trend has been that of exposing the interested nature of scientific rationality, after the acknowledgement that in laicised societies it is science which is the privileged vector of truth. But one must ask oneself on what basis, in the name of what principle, such an exposition has been carried out.

Current discussions concerning subjectifying or objectifying tendencies in rationality – whether in a Foucauldian optic, feminist philosophy, the grand pessimism of a 'dialectic of enlightenment' – suggest that questions concerning truth, value and so on, must be grasped within a firmly historicist framework. Indeed the limit situation described above offers one extreme example of this trend in thought. The exact manner in which the historical – not to mention social, racial and gender – specificity of truth and value is to be conceived is a matter open for debate. But once the historical specificity of truth has been acknowledged, and the limitations of the concept of identity exposed, the question arises of what one is to do and how one is to do it without replicating the very structures of domination which one has already so convincingly criticised. In general the current appeal to the ethical is invoked on the basis of a 'recognition' of difference. The ethical, in this sense, is about an ostensible right to difference. But what exactly might the content of such a notion be? And how exactly can one guarantee that differences are 'respected' or 'recognised'? Wouldn't this listless relativism fall over with the first newcomer who proclaims, as his or her difference, a refusal to acknowledge the other's difference?[3] This is not to suggest that the intentions motivating an appeal to ethical criteria are misplaced, as it is not at all a question of intentions, for the real issue lies somewhere else entirely. What point alleviating the alleged pessimism or cynicism of a Foucault if it is by an appeal to 'real' feelings; or what point attacking the destructive capacity of science for its will to dominate nature if it is by an appeal to some individualist criteria of common sense? For, as Deleuze showed nearly thirty years ago, difference is something which no amount of representation, no amount of mediation by subjective consciousness, will ever manage to pacify, and the inconvenience with which any ethics has to deal is precisely that.

why spinoza?

So why Spinoza? Centuries before issues of all sorts – euthanasia, abortion, the environment, capital investments, consumerism – started to be framed in 'ethical' terms, Spinoza endeavoured to set out an ethics of far more positive ambitions. His ethics was one that would not fall into the mealy-mouthed respect for difference which so frequently demonstrates only its inability to think of anything in a positive light.[4] Spinoza's *Ethics* develops a 'monist' ontology in which nature is defined as an absolutely infinite substance consisting in an infinity of attributes, and in which, as already indicated, humans are no longer defined in terms of some exceptional privilege with regard to nature, becoming instead modes of this single substance.[5] But why should such an argument be of interest to us today?

We noted above that the complexities of (post)modernity can easily be confused with the Hobbesian war of all against all. Such a similarity should not surprise, for Hobbes's 'possessive individualism' in which every individual pursues his or her individual self-interest is an accurate enough description of a liberal, market-oriented morality. When Spinoza describes the common order of nature he develops the concept of the *conatus* to account for the effort by which beings struggle to maintain their existence, an existence defined in terms of a certain power or capacity to act. In this his theory resembles that of Hobbes. However this theory differs from the Hobbesian war of all against all because for Spinoza this effort extends beyond the realm of the merely human: all beings are defined in terms of an effort to maintain a power of existing and acting. Furthermore, as an 'individual' is defined in terms of both body and idea, it is legitimate to argue that ideas themselves have a certain material force or power. This is a point of considerable importance given the resurgence of interest – since Foucault – in questions of power. Spinozist naturalism sets out an early theory of power in terms of a norm rather than a law, in which power is grasped as productive rather than constraining. Indeed, as the work of Gilles Deleuze and Antonio Negri has shown, Spinozist philosophy is a form of philosophy that operates entirely in terms of power.[6]

Another reason why Spinoza is of interest lies in the manner in which he constructs his ontology and the place that mathematics has in this construction. Of course Spinoza was not the first to vaunt the mathematical as such – ever since the inscription 'let none enter here who is not a geometer' made its first appearance on the entrance to Plato's academy, the mathematical has entertained privileged relations with philosophy. But when *The Ethics* sets out to demonstrate the necessary existence of an absolutely infinite substance and later to explore the ramified complications of the affective life of beings, using the definitions, axioms, propositions and so on more characteristic of Euclidean geometry, it is clear that the mathematical comes to occupy an entirely unique position which may not be found in the work of other philosophers, even Descartes, who in many senses inaugurates the modern project of a *mathesis universalis*.[7] How is the deductive rationality of the famous geometrical method to be evaluated, particularly given the well-established implication of such rationality in technical-scientific structures of domination and control, and the allegedly disembodied ideal that it promotes?

Finally there is the question of the position of Spinoza in the history of philosophy. Such a benignly academic question is less anodyne than one might think. Theorists of the decline of master narratives must be understood as setting themselves against the arch systematiser of the history of philosophy, Hegel. For Hegel, history was the process by which Spirit becomes conscious of itself in the absolute: the end of history is this point, at which the dialectical labour of the negative terminates. Hegel is also the key philosopher of the subject, for what determines the movement of history is precisely the scission of the finite and the infinite in/of subjectivity. Hegel temporalises – historicises – the development of truth. In one sense, then, the current, entirely laudable concern to situate knowledge, truth claims, and so on, in historically specific contexts inherits aspects of Hegelian philosophy[8] and in a very general way, one might interpret the current interest in ethics as resulting precisely from the absence of any clear sense of which way to go next. For the history of philosophy in the Hegelian sense, the position of Spinoza is unambiguous: Hegel says 'without Spinoza, no philosophy', because he thought that there was a continuous line of development leading from Descartes, through Spinoza, to himself. In other words, if Descartes discovers the ego, the thinking substance, then Spinoza, in making substance absolute, creates the possibility for Hegel to make the subject absolute. But Spinoza does not actually think in terms of a subject and this, according to Hegel, is his biggest defect. However, as a study by Pierre Macherey has argued,[9] Hegel completely misreads Spinoza, and this tends to imply that in fact Spinozist philosophy cannot be incorporated into the odyssey of the Spirit which forms the legacy of Hegelian thought. Spinoza's *Ethics* is a text which must be experienced if the nature of its ethics is to be comprehended.

foundation, nature, mathematics

In a broad sense, the philosophical appeal to a foundation or to a ground, to a first principle, is constituted with a decisive reference to nature. Indeed metaphysics may be understood as a science of being in which being is understood in relation to physics. If philosophy is constituted, for Aristotle, on the basis of physics, one must inevitably ask what is understood for the Ancient Greeks by physics. This, of course, is the approach taken by Heidegger in his essay on the notion of *phusis* in Aristotle. Very broadly speaking, nature or *phusis* is understood in terms of what Heidegger might call the movement of *presencing* – nature itself is the 'permanence' which subsists throughout change. Being as being present. There is therefore a sort of immediate experience of truth, certainly more evident in the pre-Socratic philosophers, in which it is understood not as a matter of the validity of judgements but in terms of the visible symmetries and regularities of movement and change, a 'phenomenology' of experience. Indeed a principle is, for Aristotle, what is at the origin of the movement of a thing.[10]

In the modern period, whilst one can still discern the same project of founding different genres of knowledge, analogous to the aims of *meta*-physics, the conception of nature has radically changed. It is for this reason that modern scientific explanations – beginning with Galileo – meet with such resistance. For since Galileo, nature is described as a book written in the language of mathematics. We no longer have the visible order of the universe such as it transpires in Aristotelian physics, but an invisible, mathematical order of 'laws'. This shift has been described very aptly by Koyre in terms of the shift from the closed world to the infinite universe.[11] The discoveries of Kepler, Copernicus, Galileo and so on may be understood in terms of an attempt to break with the phenomenological evidence of sensory perception so that what is most important, the essential, no longer figures in terms of any immediate reference. The early modern project, such as it becomes defined in the philosophy of Descartes, is a *mathesis universalis*. Mathematics provides the standard by which all truths may be measured.[12] The key point though is not simply that the mathematical is paradigmatic, but rather that the 'natural light of human reason' forms the principle locus of truth. The subject is the place in which truth is unveiled.

It has been a source of continuing wonder since the time of Kepler, Galileo and so on, that the mathematical is so infinitely exact. If mathematics can become paradigmatic of all knowledge and if nature can be deemed mathematical, it is precisely because of the necessity of which it is the guarantor. However, if for Descartes the *Cogito* becomes central, the rigorous necessity of mathematical laws required, in fear of compromising religion, a God not submitted to them. The image of a God submitted to the 'laws' of number was considered theologically ruinous: wouldn't it contradict the infinity of God's will to say that He knows the truths of mathematics in the same way as do His creatures, and for that reason is constrained by their necessity? Before Descartes, Kepler deemed mathematical truths to be univocal, which means simply that they are known in the same way by both God and His creatures. Evidently, this univocity implies the potential knowability of the absolute,[13] paving the way for the arguments of Spinoza, for whom the univocity of being is the direct counterpart of the absence of a foundational logic.[14]

Of course, it must be acknowledged that not all domains of knowledge have been submitted to the formalising rigours of the *mathesis*. The question as to whether all domains of knowledge are indeed formalisable in this way is perhaps less important than the material efficacy that such a dream possesses. In the Heideggerian optic, this dream is equated with the domination of nature by man, because man as subject appears as the foundation of knowledge. It does little to say that in the modern era God is dead, because with the Cartesian *Cogito* – and more pertinently, with the Hegelian subject – 'man' may be said to have taken over the space left vacant. The fact that all domains of knowledge are not mathematically formalised frequently makes itself felt in the teleological nature of the explanations advanced by scientists for a lack or deficiency in knowledge. Imperfections in the understanding which scientists possess of, say, genetic inheritance are explained away in terms of a knowledge not yet acquired owing to 'technical limitations'. In this way the possibility that a system may never become a closed perfect whole is conjured away in the teleology of a knowledge to come.

We can ignore the question of whether all domains of knowledge are formalisable[15] and ask instead whether or not the kind of systematic rationality exemplified in mathematics is itself complete or not. The phenomenological philosopher Edmund Husserl argued some time before the famous theorem of Kurt Gödel that the *telos* of perfection enveloped in mathematical reason was immanent to human subjectivity and thus that one could indeed make formally explicit the complete deductibility of a logical system. If Gödel's theorem shows that with regard to mathematics no system can ever prove itself by itself, Husserlian phenomenology could claim that the ideal of perfect deductibility was nevertheless entirely valid as ideal. Such a possibility is extremely reminiscent, on an epistemological plane, of the position of inherent culpability in which the Kantian conception of the moral law places the subject.[16] In general it suggests that systematic rationality, incarnated by mathematics and founded in the subject, is inseparable from a horizon that we are always approaching but that is always receding.

the a-subjective

Spinozist philosophy is usually held to be in continuity with the Cartesian project of a *mathesis universalis*, an argument which is superficially borne out by Spinoza's early endeavour to demonstrate the principles of Cartesian philosophy in a more rigorous and systematic way. This is a view confirmed not only by Hegel in his scattered writings on Spinoza but also by Heidegger, in his essay on Schelling.[17] Now whilst Descartes can be seen as setting out from the intrinsically modest nature of the human subject which is, as finite being, unable to know anything of God, Spinoza – in a manner analogous to Leibniz – sets out, more or less, from infinity and affirms the integral knowability of God, or 'an absolutely infinite substance'. Some of the implications of this move only become apparent if we consider Kantian and post-Kantian philosophy. Kant criticised what he saw as a dogmatic pretension to know things as they are in themselves,[18] a criticism which, if not always aimed at Spinoza, could certainly be inflected in this direction. But the paradox of Kantian philosophy is that the knowing subject which for Descartes was defined as a thinking substance (irremediably split from the body as extended substance), is little more than a regulative idea, a sort of function inexplicably organising sensory intuition and conceptual understanding, but of which in itself there was no possible intuition. Little surprise then that Romantic aesthetics takes its impetus from this peculiar absence in subjectivity. As Lacoue-Labarthe and Nancy have argued in their study of German Romanticism:

> in default of a subject present to itself in an originary intuition and capable of organising *more geometrico*, from the mathesis of its initial evidence, the totality of knowledge and of the world; the system proper, nevertheless called for by Kant with all his might (as the notes gathered in the *Opus Posthumum* testify) doesn't cease to lack in the very place where it would be required. The hiatus introduced into the heart of the subject itself will have exacerbated, but in vain, the will to systematicity.[19]

Such an appeal to subjectivity in the endeavour at founding knowledge is argued to be an acknowledgement of 'man's' 'constitutive finitude'. Indeed, recent philosophy has made a great deal of the finite nature of human existence: taking his cue from Kant's view that it is impossible to know things as they are in themselves, Heidegger – from whom the phrase 'constitutive finitude' comes – endeavours to show how accepting the fact that we will die is what makes for the possibility of authentic existence. Conversely, the 'threat' inherent in techno-science is that ignoring limits is said to induce disastrous consequences. One may find many versions of the fatal errors which a thirst for knowledge with a disregard for limits incurs: think of Goethe's Faust, for example. At the same time, however, one must also note that the Heideggerian optic led to a disastrous identification of authentic experience with Nazi ideology. It would be relatively easy to show how the 'noumenal' status of the subject in Kant's work – the fact that, as we have mentioned already, its status as an in-itself prevents it from being known – simply replicates the theological gesture that separates this world from the beyond, such that any ethical injunction to 'know thyself' can only be construed as a Nietzschean will to nothingness. Given the appeal in Spinoza to the knowability of the absolute, does it not simply repeat the errors which find so many representations in modern science?

As previously mentioned,[20] Spinozist philosophy demonstrates a remarkable hostility towards manners of thinking which conserve a central place for the subject, which make the universe revolve around the human, and which would see in the mathematical the fundamental expression of subjectivity. One does not have the sense that, with Spinoza, there is something special about 'man' which would give him some sort of privileged point of view on the universe. Indeed, the taken for granted distinction which is usually made between events that occur outside us in the world and the manner in which the mind comprehends them internally is a distinction with a merely relative status. The image of the supremacy of the subject encoded in, for example, Quattrocento perspective space, is not one that would find a theoretical counterpart in Spinozist philosophy. But what constitutes the real difficulty is precisely the key point of Spinoza's philosophy: that of thinking how we are a part of nature, open on all sides, rather than an 'empire in an empire'.

Spinozist nature is absolute, it is an absolutely infinite substance, this absoluteness consisting in its 'possession' of all attributes. We know two of these attributes – thought and extension, precisely those which Descartes hypostasised in his conception of humans as being thinking and material things. But there Spinoza differs radically: the clear distinction introduced by Cartesian dualism disappears in Spinoza's nature, and the moral superiority of mind over body ruled out in advance, because there is no superiority of one attribute over another. Humans are considered modes of this substance, modes of extended matter and of thought, at the minimum. One of the implications of Spinoza's conception of nature is obviously then that humans are inextricably caught up in infinite chains of cause and effect, 'everything' in nature thus being connected. But because of this situation, finite beings find themselves determined from the outside *ad infinitum* with all the necessity usually associated with a rigorous mechanical determinism.

How, under such conditions, are humans ever to be considered free? If they are determined from the outside *ad infinitum*, can they ever say that they are the 'authors' of their own actions, thoughts, etcetera? In fact, Spinoza suggests that it is possible for them to form adequate ideas about their situation. This suggests a somewhat idealist position, but such is not the case, because for Spinoza every idea has its exact corporeal correlate: there is a mind–body parallelism. Thus to a state of mechanical causality in which one is determined from the outside, there corresponds inadequate ideas (imaginary ideas), whilst to adequate ideas there must, logically, correspond a state of internal self-causality. Now Spinoza tells us that only an absolutely infinite substance exists of its own accord, is *causa sui*. This suggests that if 'humans', or modes of substance, can have adequate ideas it is because they can, in some sense *know* the absolute. The whole question is *how*, because as already suggested, the drive to know the absolute is formally similar to what Freud understands by the death drive – or even to what Nietzsche thinks of as nihilism.

How is one to grasp oneself as part of nature? One thing is certain: because the distinction of mind and body with Spinoza is merely relative and because there is no foundational subject, the usual ascetic process which consists in disengaging thinking from affectivity will not work. But this does not mean there is no process of abstraction at all. We should use Spinoza's term 'mode' as a guide: it is deliberately impersonal because one of the obstacles to having adequate ideas is a kind of anthropologising tendency to separate subject and object. Here is a paradox: emotion, affect, is experienced as the most intimately personal of things and yet, Spinoza implies, it is also objective. Topologically speaking, the inside is a fold of the outside.[21] One can also understand why Spinoza might deem the mathematical appropriate for the construction and exploration of the abstract plane of thought which forms an infinitesimal part of absolutely infinite nature: it is precisely because it forces humans to change their habits of thinking which – implicitly or explicitly – situate them apart from nature, an empire in an empire.

x = nature, ethics = f (x)

The aim of Spinoza's *Ethics* is to liberate humans from the situation in which their finitude seems to place them. That this project takes the form of an ethics might surprise, given the necessity which reigns everywhere in nature. The fact of the matter is, says Spinoza, that if we were born free we would never form an idea of what is good or bad. Whilst nothing guarantees that our ideas of good and bad are themselves good or bad, the fact that we form such ideas testifies to the importance of maintaining a margin or latitude in a capacity to act. The whole question is whether the ideas we have are adequate ones. The brief answer is in general no: the fact of finitude means that our ideas fail to express their causes which must in fact be considered immanent to them. For this reason, it is 'natural' for humans to confuse ethical problems with the morality of absolute values, Good and Evil, and the moral law which accompanies such notions. But a naturalism of the Spinozist type, on the other hand, has no room for the morality of a law, such that even if one can acknowledge the existence of a natural tendency to form such ideas, the Spinozist conception of nature offers a way of grasping why these ideas come about, and thus why they are not absolutely necessary, as adequate ideas must be.

As Deleuze has argued in *Spinoza Practical Philosophy*, Spinoza energetically combats the Adamic idea of original sin and the entire theology of culpability which it inevitably implies.

From the point of view of the discussion here, this necessitates that Spinozist philosophy is not one that holds 'constitutive finitude' to define anything essential about humans. To feel oneself a part of nature, and not an empire in an empire therefore implies an entirely different relation of finite and infinite. The fact that Spinoza considers there to be a parallelism between mind and body is vital here, because if adequate ideas correspond to a certain affective state of the body, and if this state must be grasped in terms of the immanence of a cause (which cause, as we have seen, can only ever be nature), then the usual negative relation between finite and infinite and the conception of morality it implies, ceases to pertain. It is no longer pertinent to specify in advance what is good and what is bad. Evidently then, if humans cannot help but make ethical distinctions between good and bad, our sense of ethical behaviour is a function of the kind of experience which we have of nature.

'We experience ourselves as eternal.' Spinoza's formulation of the manner in which we apprehend ourselves in nature suggests an end to all movement and change. Why? It was argued above that mathematical idealities could be characterised by their infinite exactness or their infinite identity, which means their absolute indifference to spatial and temporal locatedness. 2 + 2 = 4 everywhere and for all time. This infinite identity can be read as a thoroughly laicised version of eternity. Movement and change, becoming, tends to imply at most finite identity – something is the same for a period, it endures and then changes state. If one imagines that the substance of something is what enables it to be identified as being the same throughout a series of changes, which is to say if one maintains the traditional conception of substance, one will also realise that it indicates a state of potential mathematisability.

Is Spinozist substance, and thus nature, to be understood in this way? Certainly the geometrical method invoked by Spinoza lets us think that this might be the case. Is the absolute infinity of substance the same thing as the infinite identity of mathematical ideas? But from our more limited point of view the question is that of knowing whether having adequate ideas is, analogous to Descartes, equivalent to thinking mathematically? The answer here too is a strict no. As has already been suggested, Spinoza's geometrical method offers a manner of constructing an abstract plane of thought which envelops nature. This is not the same thing as grounding nature in the mathematical. Indeed, Spinoza himself says that number is a poor way of imagining the *quantities* which define nature.[22] Why is this so important? It is because we completely fail to grasp the singularity of anything at all if we say that one thing differs from another numerically.[23] The difficulty which mathematics poses then becomes this: it is acknowledged that mathematics is possessed of extreme exactitude and yet we do not want to say that it defines the essence of things. This makes numbers into names of things and it makes the efficacy of maths derive from something else. Since Descartes this efficacy is determined as deriving from the subject.

For Spinoza, rather than seeking to base mathematical rationality in a subject, the problem is that of having an adequate idea of quantity, which is to say too, of experiencing the power or potential which constitutes the essence of substance. The geometrical method and its formal procedure of deduction derives its own power from the fact that it forces thought to develop a conception of God or nature which goes against the most deeply ingrained of habits of thought. Such is the role of the mathematical: it is not at all a question of identifying something but of differentiating – intransitively. This procedure is what may be called a procedure of *individuation* or what Deleuze and Guattari call the construction of a body without organs, becoming or multiplicity.[24] Indeed, Deleuze and Guattari themselves ask, in *A Thousand Plateaus*, 'is not Spinoza's *Ethics* the great book of the B.w.O.?'.[25] The paradox of the theory of Bodies without Organs – which is, likewise, the paradox of Spinoza's *Ethics* – is that one must maintain both that it is an entirely artificial construct, the product of an extreme formalism and that it is entirely unformed, natural.

The whole of Western philosophy demonstrates a remarkable tendency to conceive of God by analogy with 'man'. When applied to nature, such a tendency simply amounts to its anthropomorphisation. If, as Spinoza maintains, to every idea there corresponds a body, and if the error of philosophy is of thinking God in terms of the (male) human, then an adequate idea of God – and thus of nature – will correspond to a body without organs. If Spinoza uses the geometrical procedures in the construction of his philosophy, this is only because it offers the surest manner of not conceiving nature according to in-built prejudices. But does it not amount to the sanctioning of mathematical formalism, the complete indifference to the matter out of which truths are constructed? Not if one bears in mind the reference to individuation rather than to individuals. This is perhaps the most difficult point to grasp.

The absolute immediacy of sensory experience, its rich and diverse complexity, is what defines it as 'individual'. We always set out from this experience. Funnily enough the sensory-certainty of *this* experience, the most immediate and individual of experiences, is also argued – by Hegel in the *Phenomenology of Spirit* – to be the hollowest and emptiest of experiences. Why? Because, he tells us, of the formal replicability of the deictic shifter:[26] *this* experience could be no matter what experience. Now from this formal property of language, one could argue, as does Hegel, to a dialectical relation of the individual and the universal (i.e.. from the particular specificity of this (sensory) experience to its intelligibility under the universality of reason). All determination, says Hegel, is negation. How are things from the point of view of individuation or becoming? As already seen, with Hegel, the movement of thinking refers back to a subject, such that any experience testifies to a split between the objective, what exists outside, and the subjective, or what exists inside. There is no such subject in Spinozism: *this* experience introduces an infinitesimal differentiation of substance. One might say that thoughts are subject to being formed – not relatively to a subject which as it were pre-exists them as form-giver but *absolutely* as the ideas which 'subjects' are in the attribute of thought, and to which bodies correspond in the attribute of extension (to name but one other of the infinity of attributes of which nature is composed). It would be more accurate to make this thought and this body lie in an impersonal and inappropriable zone of interference between other thoughts and bodies. This is to say that even the thought which we are is inseparable from every other thought, and so on *ad infinitum*. There is an imperceptible movement from one to another, with no rigid limit between. *This* experience is always an encounter, but nothing guarantees in advance that the encounter of two bodies or two ideas will produce a change or movement. That depends on the degree of power each envelops.

Emmanuel Levinas[27] has argued that nothing could be further from his own efforts to reverse the metaphysical – and ethical – prioritisation of the Same over the Other, as Spinozism. It is not clear how the transcendence of the Other, described by Levinas in terms of its incarnation in the face, could distinguish an other from Other, most particularly because it is so easy to extract a few sensible resemblances from a face, thus crushing its alterity under a wave of sameness. But can we say that Spinozist nature marks the death of others? If we forget that Spinozist substance doesn't ground anything in the sense which has been analysed above, then the answer is yes. On the other hand the formal dissimilarity of Spinoza's conception of substance to that held by Descartes, for example, prevents us from considering its absolute infinity as the infinity of identity, such as it is understood by Husserl, for example. Thus it cannot be considered in terms of the formal replication of the same everywhere but in terms of the purely immanent experience of difference. And more precisely, as Spinozist substance is quantity, and as it is not quantity in the sense of the extensive magnitudes dealt with by geometry, it must be an intensive quantity – a continuum of intensities. *This* experience forces thought by virtue of its unannullable intensity.

Spinoza's *Ethics* doesn't offer a prescriptive sense to ethical behaviour: deducing what is the best way to act in any situation belongs to another philosophical vocabulary. Defining experience or situations in terms of intensities makes the ethical a matter of thinking the continuum of events of nature, and this is asymptotic to representation.

notes

1. This is not to suggest that Lyotard is a kind of postmodern Hobbes – although recent discussions of his work occasionally tend to point in this direction. See, for example, Arthur Kroker's *Possessed Individualism*, London, Macmillan, 1992. It would be more pertinent to consider Hobbes's own theory of language and the extreme conventionalism it implies if the comparison were to be seriously made. See on this point Étienne Balibar, *Lieux et noms de la vérité*, Paris, L'aube, 1994, Ch. 1. The notion of possessive individualism comes from C.B. Macpherson, *The Political Theory of Possessive Individualism: Hobbes to Locke*, (Oxford, Oxford University Press, 1975).

2. The reader is referred to Reiner Schurmann's work on Heidegger's *Being and Acting: On Principles and Anarchy*, Bloomington, Indiana University Press, 1990. The author's main thesis is that the constitution of philosophy as the discourse on first principles maintains the ethical under the yoke of the metaphysical. An-archy is thus the name for a kind of acting without reference to any sense of an origin.

3. On this point see the wonderfully incisive essay by Alain Badiou *L'éthique*, Paris, Hatier, 1993. It is worth noting here that the very terminology of the 'ethical' implies a relation with philosophy, even as one proclaims to have left the latter behind.

4. In truth this is a very delicate question which requires much more in-depth discussion. The respect of difference falls into the trap of representing difference, which is to say understanding it in terms of 'the same'. The Nietzschean conception of difference developed by Deleuze shows very clearly that it is precisely the difficulty of thinking difference which produces morality in the first place. It is this which constitutes the nihilism of representation. See especially Gilles Deleuze, *Nietzsche and Philosophy*, London, Athlone, 1983 and *Difference and Repetition*, London, Athlone, 1994.

5. Such a monism cannot really be understood – as Hegel suggests – in terms of the ancient 'monism' of Parmenides, in which what is and what is not is not, because strictly speaking God or Nature is not the subject in a subject–predicate relation. See on this point Macherey's article on Russell and Spinoza in Pierre Machery, *Avec Spinoza*, Paris, PUF, 1992, pp. 229–230

6. An exhaustive list of the recent publications concerning Spinoza would perhaps be redundant here. In particular see: Gilles Deleuze, *Expressionism in Philosophy: Spinoza*, New York, Zone, 1990; G. Deleuze, *Spinoza, Practical Philosophy*, City Lights, San Francisco, 1988; Antonio Negri, *The Savage Anomaly*, Minnesota, Minnesota University Press, 1991; Etienne Balibar 'Spinoza, the anti-Orwell: Fear of the masses', in *Masses, Classes, Ideas*, London, Routledge, 1994; Pierre Macherey, 'Towards a natural history of norms', in T. Armstrong ed. *Michel Foucault Philosopher*, Hemel Hempstead, Harvester Wheatsheaf, 1992; Christopher Norris, *Spinoza and the Origins of Critical Theory*, Oxford, Blackwell, 1991. See also Alexandre Matheron, *Individu et communauté chez Spinoza*, Paris, Minuit, 1969, and the incomplete series of readings by Macherey; *Introduction à l'Éthique de Spinoza*,' Paris, PUF, 1994–. Other references will be made through the course of this discussion. It is noteworthy that some of the philosophers in France who are still interested in the political project of emancipation since the waning of Marxism have pursued this interest by an invocation of Spinoza.

7. The term *mathesis universalis* is used by Descartes to designate the paradigm in which all knowledge is deemed expressible in the language of mathematics.

8. This is not the place to enter into a discussion of the sense of the Hegelian dialectic. It is clear, however, that the view of the dialectical process of thesis–antithesis–synthesis as inevitable correlative to a conception of history as having a predetermined outcome is not one that can easily be ascribed to Hegel. The merit of Slavoj Zijek's work is to have underlined the contingency of the dialectic. See also Alain Badiou, *Théorie du sujet*, Paris, Seuil, 1982.

9. P. Macherey, *Avec Spinoza*, Paris, PUF, 1992.

10. See Aristotle, *Metaphysics*, D 1012b 32–35.

11. Alexander Koyre, *From the Closed World to the Infinite Universe*, Baltimore, Johns Hopkins University Press, 1957.

12. Another way of looking at the change is that offered by Gilles Deleuze in his work on cinema. In modern science, movement, change, is grasped in its relation to 'any instant whatever', whilst in Ancient Greek physics, there are privileged moments. On the other hand, with Aristotle and his struggle against the Sophists, one also finds inexplicable aberrations of movement, movements which can only be grasped in relation to abstraction procedures. See Gilles Deleuze, *The Movement-Image*, London, Athlone, 1986; *The Time-Image*, London, Athlone, 1989; and the discussions of Aristotle in Eric Alliez, *Les Temps capitaux*, Paris, Cerf, 1990.

13. Or, of course, that God is imperfect or finite. This is the reading which leads Descartes to maintain the analogy of being. See Jean-Luc Marion, *Sur la théologie blanche de Descartes*, Paris, PUF, 1981.

14. See on this point the argument of Gilles Deleuze in the first part of his *Expressionism in Philosophy: Spinoza*, op. cit.

15. And the parallel debates on the distinction of human and exact sciences, the natural and the historical, the explanatory and the interpretative.

16. Thus Law = Infinite, Subject = Finite. What is good is what conforms to the law. Finite is incommensurable with infinite, thus one never reaches the ideal state of perfection. Original sin.

17. See in particular Heidegger's essay 'Schellings Abhandlung über das Wesen der menschlichen Freiheit' [1809], Tübingen, Niemeyer Verlag, 1971.

18. Hence the distinction made between the realm of phenomena, or things as they are for us, and that of noumena, or things as they are in themselves. For Kant knowledge is only valid when it concerns itself with the former.

19. Phillipe Lacoue-Labarthe and Jean-Luc Nancy, *L'absolu littéraire*, Paris, Seuil, 1978, p. 46.

20. In addition to Macherey's study, see also Jean-Marie Vaysse's, *Totalité et subjectivité*, Paris, Vrin, 1994;

Sylvain Zac, *Spinoza en Allemagne*, Paris, Klincksieck, 1989. It is not just that Spinoza has a negative role for Hegel, Schelling *et al.*, but also that his ideas also have a certain unacknowledged role in their systems, a point which seems to have escaped the attention of Heidegger.

21. Gilles Deleuze is the theorist *par excellence* of the operation of folding. See his books: *Foucault*, translated and edited by Sean Hand, London, Athlone, 1988; *Expressionism in Philosophy: Spinoza*, translated by Martin Joughin, New York, Zone Books, 1990; and *The Fold: Leibniz and the Baroque*, foreword and translation by Tom Conley, London, Athlone, 1993.

22. In this regard one should consider the famous Letter XII of Spinoza's correspondence, to Meyer, with its discussion of modal infinity.

23. Why? Because if we distinguish things only by number, the difference of the thing is understood in relation to a more general category.

24. On all this the indispensable reference is, of course, Gilles Deleuze and Felix Guattari, *A Thousand Plateaus*, London, Athlone, 1988. It is worth noting that Deleuze's Spinozism has been discussed in several chapters of the *Deleuze Critical Reader*, ed. Paul Patton, London, Blackwell, 1996.

25. Gilles Deleuze and Felix Guattari, *A Thousand Plateaus*, London, Athlone Press, 1988, p. 153.

26. In linguistics deictic shifters are terms the sense of which is entirely related to the context of enunciation: I is whoever says I, this is whatever is indicated as the case, etc.

27. E. Levinas, *Totality and Infinity*, Pittsburgh, Duquesne University Press, 1969, p. 105. The work of Levinas is famous in philosophical circles for its endeavour to theorise the role of ethical experience as prior to metaphysical distinction such as that between Same and Other. In the metaphysical conception, difference and alterity is always grasped for the position of the Same: another is always a bit more of the same. However, Levinas argues that it is in the face of the Other that we can experience the other as Other.

chapter 5

embodying virtue

a buddhist perspective on virtual reality

damien keown[1]

introduction

The concept of 'virtual reality' is a product of late twentieth-century technology, and this technology, some would argue, is the product of a cultural tradition steeped in assumptions – typically characterised as 'dualistic' – concerning the relationship between the self and the external world.[2] This chapter is about the ethical implications of virtual reality as viewed from the standpoint of a non-Western cultural tradition. The discussion will be orientated around two main issues. The first concerns the concept of virtuality and its ethical implications. The semantic overlap between the terms 'virtue' and 'virtual' is of particular interest here, since there is a fundamental and important sense in which the incarnation of the virtual through virtue is the primary aim of Buddhist teachings. The goal of Buddhism[3] is to make that which is at present virtual (the as yet unrealised potential for self-realisation) real and embodied in the individual.[4] This is what is meant by nirvana or 'enlightenment'. The goal of the spiritual life, as conceived by Buddhism, is increasing participation in human goods (such as wisdom and moral concern) by means of a set of practices known as virtues. The virtues, we might say, are the progressive ethical embodiment of the virtual, the latter conceived of as a set of abstract possibilities which marks the parameters of human well-being or flourishing (Aristotle's *eudaimonia*). Discussion of this point involves some consideration of Buddhist ideas concerning the status of the phenomenal world and the deconstruction of the human subject in the doctrine of 'no self' (*anattā*), a topic which has recently attracted the attention of Western philosophers such as Derek Parfit.[5]

The second point to be discussed relates to the way in which ascetic or meditational virtual realities differ from technologically generated ones and asks what (if anything) the meditating monk has in common with the teenager in the video arcade. Ascetic practices such as meditation play an important part in the process of spiritual development in Buddhism. Meditation may be thought of as one of the earliest techniques for the creation of virtual reality. It is a spiritual technology of considerable power and sophistication, allowing control and mastery of the internal modes of representation (auditory, visual, kinaesthetic, olfactory and gustatory). The chapter concludes with some reflections on the morally significant differences between reality and virtual reality.

virtue and virtual

How are the terms 'virtue' and 'virtual' related? Both (the former in particular) are etymologically complex terms. According to *The Shorter Oxford English Dictionary*, 'virtue' comes to us via old French *virtu* from the Latin *virtus* meaning 'valour, worth, merit, moral perfection'. In English the term has two principal senses which overlap at certain points. The second, and now less common sense, is that of virtue as a quality or power of things. This sense lingers on in the phrase 'by virtue of' meaning 'through the power of'. While this second sense of the term can have a moral aspect, such usage is now rare and tends to be associated exclusively with the first or primary meaning of 'virtue', namely as a moral quality. If we try to link these two senses of the word together, we arrive at the idea of virtue as the intrinsic power or potency of a thing which when actualised manifests an affirmatively valued (moral) quality. To go back to the root meaning – that of *vir* or a man – the 'virtue' of a man is to act with valour, courage and so forth. This virtue lies dormant until exercised and through exercise becomes more pronounced.

Turning now from virtue to virtual (which comes from medieval Latin *virtualis*) we find very little to do with morality. Although the word can mean 'morally virtuous', such usage is rare, and the term appears to have been appropriated by the natural sciences such as optics, dynamics, nuclear physics, particle physics and computing. These various meanings come together under the following generic definition: 'That is so in essence or effect, although not recognised formally, actually, or by strict definition as such; almost absolute.' The final two words contain the essence of the contemporary meaning of 'virtual' as that which is 'almost' real, or which appears real but is not. In the context of computing, *The Shorter OED* defines this as 'Not physically existing but made by software to appear to do so from the point of view of the programme or the user.' As noted above, in the move from 'virtue' to 'virtual' the moral dimension of the term has all but disappeared to be replaced by a neutral scientific or technical one. While it is clear how human beings can – through actualising their potential – develop moral qualities (virtues), it is less clear how this can apply to atomic particles, for example. Such particles are not moral agents and it seems absurd to think of them as being subject to moral judgements. Does the same apply to computing? Computers as artifacts are nothing more than silicon chips and other components arranged in a certain configuration, so at first glance it is difficult to see how a moral assessment could be relevant. Clearly, when they are used in certain ways – for example as tools to perform tasks devised by human operators – it does not seem inappropriate to enquire into the moral aspects of their use. It may also be the case that certain usages have an intrinsic moral dimension. In connection with the generation of virtual realities, in particular, it may be appropriate to ask whether 'virtue' should not be put back into the 'virtual', a point to which I shall return below.

Alasdair MacIntyre has been influential in redirecting the attention of moral philosophers to the important role the virtues have played in Western ethics. His major work on this theme is significantly entitled *After Virtue*, since he regards the Western moral tradition as having lost or discarded the pre-Enlightenment moral framework within which the virtues operated. In the course of his philosophical analysis, MacIntyre vividly compares contemporary moral life to the situation of a civilisation in the aftermath of a nuclear war. A few generations on, the survivors of the holocaust preserve different bits and pieces of the tradition that went before, but no one has a clear understanding of how the parts fit together. All that remains are interesting fragments of debris. This is a metaphor for the collapse of the Aristotelian and medieval Christian tradition of virtue ethics, within which a common understanding existed of the nature of human good and human destiny. Virtues are acquired properties, and in the absence of a consensus as to which properties should be acquired, the virtues have no clear role to play in either social life or in relation to metaphysics. MacIntyre notes: 'This notion of the political community as a common project is alien to the modern liberal individualist world.'[6] 'Unsurprisingly', he adds later, 'it is the lack of any such unifying conception of a human life which underlies modern denials of the factual character of moral judgements and more especially of those judgements which ascribe virtues or vices to individuals.'[7] It would not be surprising if this shift had contributed significantly to the semantic drift from 'virtue' to 'virtual' noted above.

virtues in the east

The above describes the situation with respect to virtues and the virtual in the contemporary West. But what about the East? I think the situation in Eastern cultures is similar to that of the pre-Enlightenment West. I shall be concerned here only with Buddhism, but I believe the conclusions reached about Buddhism could be generalised to apply to other Eastern ethico-religious systems such as Hinduism, Confucianism and possibly Taoism. What is interesting about Buddhism, however, is that while (in my view) it shares a common moral foundation with the pre-Enlightenment Western tradition of virtue ethics,[8] it differs significantly in certain of its metaphysical and philosophical presuppositions from both the West and other traditions of Eastern thought. Recurring themes in discussions of the virtual and the embodied concern human nature, mind–body dualism, and the ethical implications of individuals immersing themselves in VR technology. What I would like to do for the remainder of this chapter is consider these questions from the standpoint of Buddhist thought.

The Buddha's philosophical reflections on the nature of the human condition are contained in a set of propositions known as the Four Noble Truths. These assert that:

1.   Life is shot through with pain and suffering

2.   The cause of this suffering is selfish desire

3.   There can be an end to suffering and

4.   The way to put an end to suffering is to live in conformity with the principles set
      out in the Eightfold Path.

The First Noble Truth points to the physical and mental sufferings experienced by everyone
from time to time, and which are an inevitable part of the human condition. These include
birth, sickness, old age, death, and being separated from the things and people we love. If
the problem were simply that life is 'nasty, brutish and short', it would at least only be a
temporary condition to which death would put an end. Since Buddhists believe in reincarnation, however, the scale of the problem is greater. An individual goes from one life to another,
repeatedly experiencing the pain and distress inherent in physical existence. While the
unpleasant aspects of life are often masked by pleasant ones, the problem is that as human
beings we are ultimately powerless in the face of these realities and cannot escape the
vulnerability inherent in our natures.

The First Noble Truth also makes reference to a theory of human nature which is distinctively
Buddhist. This theory (known as the doctrine of *anattā* or 'no self') claims that human beings
can be analysed into their component psycho-physical parts without anything corresponding to
a metaphysical principle such as a 'self' or 'soul' being found. The Buddha taught that human
nature consists of five component parts, namely

1.   its visible form (roughly equivalent to the Western concept of 'matter')

2.   feelings and emotions

3.   cognitions

4.   dispositions and character traits, and

5.   consciousness.

He saw these components as interacting in a complex way and as constantly in a state of flux,
changing even from moment to moment. In rejecting the existence of a 'soul', the Buddha was
reacting to the teachings of Brahmanism (the ancestor of what is now known as 'Hinduism')
which, in a manner similar to the Platonic strand of Western thought, conceived of the soul as
an eternal spiritual principle 'entombed' within the physical body and longing for release and
reunion with its transcendent parent or source. Rejecting this dualistic conception of human
nature, the Buddha preferred a vocabulary of process, change and dynamic interaction, and
grounded his anthropology (and metaphysics) in notions of this kind. Given such a conception of
human nature, the problem of embodying the virtual (understood as that which is not yet
real) is less acute, since there is no sharp contrast between that which is and that which is
coming into being. The goal for Buddhism is not the replication or embodiment of pre-existing
transcendent essences or 'forms', but the shaping of the given in accordance with the

conception of a specific end. The more appropriate metaphor for this process is not that of the production line but of a potter gradually giving form to wet clay in accordance with his aesthetic vision of a final end.

Although Platonic dualism is commonly regarded as the dominant anthropological Western model, it is worth bearing in mind that there is an important countervailing tradition which has understood human nature in a very different way, one much closer to the Buddhist conception. I refer here to the tradition of thought that goes back to Aristotle, who conceived of the 'soul' not as a divine spark (as did Plato) but as the 'form' of material things. For Aristotle, human nature meant essentially the possession of a human form with its distinctive powers and abilities, notably the faculty of reason. According to his views in the *De Anima*, the soul was not some mysterious 'ghost in the machine' but the sum total of human (or other) capacities which an organism possessed. Human beings, he taught, successively acquired souls of three kinds while still in the womb. First came the vegetable soul (the power to ingest nutriment and excrete waste products), next the animal soul (the power of movement), and finally the rational soul (the ability to cogitate and reason which distinguishes human beings from other animal species). While Buddhism would be unlikely to accept this notion of the successive infusion of souls, it would have no quarrel in principle with Aristotle's basic anthropology, in terms of which different capacities become manifest at different stages of evolution. The embodiment of the virtual is once again more a case of allowing what is already present *in embryo* to manifest itself rather than cloning from a paradigm. The Aristotelian model has long rivalled the Platonic one, and was dominant in the Latin West from the rediscovery of Aristotelianism in the high Middle Ages. Thomas Aquinas and other theologians of the period provided readings of Christian doctrines which incorporated Aristotelian teleology. The more familiar dualism stems from the rejection of medieval learning from the Reformation onwards, and is linked to philosophers such as Descartes. One does not have to scratch the surface of Western thought too hard, however, to find Aristotelianism alive and well and arguably headed for a comeback which will eclipse the mind–body dualism which science seems to have embraced just as many philosophers prepare to abandon it.

Associated with the Second Noble Truth of Buddhism (the claim that all suffering is due to selfish desire) is a doctrine of equal importance to the teaching on no-self, and a corollary of it. This doctrine is known as 'dependent origination', and it holds that all phenomena that come into being do so in dependence on one or more causes and conditions. In brief, the doctrine teaches that anything that 'originates' is 'dependent' on something outside itself. Nothing is ontologically autonomous. The specific teaching in the Second Noble Truth that suffering is caused by selfish desire is an application of this doctrine to human psychology. The Buddha believed a causal connection could be traced between craving and suffering, and his solution to the problem of human suffering was therefore to remove its cause. By reducing and eliminating selfish desire (falsely predicated on the notion of an independent self as the owner and consumer of objects and experiences), many of the painful experiences of life (dissatisfaction, frustration, envy, jealousy, anger, etc.) can be attenuated and finally eliminated. Since according to Buddhist teachings it is the accumulated momentum of desire which fuels rebirth, once desire is eliminated, rebirth ceases and the individual is not reborn. Instead of rebirth one attains nirvana, the state free of suffering announced in the Third Noble Truth.

The Fourth Noble Truth sets out the practical methods to be followed by one who wishes to attain nirvana. These are summarised in a formula known as the Noble Eightfold Path which consists of the following eight factors:

1.   Right Understanding

2.   Right Resolve

3.   Right Speech

4.   Right Action

5.   Right Livelihood

6.   Right Effort

7.   Right Mindfulness

8.   Right Meditation

It can be seen that the Eightfold Path is a life plan that emphasises ethical living and mental cultivation. It begins with a proper understanding of the nature of things as set out in the doctrines mentioned above. For example, there are ultimately no discrete, monadic separate 'selves': all phenomena are dependently produced, and everything that comes into being sooner or later ceases to exist. Although this denial of permanent substances seems at first to undermine human endeavour, Buddhism sees it as a liberation from the bondage of 'essentialism' or the idea that there are fixed and unchanging realities. In other words, it is because there are no static frozen 'selves' that human nature can fulfil its potential. The individual subject comes to be regarded not as a fixed datum but as a repository of virtually unlimited potential; an ongoing project that can always evolve beyond its present state. The 'self' is thus not so much an entity as a narrative.

Another way of regarding the Eightfold Path is as a modelling process. The Path provides a template which defines the Buddhist conception of where the scope for human flourishing lies. Traditionally, the Path is divided into three categories known as Morality, Meditation and Wisdom. This tells us (to draw on Western terminology for the moment) that 'the good life for man' lies, according to Buddhism, in the cultivation of ethics and knowledge. Meditation in Buddhism may be regarded as an instrumental means to developing moral conduct and of coming to understand through personal experience that the world is indeed as described in doctrines such as the Four Noble Truths. For example, through meditation on the body and mind, the meditator comes to see that the human subject is a constantly changing flux of experience. Thoughts arise and disappear, sensations come and go, all without any connection to a permanent locus beyond the ever-changing subject. There is no 'thinker', just the thought; there is no 'self' which 'has' sensations, just sensations which arise within a field of consciousness. Through meditation one gains empirical verification of the deconstruction of the 'self' postulated in doctrine. Through the emptying of self, it is taught, comes heightened concern for others; as the ego wanes the interests of others come more fully within our ethical horizon. Metaphysics and ethics thus coincide.[9]

meditation

As noted above, meditation (*samādhi*) is one of the three divisions of the Eightfold Path, and thus occupies a central place in Buddhist practice. The importance of meditation in Buddhism can be appreciated by noting that it was while meditating that the Buddha gained enlightenment. The image of the Buddha seated cross-legged in meditation is one of the most popular themes in Buddhist art, and a constant reminder of the close association between meditation and enlightenment. Freud saw dreams as 'the royal road to the unconscious', and virtually all schools of Buddhism see meditation as the royal road to enlightenment. The general term for meditation in Buddhism is *bhāvanā*, which means 'cultivation' or literally 'making become'. The literal meaning is quite appropriate, for meditation is the principal Buddhist strategy for making oneself what one wishes to be. The Buddha did not invent meditation, but, as we shall see below, he did introduce significant modifications to the methods of his contemporaries which make Buddhist meditation distinctive in both theory and practice.

But what exactly is meditation? Meditation may be defined as an altered state of consciousness which is induced in a controlled manner. There is nothing very mysterious about it, and people slip in and out of trance-like states akin to meditation spontaneously in the course of waking life. A good deal of waking life is punctuated by daydreams, reveries and fantasies in which the mind withdraws to contemplate an interior landscape. Sometimes these reveries can be quite absorbing, as when driving a car one suddenly finds oneself at the destination with very little recollection of the trip. Taking drugs may also produce effects not unlike those experienced in meditation.

The main differences between meditation and the states mentioned above are the degree of control exercised and the depth and duration of the experience. Also – unlike drugs – with meditation there are no side effects or 'bad trips', and the benefits are cumulative and sustained. In the normal waking state the mind meanders in and out of trance states continually. Someone interrupted in the course of a reverie may remark that his mind was 'elsewhere'. The goal of meditation is not to be 'elsewhere' but to be right here, fully conscious and aware. The aim is to 'get one's head together', and become mentally concentrated rather than fragmented. A laser beam provides a good analogy: when light is diffuse it is relatively powerless, but when focused and concentrated it can cut through steel. Or, to use sound as a metaphor rather than light, the aim of meditation is to screen out mental 'static' and reduce the mental 'chatter' which dissipates psychic energy.

An interesting feature of the non-dualistic Buddhist (and Indian) cosmology is that the topography of the spiritual and material worlds overlap. The Buddhist universe may be thought of as kind of tower block wherein human beings inhabit one of the lower floors with the upper floors occupied by gods, spirits and supernatural beings of many kinds. The higher one goes, the more subtle and refined the levels become, until at the top exist noetic realms in which matter is absent. The different levels are linked to the stages of meditation. The beings who dwell in the various levels of the universe thus abide in the same state of mind as the meditator in the corresponding level of trance. The corollary of this is that meditation provides a means of accessing different levels of reality, and in particular the more sublime ones.

According to Buddhist sources, in the higher levels of trance the meditator can develop psychic powers corresponding roughly to what in the West is known as extra-sensory perception (ESP). These include the power to see events occurring in remote places (clairvoyance), to hear distant sounds (clairaudience), to recall previous lives (retrocognition), and to know the thoughts of others (telepathy). A collection of miscellaneous psychokinetic powers are also acquired such as the ability to fly through the air (astral projection), walk on water, and create duplicate bodies. The mind in profound trance is likened to purified gold in the malleable and pliable state from which precious objects are formed by a skilful artisan. In this case the artisan is the meditator who, having access to the deep levels of the psyche, is equipped to undertake the task of remodelling himself. At this point, given the non-dualistic ontology of Buddhism, the distinction between reality and virtual reality becomes blurred, and it appears that the mind begins to act on reality itself such that what was at first only imaginary now becomes real. The implication seems to be that the mind has the capacity to operate in a quantum mode which bypasses the physical limitations of the embodied state. To use a metaphor from computing, it is as if the virtual is the gateway to the program code for reality. In a reversal of our normal assumptions this implies that the reality we are familiar with is the virtual one, since it is contingent, whereas the reality we gain access to through virtual mental states is of a qualitatively higher order.

The Buddha came to see, however, that entering into a state of trance, however blissful and serene, was only a temporary diversion and not a permanent solution to suffering. Meditational states are impermanent and do not last. What these meditational techniques failed to provide was the kind of deep philosophical insight into the nature of things which is needed for enlightenment. He therefore developed a completely new meditational technique to supplement the traditional Indian practices. To the kind of techniques already described, which in Buddhism go by the generic name of 'calming meditation' (samatha), the Buddha added a new one called 'insight meditation' (vipassanā). The goal of this was not peace and tranquillity but the generation of penetrating and critical insight (paññā). Whereas in calming meditation intellectual activity subsides at an early stage, in insight meditation the object of the exercise is to bring the critical faculties fully into play in a meticulous reflexive analysis of the meditator's own state of mind. In practice, the two techniques of calming and insight are normally used back-to-back within the same session: calming may be used first to concentrate the mind and then insight to probe and analyse.

In insight meditation, the meditator examines every aspect of his subjective experience, breaking this down into four categories: the body and its physical sensations; feelings; mood; and mental patterns and thoughts. Through detached observation it gradually becomes clear that even one's conscious mind is but a process like everything else. Most people regard their mental life as their true inner essence (one thinks of Descartes' famous statement 'I think therefore I am'), but insight meditation discloses that the stream of consciousness is just one more facet of the complex interaction of the factors of individuality, and not what one 'really is'. The realisation that there is no hidden subject who is the owner of these various sensations, feelings, moods and ideas, and that all that exists are the experiences themselves, is the transformative insight that triggers enlightenment.

meditation and virtual reality

The practice of meditation is a way of manipulating reality through the generation of virtual realities. Does virtual reality have a similar effect in being a shortcut to virtue? And to what extent is the monk or other meditator who spends years in the practice of generating psychological fictions different from someone who dons a headset and enters instantly into a computer-generated virtual reality zone?

I think there are important differences between meditation and VR, and that there are potential dangers in prolonged exposure to the latter. To see where such dangers might lie, consider the scenario sketched by the philosopher Robert Nozick. Nozick asked what it would be like if scientists one day developed an 'experience machine' which was capable of simulating all human experiences perfectly on demand. The user would be put into an immersion tank and hooked up to the machine which would then generate whatever experiences the subject required. His body would be serviced by tubes, which would supply nourishment and drain waste products. The person floating in the tank would have exactly the same sensations as a person living life in the conventional way outside the tank. As part of his scenario, Nozick suggested that the decision to connect would be once and for all with no disconnection allowed. Such an idea seemed purely hypothetical when Nozick[10] proposed it in 1968, but today it seems less far-fetched and could be entirely feasible within decades. The moral questions which arise from this thought-experiment may be put as follows: What does it mean to us as human beings that technology may one day allow us to experience a simulated reality which will entirely replace the real world?

In commenting on Nozick's thought-experiment, John Finnis[11] suggests three reasons why it would be wrong to connect to the machine:

1   Activity has its own point

This point can be prefaced by noting that what is important in our lives is not just how things feel 'from the inside'. Human good is not defined solely by feelings, as Aristotle implied when he said 'No one would choose to live with the intellect of a child throughout his life, however much he were to be pleased at the things that please children.'[12] Aristotle further recognised that the fulfilled human life is a life of activity, of active participation in human good. It is a life of *doing*, and of achievement as expressed in the tag *Omne ens perficitur in actu*: 'Flourishing is to be found in action.' Action need not necessarily mean aggressive physical activity, and even the contemplative life is an active one since the faculties are actively deployed in the pursuit of an intelligible good (to make spiritual progress through meditation requires virtues such as effort, perseverance and self-control). Worthwhile activity certainly includes feelings, for example of pleasure and satisfaction, but crucially these are generated as a by-product of the activity engaged in (study, labour, play). What a virtual experience provides, on the other hand, is the feeling without the action. As Finnis notes, it is the counterfeit of worthwhile experience.

> The experience machine could give you the experience of writing a great novel or of overcoming danger in company with a friend; but in fact you would have done nothing,

achieved nothing. When, in the end, your brain rotted in the tank, it could be said of you that from the time you plugged in until you died 'you never lived'.[13]

2   Maintenance of one's own identity is a good

The second point concerns the threat which virtual reality poses to personal integrity. How does immersion in virtual reality (I am thinking of long-term usage) affect one's personality and identity? The problem here is pointed out by Nozick when he offers a further reason for not plugging in to the experience machine:

> A second reason for not plugging in is that we want to *be* a certain way, to be a certain sort of person . . . There is no answer to the question of what a person is like who has long been in the tank. Is he courageous, kind, intelligent, witty, loving? It's not merely that it's difficult to tell; there's no way he is. Plugging into the machine is a kind of suicide.[14]

A person immersed too long in virtual reality would be little more than a cypher. Experiences of all kinds would wash over him but leave no trace, for nothing would be worth retaining. A person's character is formed by the free decisions and choices made in the face of challenges and conflicts. The history of our choices is what we are: each choice leaves a trace and cumulatively they define us. Moreover, what is done is done, and in the real world we have to live with the consequences of our decisions. But for the person in a virtual world major choices never arise. Nothing would be worth fighting or dying for. He can marry one woman today and another tomorrow; be a doctor on Tuesday and a rocket scientist on Wednesday, a composer in the morning and a poet in the afternoon. But all this is undermined by the fact that since none of these achievements has been paid for (nothing has been sacrificed for any of them), none of them has any value. What kind of symphonies would the virtual composer produce? What passion would his love poetry contain? It is hard to see what value there could be in the works of a person whose mind was little more than a blank screen for the projection of fantasies. In real life our most fundamental accomplishment is the creation of our own identity whereas virtual reality acts like a character-solvent.

3   Appearances are not a good substitute for reality

Although Plato's dualistic ontology seems alien to the tenor of much contemporary thought, it embodies an important truth for ethics: *reality is to be preferred to appearances.* Developing this point with reference to the experience machine, Finnis writes:

> Opting for such a simulation would be to bury oneself in a tomb far deeper than Plato's Cave. The experience, would, *ex hypothesi*, be more veridical than that of Plato's prisoners, but the actual divorce from reality would be more total than theirs, since they could actually communicate with, for example, those who, having ascended to a clear view of reality, had returned to tell them about it.[15]

At one level – the level of experience (feelings, sensations) – there is no difference between reality and virtual reality. What one sees, hears and feels is identical in either case. Indeed, the very point of generating virtual realities is that they should be veridical. The difference between them, therefore, will always remain opaque to our senses since there is no way to tell what is real and what is not *from within the experience itself.* Yet we *know* there is a profound and important distinction between 'a real life really lived', and 'the self-immolating passivity of the "indeterminate blob"'.[16] This distinction is one that can be grasped only by our critical understanding, by pre-experiential reflection on the nature of genuine and counterfeit human goods. Finnis puts it as follows:

> When we reject ... the option of plugging in, we are grasping (understanding) that certain possibilities – the possibility of activity (as distinct from the mere experience of it), of shaping and maintaining one's identity (instead of merely seeming to), and of knowing and communicating with reality and real persons (not mere semblances) – are more than bare 'factual' possibilities. We understand them instead as the sort of evaluated possibility that we call opportunities. That is, we understand those possible states of affairs as desirable, i.e. as important, and perhaps, in the instance under consideration, as basic, human good(s).[17]

In other words, reflection on what constitutes human good teaches us that it is only in and through activity itself (and not a simulacrum of it) that human beings can flourish. A virtual existence is a life without a *telos*, a life spent going nowhere. As far as meditation is concerned, the difference is clear. Within Buddhism, meditation is a central part of a programme for life, a programme aimed at producing real change by encouraging human beings to participate in real goods. In this respect it is the very opposite of the stasis of a virtual experience, wherein however much the wheels spin, nothing ever moves. The Buddha's dissatisfaction with purely transic meditation referred to above suggests that were he alive today, he would find VR inadequate for the same reasons. Lest this conclusion sound unduly negative, let me conclude by pointing out that these comments apply mainly to the abuse of VR, or what might be called VR-for-its-own-sake. When used within a meaningful context to enhance human capabilities (for example in training simulators and the like) VR can be a productive tool. The dangers of VR lie in its awesome power to seduce, to become an addictive technology – perhaps the opium pipe of the next millennium.

notes

1. This chapter was written during my tenure of the Spalding Trust Visiting Fellowship in Comparative Religion at Clare Hall, Cambridge, 1996–1997. I wish to record my gratitude to the Trust and to Clare Hall for the financial support which made it possible for me to contribute to this volume.

2. Many implications for ethics flow from this ontology. A culture based on or influenced by dualistic premises in terms of which the self stands over and against nature will tend to emphasise the importance of the individual and give prominence to concepts such as 'autonomy' and 'rights'. In the moral discourse of Buddhism, however, like many traditional non-Western societies, it is duties and the common good which are emphasised more than the claims of individuals. For a further discussion of these points see Keown, Damien, 'Are there human rights in Buddhism?', *Journal of Buddhist Ethics* 2, 1995, pp. 3–27.

3. Buddhism is a vast and complex tradition which has spread to and influenced almost the whole of Asia. For the purposes of this chapter, however, I shall be referring solely to ideas associated with Buddhism in its early Indian form. Buddhism is neither monolithic nor homogeneous and is made up of many

strands consisting of different schools, sects and ethnic groups. What I will say here, therefore, while generally holding true of the mainstream, should not be regarded as necessarily applicable to all forms of Buddhism.

4. For a simple introduction to Buddhism see Keown, D., *Buddhism: A Very Short Introduction*, Oxford, Oxford University Press, 1996.

5. For example in *Reasons and Persons*, Oxford: Clarendon Press, 1984.

6. MacIntyre, A., *After Virtue. A Study in Moral Theory*, London, Duckworth, 1981, p. 146.

7. Ibid., p. 209.

8. For further discussion of this point see Keown, D., *The Nature of Buddhist Ethics*, London, Macmillan, 1992.

9. Note that ethical values in Buddhism are not derived from metaphysics (as in the 'Naturalist Fallacy') but are established independently on the basis of a conception of human good which looks beyond the facts of human nature to its *telos* or fulfilment. In other words, the postulate that knowledge and moral concern are goods worthy to be pursued is an underived axiom, not the conclusion of a syllogism premised upon one or more facts about human nature.

10. Nozick, Robert, *Anarchy, State, and Utopia*, Oxford, Basil Blackwell, 1968.

11. Finnis, John, *Fundamentals of Ethics*, Oxford, Clarendon Press, 1983, pp. 37–42.

12. *Nicomachean Ethics* X,3:1174a1–3, quoted in Finnis, op. cit., p. 38.

13. Finnis, op. cit.

14. Ibid., p. 39.

15. Ibid., p. 41.

16. Ibid.

17. Ibid.

chapter 6

redesigning the present

john wood

introduction

This chapter[1] consists of a series of notes and remarks that offer an environmentalist perspective on globalised capitalism, which it characterises using terms such as 'speed' and 'comfort'. It highlights the way in which consumerism claims to enhance, but in practice reduces, our awareness of the 'immediate now', or temporal present. This happens because of an increasing pace and frequency of exchange which places us in deference to an always imminent space–time. This loss of situated presence is referred to here as 'temporal alienation'. Ironically, this dislocation from a more fully situated and embodied experience also reduces our enchantment with the stockpile of designed products that mediate our busy lives. This outcome affects designers and consumers in similar ways. Whereas the 'time' of design practice is dependent on the Western idea of a confidently predictive 'future', the 'time' of nature should, I propose, be assimilated from our experiences in the situated, embodied 'now'. This can be justified as follows: if the idea of nature were to be defined exclusively in the past tense it would eventually become inseparable from art, and thereby sentimentalised and lost. If it were to exist only in the future, it would become inseparable from our arrogant faith in technology[2] and this would erode its authenticity. If we consider ourselves to be part of nature, then our 'presence' is part of the immanence[3] of everything else. Unfortunately, whilst it would be desirable to look for the authenticity of (our) nature in the present, consumerism is increasingly tempted to offer us a virtual and unattainable 'future presence'. In reconciling the practical and theoretical aspects of these ideas, the chapter concludes with some concepts for the design of a series of novel wristwatches. These ideas are offered as provocations intended to highlight the predicament of designers in the age of entrepreneurship and consumption.

'green' consumerism

For many years, environmentalists have warned that capitalism is only sustainable when we set its controls for permanent economic growth.[4] That is why, in the clamour for 'productivity', we have learned to elide 'quality of life' with 'standard of living'. More recently we have tended to confuse ecological 'sustainability' with a desire to keep things as they are, economically. As we all know, if perpetual economic growth is necessary for the stability of capitalism, marketing campaigns must strive to become ever keener and intrusive, resorting to any, and every, available technique at every conceivable point in the transactional cycle. Advertisers and designers have traditionally been employed at the most persuasive parts of this ceaseless process of rhetoric and novelty, and it is almost three decades since the late polemical designer Victor Papanek made his famous statement:

> There are professions more harmful than industrial design, but only a very few of them. And possibly only one profession is phonier. Advertising design, in persuading people to buy things they don't need, with money they don't have, in order to impress others who don't care, is probably the phoniest field in existence today.[5]

factor 20

Since Papanek first launched his attack upon a bemused design profession, a more pervasive strain of capitalism has infiltrated a popular awareness of environmentalism. In ecological terms this has been a mixed blessing. Whilst we have seen the welcome introduction of so-called 'green products' and notions of 're-usability', and 'recycling', these innovations have also been used to revive flagging sales figures, or even to promote major new markets. Where we have seen a popular conflation between adjectives such as 'environmentally friendly' and 'user-friendly', it is hardly surprising that many people have come to believe that a few minor technical adjustments are all that is required to achieve permanent 'ecological sustainability'. Unfortunately, more pessimistic observers[6] conclude that unless the developed world reduces its consumption of energy and materials to between a tenth and a twentieth[7] of current levels, perceived inequalities of well-being will lead to dangerous conditions for everyone.

In recent years, there have been renewed calls for an end to economic 'short-termism'[8] which puts immediate financial profit before social and ecological well-being. Dramatic consequences of such policies became infamous in the UK at the beginning of 1996 when we learned that reckless expediencies in the meat industry had led to the so-called BSE 'beef crisis'. Equally symptomatically, the last days of 1996 were commemorated by experiments to keep certain supermarkets open twenty-four hours a day. Elsewhere, wasteful processes of economic globalisation, and the rise of massive new economies have hastened developments that are unprecedented in scale. Despite this, all the main political parties spend much of their time reassuring us that, although we may expect to 'do the decent thing' for the global environment, nothing will actually change; and although governments promise us a 'future' in which advanced technologies will do more and more work for us, they still refuse to challenge the old concept of 'jobs'. They act as though local communities could never be self-sufficient, and that every citizen needs to be a producer. Whilst they endorse a vision of full employment, they also deny that many people are damaged and disenfranchised by our technological culture of overworking and speed, in which the symbolic act of transaction must be streamlined and forced into every last nook and crevice of human activity.

technology and comfort

An important counterpart to the industrialised idea of 'speed' in consumerism is the notion of 'comfort'. If, as late twentieth-century consumers, we were to reflect upon the history of our species, we might conclude that environmental conditions must have been the determining factor in balancing human comfort with the possibility of its gratification. Over the last few hundred millennia, successive waves of technology have reduced the tension between humanity's desire for comfort and the possibility of its being satisfied. Very recently, technology has joined forces with consumerist modes of capitalism in the unsaid hope that comfort will be dispensed on a more or less utilitarian basis.

Where early capitalism sustained the production of only a few commodities, consumerism has staked out a more comfortable utopia in which – we are assured – everyone will be able to shop for anything, at any time, anywhere. On the other hand, the consumerist rhetoric of 'instant' gratification is often more vicarious and anticipatory, offering the pleasure of an experiential 'present', or 'satisfied presence', at some unspecified time in the future.

Today, the manipulation of consumerist desire can be seen at its most theatrical in vast shopping malls where artificial skies change ceaselessly and where safety and comfort are regulated as meticulously as the ambient air temperature and humidity. Pandering to escapist fantasies of their visitors, these virtual comfort zones boast the highest retail profits per square metre of anywhere on earth. Shopping malls are designed to mollify the shopper's presence at the moment of the product's appearance. Their hugeness and vapidity are a part of their strategy of delay; giving consumers the illusion of suspended animation. Current modes of design, production and marketing ensure that the product is shown in prime condition; just prior to, or in the first moments of, acquisition and consumption. For this reason we could say that, in terms of late-capitalist design, the mythical 'origin' of the designed object is that it is forever 'brand new' in its state of 'always just ready'. A product's accompanying narrative invariably conceals and displaces its actual origin[9] or contents, and which implies that we should see it *only* in this 'virtually authentic' state.

the shoppers' continuum

In short, most consumer products are designed to create a feeling of dissatisfaction at the moment they are unwrapped for 'consumption'.[10] This means that our embodied relationship, or empathetic concern, for them in this state is difficult to sustain for more than the briefest moment. Up until now, the large and ever-increasing centralisation of our shopping malls has been necessary because we have yet to match their commercial effectiveness at a more modest, one-to-one level. This will probably change as interactive technologies learn to reproduce the marketing forces of the 'mall' and to redeploy them in virtual 'home shopping' zones that are targeted to individual predilections and incomes.

New technologies of 'customer targeting' are already automating the tailoring of services or products to individual desires and 'needs', and it would be rather optimistic to expect these advances to reduce the net throughput of materials, energy requirements, or proliferation of toxic wastes. A likely scenario is that information technologies will become the catalyst in some form of 'shoppers' continuum'[11] – a self-sustaining cybernetic cycle of increasingly individualised production and consumption. Where certain television genres already cause psychological dependency for some individuals, interactive modes of narrow-casting could eventually resemble 'black holes of human presence' in which vulnerable consumers act as hostages to self-reinforcing gravitational forces of financial speculation, comfort and role-play. The strong appeal of such 'virtual products' is likely to increase their number, but it is also likely that they would precipitate a significant increase in the net consumption of other, more 'material' commodities.

working through without stopping

As we have claimed, consumerism within an increasingly globalised economy has led us into a restless age of innovation in that technological 'advances' encourage designers and managers to shorten design-to-production cycles, at the same time as kindling the consumer's desire for trends which have yet to happen. The success of this process, and its side-effects, derive from a profound integration of technology into our everyday lives. It is therefore socially and economically contagious, even though it is not essential to our well-being.

We use the term 'working against the clock' when rescuers work day and night to reach victims buried beneath a collapsed building. Likewise, we are not surprised to hear of people in subsistence economies pushing themselves to extreme physical limits in order to sustain their survival. For many workers in the rich economies, however, overworking for competitive monetary success has become an operational imperative of industrial practice, even where there is no immediate threat to their survival. Walter Benjamin[12] wrote about capitalism's 'transformative and continually destructive power' which had led to the arrival of what he called 'now-time'.[13] As we design machines to run increasingly fast, humans must keep up with them to maintain the possible throughput of work. In short, the accelerating pace of competitive practices, the downsizing of workforces, coupled with the wholesale automation of information and communication systems, all combine to promote a self-organising mode of Taylorism. This phenomenon continues to narrow the width of the experiential and actative present, both for the 'creator-producer' and for the 'consumer'.

'euphoric loss of the present'

For consumers, many activities are deliberately 'streamlined' to give us a 'buzz', and therefore to narrow our temporal focus for a short period of 'now-time'. 'Buy now pay later' schemes, and 'forget it all for an instant' products are likely to become increasingly popular whenever consumerist economies reach higher temperatures and a sense of alienation becomes more widespread. Where late twentieth-century consumerism assures gratification in the rhetorical promise of 'now-time', the perpetually renewed imminence of that which is promised tends to eclipse the consumer's 'actual present'.

In monetary terms, boundaries between the present and the immediate future are deliberately made unsteady, and we may find that each temporal tense calls for the other in a transactional continuum. Advertisers entice us into a redefined present which incorporates reimagined futures and pasts, and away from our situated presence. Banks tempt us to postpone the implications of our current financial state through the 'present-deferred loss' of a credit card. Similarly, for producers and designers, the pace of work encourages us to defer our experiential existence to a permanently imminent future rather than to a more convivial[14] present. For many creative professionals, this projective process is often enticing and addictive, and I have described this as a 'euphoric loss of the present'.[15] Sometimes, designers may justify ethically dubious practices in the present because they seem to promise ecological benefits in the future. Here, we must find a new balance. Although projected planning is endemic to our societies, we also use the 'economy of scale' argument to justify living *for* the future, rather than *in* the present. This 'present/s-denying' deference to an impending consumerist utopia may also be shared by consumers and producers of commodities because most of us occupy both roles. We may assume that these economic factors will continue to become increasingly prescriptive, perhaps combining with new technologies of commercial advertising and 'intelligent business agents', which seek out and colonise every last moment of our unscheduled free time.

deep ecology

Inspired by Ghandi's and Spinoza's[16] ideas, the Norwegian philosopher Arne Naess[17] coined the term 'deep ecology'.[18] In developing his ideas, Naess retreated to a hut in the mountains where he found 'contraries indistinguishably blended'.[19] These 'contraries' confound the Western consumerist notion of 'speed' and 'comfort' which has developed alongside the logic of stridently individual (consumer) rights, and which has come to imply that any discomfort or deprivation should be avoided or denied. If alienation can be understood as the rational denial of direct sensory experiences – e.g. bodily pain – in the situated and changing present, then it can be interpreted as being opposite to the 'glow' of presence and well-being. Naess's equation takes the subjective idea of 'glow', or 'passion', as an index for well-being:

$$W = \frac{G^2}{Pb + Pm}$$

where:

W = well-being
G = 'glow' (passion)
Pb = bodily pain
Pm = mental pain

how can designers help?

How can responsible designers evaluate what is going on? How can they increase this 'glow' factor whilst drastically reducing the net throughput of materials and energy? Since the seventeenth century we have come to accept analytical methods in which statistical and other data are accepted as evidence of 'how things really are' in human society. Originally developed for science, these rational and divisive approaches are increasingly used in the mass media to synthesise impressions of many criteria, ranging from large demographic changes to evidence of individual well-being. When asked by journalists about his state of health during the Watergate trial, Richard Nixon quipped: 'My doctors tell me I feel fine.' Philosophically speaking, this technique of thinking can be described as 'noumenal', as opposed to 'phenomenal'. Arguably, an increase in noumenal values at the expense of phenomenal values contributes to our general feeling of alienation. Even today's discourse of 'eco-design' is couched in the quasi-scientific languages of managerial control; tending, therefore, to detach the observer from relevant local situations by establishing and applying increasingly 'disembodying' theories.

In Erlich's famous equation for environmental impact, collective human actions are expressed in a noumenal form as:

$$I = P \times C \times T$$

where:

I = environmental impact
P = population
C = consumption per head
T = 'environmental intensity', or environmental impact per unit of consumption

Here, the destructive aspect of technology may be found in the noumenal 'T' of the above equation because we may assume that human beings cannot cause excessive environmental damage unless aided by technology.

sustainable consumerism

Marketing claims often comfort us with noumenal, technological evidence that assures us how 'safe', 'responsible' and 'eco-friendly' we are, as intelligent consumers. The commercially driven rhetoric of eco-rationalism therefore tends to shield us from our individual responsibilities, and has often been rather mischievous in its claims. We are assured, for example, that our disposable tissues are 100 per cent recyclable, our electric water heater has a 100 per cent conversion rate, and our fluorescent 'eco-lamp' uses only 15 per cent of the energy of an incandescent bulb.[20] The appeal to 'green consumerism' has too often been applied as a protection against declining sales figures, or even as a way to increase sales.

An important method of eco-design is LCA, or 'life-cycle assessment', which makes a quantified evaluation of manufactured products throughout their expected history from 'cradle to grave'. Typically, this technique seeks to harmonise adverse features of numerous factors such as energy requirements (in manufacture and total usage), availability of raw materials, number of potential users, and the effects of pollutants which find their way into sensitive parts of the ecosystem. However, as we shall show, whereas LCA techniques address the net environmental cost of products in terms of actual materials and energy used, the 'speed' factor tends to reduce the received, or experiential, qualities of the products when they are consumed.

I would not deny that 'eco-design' is the acceptable face of responsible capitalism. As such, it is designed to sustain consumerism at 'acceptable' levels of economic growth. However, what it may fail to do is to help individuals to reconcile data about natural resources with their lived experiences as human beings. Consumerism widens this gap in several ways. For example, it seeks to increase the product range and to broaden the repertoire of manufacturing methods. It deliberately conceals the origins and essences of commodities from their purchasers, and gives products an arbitrary (i.e. market value) price-tag. In doing these things it diminishes their 'true' cost, or meta-economic value, by detaching them from their ecological context and meaning. Each year, the human race consumes fossil fuels which took a million years of sunlight to produce. Yet when, as consumers, we switch on a domestic fan heater[21] we are unlikely to have any intuitive, or embodied insight about the amount of energy required to keep the element hot. The nearest we come to making 'actively embodied equivalents' is to measure the energy of car engines in 'horsepower', rather than in 'person-power'. Even if we happen to understand about technical 'units' of energy, we are unlikely to know whether, for example, our own body has the muscle power to run the electric fire from a pedal-generator – even for the briefest moment. Buckminster Fuller proposed the term 'energy slaves' to remind us of this problem. Ironically, the age of the exercise-bike has done nothing to change this situation.

space versus time

Our familiar notion of 'speed' did not exist before scientists decided to separate time from space in order to invent a new physics of heat and movement. This technique, refined since the Enlightenment, distanced critical observers from the time of their own situated present (i.e. their own 'presence'). It has become so prevalent that our concept of design is now virtually meaningless without a confident and predictive sense of 'future'. Where did this particular temporal idea originate, and how can we begin to evaluate it? Historically speaking, the Western idea of time can be generalised into two distinct categories. On the one hand, 'clock-time' evolved from Aristotle's idea of 'astronomical time'.[22] It informed Newton's vision of an 'absolute, true, and mathematical time' which was believed to exist independently of human presence. On the other hand, St Augustine's revision of Aristotle's concept became known as 'lived time', because it recognised the importance of the phenomenal realm, and therefore put human subjective experience at the heart of temporality. Since the fourteenth century, technology has evolved co-dependently with our ability to synthesise an increasingly dependable 'clock-time'. This technique became central to the regulation of industrialised society.

The competitive nature of today's service culture appears, on the face of it, to make 'instant' gratification the ubiquitous aim of consumerism. Yet, in dignifying the always impending moment of transaction at the expense of all other human institutions, we risk becoming oblivious to, or at odds with, our own presence, and which is strongly allied to what we have come to know as nature. Although today's product advertisements often characterise the consumer as an individual who wallows in her own 'lived time', or 'social time' to enjoy, say, a certain brand of chocolate or a proprietary bath oil, our technological culture increasingly encourages us to put our faith in instruments and systems rather than in our own subjective judgement. Clock-time is more authoritative than lived time because it appears to punctuate our experience in precise, infinitesimal increments; i.e. in 'instants' rather than in 'moments'. Often, the technological authority of 'clock-time' tends to outweigh the awareness of our own presence. For this reason we have learned to trust it in preference to our personal sense of duration. Even today we commonly speak of the condition of 'absent-mindedness' to denote a state of conscious abstraction from, or a disavowal of, the 'situated actual'. We speak of being 'distraught' when we mean that a condition of stress makes us ineffective through alienation from the business at hand. Conversely we also talk of being in the present as 'presence-of-mind' when we refer to unplanned actions which are both situated and effective. Perhaps 'presence-of-mind' can be identified as a sudden 'readiness-to-hand' of fluency in thought and action, similar to Donald Schön's idea of 'reflection-in-action'.[23]

embodying 'clock-time'

A salutary project for designers is one that asks them to imagine a world in which every single mechanical and electronic timing system has been destroyed by a mysterious virus. In this scenario, clocks cannot be rebuilt and the design brief asks them to devise a system that would help everyone to celebrate the new millennium. Obviously, this would entail finding a way to choose the appropriate moment at which as many people as possible can agree to celebrate the first moments of the new century. The system must be designed to minimise bad feelings, diplomatic embarrassments, confusion, and wasteful exploitation of the event by politicians. The project reminds us how much we rely on mechanisms to regulate our lives.

In technological terms, 'clock-time' can be regarded as a form of temporal data which has yet to be embodied as 'lived time'. We embody clock-time in many ways. The athlete who glances at her stop-watch whilst running is choosing to embody clock-time as a 'pace-pusher' in place of a human competitor. Usually, we choose how frequently to look at our clocks and wristwatches, and therefore how much to embody mechanical time as information. Different strategies in the design of clocks offer different levels of intrusiveness. These are governed by the extent to which inescapable stimuli, such as 'ticking', or alarm sounds, are used. At the cognitive levels, this aspect of clock-time gives us a certain degree of freedom to reinvent our presence by incorporating it into immediate discourse. For example, we may wake up and talk to the alarm clock and/or to ourselves. We may try to appease the alarm clock, or to defy the fearful moment when it rings. We promise it/ourselves that we will wake up properly, but demand a short extension of time. 'Five more minutes!?' we mumble, then go back to sleep. When these phenomena work at a more metabolic level they are less avoidable. For us, the diurnal rhythm of 'solar time' is a class of metabolic 'time' and we may notice its unwelcome effects as 'jet-lag' when travelling with, or against, the Sun's motion.

Richard Buckminster Fuller[24] described global patterns of working as 'continuous man' because the daily arrival of sunlight determines the major work-times of human life as it illuminates half of the globe at a time and wakes us up on a 'rota' basis. Compared with solar time, digital clocks sometimes seem to display a particularly intrusive mode of idealised Aristotelian time, in that they purport to show successive instants without revealing any transitional change in between.

The same denial of bodily travel can be found in the design of modern lifts, especially those with mirrors to focus our attention inwards, and digital displays to tell you the 'instant' you reach the next floor. As such, they lay claim to the rhetoric of our digital age, i.e. the perfect square wave form, which seems to defy material (embodied) logic by travelling instantaneously from one state to another. Inherent in the idealised digital form is the dubious promise of travel at the speed of light.

temporal alienation

The painful mismatch between rational and experiential understanding can be seen as a condition which can be described as alienation. Where alienation commonly refers to a feeling of withdrawal or estrangement from our sensibilities or surroundings, Marx applied it more specifically to emphasise the dehumanising conditions of modern capitalism. In part, this process is characterised by the modes of technology that have most influence on our lives, and therefore it manifests itself in new, and sometimes unexpected ways. It is surprising, for example, that information technology has helped to blur the boundaries between work and leisure. At one time, we would have been immune from 'work-time' when geographically separated from our workplaces. Today, an increasing number of workers are connected, albeit indirectly, to a 24-hour networked communication system in which work-time quickens the pace of social time via pagers, telephones, faxes, computers, Walkmans and broadcast signals. At times, the pace and pressure of globalised capitalism may make life in the 'fast lane' seem unbearable for some. They may feel, for instance, that they are expected to be in two places at once, or that there are an insufficient number of hours in the day.

Harold Ramis has satirised temporal alienation in several of his films. In one – *Groundhog Day* (1993) – a television journalist finds himself trapped in a repetitive 'rerun' of a particular day's events. After a while he learns to focus upon many of the nuances and opportunities which he would otherwise have missed, so that he can exploit them to unique advantage. In another film (*Multiplicity*, 1996) an overworked site manager is given the chance to clone himself as a matching set of specialist individuals; i.e. loving husband, attentive father, exemplary employee, DIY consumer, and avid follower of leisure pursuits.

Where we may usually understand alienation as a feeling of estrangement from our surroundings, it is also possible to reflect upon the temporal aspects of this predicament, perhaps by comparing an individual's compulsive interest in clock-time, or mechanical time with a reposeful awareness of her own 'lived time':

$$\text{temporal alienation} = \frac{\text{obedience to clock time}}{\text{sense of one's own presence}}$$

Psychoanalytically speaking, it may be argued that, although we may be able to moderate our actions through rational plans and schedules, we cannot satisfactorily postpone our feelings and emotions.

If we examine received ideas of technological performance we can find that they conform to the mechanistic domains of 'clock-time' rather than to the human domains of 'lived time'. The technological concept of power, for example, can be expressed as mechanical work which lasts for a given period of clock-time. Could we, then, redefine calorific energy in terms of a given work level which is sustained throughout an equivalent period of 'lived time'? This could have an important outcome in terms of reducing our careless dependency on automatic systems such as domestic space heaters, and may also help us to become more in touch with our surroundings. Instead of heating systems being regulated by autonomous control circuits which use Aristotelian time to maintain arbitrary parameters such as temperature, they could be developed to remind consumers of their own presence and role in the situation. In a limited sense this happens with, for example, camp fires because their low level of technology makes precise temperature regulation difficult to achieve. A sense of time around the fire is usually quite inseparable from the (space–time) actions of its keepers and revellers. Hi-tech alternatives could monitor our responses to ambient conditions and encourage us to reduce our threshold of demand. For example, whenever we lose our immediate awareness of a particular energy-consuming appliance, it could be trained to withdraw[25] from us and, perhaps, to offer us mocking representations of ourselves.

There are many everyday examples of temporal alienation. When driving to an appointment we may find ourselves accelerating towards traffic 'stop' lights or a queue of cars, even though we know, rationally speaking, that we will very soon have to step hard on the brakes. Another way to consider temporal alienation is the individual relationship between the cognitive and metabolic pace of living. We suffer temporal alienation because our metabolic pace is being driven too hard by our cognitive pace; i.e.

$$\frac{\text{individual cognitive pace}}{\text{individual metabolic pace}}$$

An example of this is when the industrialist culture encourages us to maximise our lifestyle with caffeine 'hits', 'working breakfasts' and television dinners, because our (unstimulated) bodies would tend to run at too slow a metabolic rate for the work rate expected. Fast-food retailing tries to harmonise the dissonance between the two rates of change, employing cunning advertising strategies to wake up our appetites (metabolically), and to persuade us (cognitively) that speed-eating would be fun! This is co-ordinated with design strategies that enable fast-food customers to choose, order, receive and consume their food as quickly as possible. The sales of antacid tablets are a lucrative complementary market for the snack industry. Given the competitive nature of fast-food retailing in the high street, it would be reasonable to assume that the rational design process is focused on the task of consumer gratification. Ultimately, however, there is always an irreconcilable conflict between speed of service and our individual comfort. For example, if each company's primary aim is to increase sales and to promote brand loyalties, this may lead to a net reduction in the customer's sensory pleasures over a given (calendar) time-scale. In short, the cardinal and systematic pursuit of individual 'comfort' will ultimately lead to an erosion of convivial experience.

ideas for the design of convivial wristwatches

1 ©the 'lovers' clock'

When we play 'catch the ball' with a partner, we create a negotiated form of 'lived time', or 'social time'. This was an inspiration for my invention of a conceptualist artwork, 'the lovers' clock'[26] in which a single clock is constructed in two halves, each located in a separate physical place and linked by radio, or light signals. A pulse of standard length is generated by each individual half, and after a characteristic period of delay, is triggered by receipt of the other's signal. An aggregate or 'shared' time is displayed on identical dials of the clock faces, which may be placed at great distance from each other. In theory, the basic lovers' clock mechanism will run slower, the further apart its halves are placed.

i.e.

$$R = \frac{M1 + M2}{2D}$$

where: R = clock rate
C = velocity of 'prompt' link medium
D = distance between clock halves
M1 = delay period of clock half 'A'
M2 = delay period of clock half 'B'

If their time were to be monitored whilst travelling away from each other, this effect would increase until their combined speeds attained the velocity of light at which point the clock[27] would stop. Einstein's work shows that when one clock/lover travels at a great velocity away from the other and returns, this may lead to temporal asymmetry which may cause serious social problems for the 'lovers'. The system only works on a phenomenological level, because we cannot 'redesign' metabolically embodied time. By contrast, when we imagine two people playing 'catch the ball' in a rural landscape, it is easy to become nostalgic for an imaginary idyll, and for the more convivial timescape with which we associate it. In today's ball games, the pressures of an industrialised lifestyle will tend to integrate fixed periods of 'social time' within the scheduling constraints of lunch times, holidays or weekend breaks. Late twentieth-century 'leisure' moments are seldom unmediated by the clock.

2 ©the 'adjustable focus' wristwatch

One of the problems with extremely large, digital display, or noisy clocks is that they leave their human subjects little respite from their mechanical pace. However, it would be easy to devise a personal watch with a variable 'time-focus' display. For example, this would, at its widest focal adjustment, merely tell the wearer that it is, for instance, 'more daytime than night-time'. Broader focus tuning would make the display go blank or, perhaps, display a holiday scene or fish-tank image. Tuning it to a narrower timescale, the watch would begin to indicate that it is 'closer to afternoon than to morning'. Increasing the fine tuning further would begin to show hours, then minutes, then seconds, then tenths of a second, etc.

3 ©the 'lived time' wristwatch

It would also be possible to redesign clocks so that they could mediate a kind of metabolic 'lived time', rather than mechanical time. Further to the idea of the 'Lovers' Clock', it would be technically easy to manufacture wristbands that monitor the pulses of computer users so that shared communication domains could become temporarily independent of global or other clock-based time. For example, wherever there is a dedicated channel of communication between a small number of users in a virtual conferencing system, we could establish a shared time-zone based on the average pulse-rate of participants. This could be used to drive the pace of communication packages in such a way that, where collective boredom would slow the system down, excitement would tend to drive it faster. This would create greater delineation between local and non-local modes of conferencing.

4 ©the 'pressure watch'

This timepiece is designed to combine clock-time with an indicator of the ambient stressfulness in the wearer's environment. In its comparative display, a secondary dial is electronically 'twinned' with a standard watch face to register the average daily incidence of inertial movements and loud noises. Miniature inertial transducers and microphones would convey their signals into integrator circuits to produce a daily average count of the number of potentially stressful movements and percussive sounds in the vicinity of the wearer. These would be combined with samples of the wearer's pulse rate. Average daily levels would cause the clock display times to show 'aggravation' times which deviated from standard clock-times. The deviation would make the 'pressure watch's' display run relatively 'fast' or 'slow', depending on whether the working environment was more or less stressful than usual. 'Space–time' pressure tables of other wearers would show them how their normal working environment compared with others in factories, countryside, at sea, etc.

notes

1. The author would like to thank his students on the Design Futures MA programme (especially Sam Deeks, Robert Wells, and Miho Ito) for the many lively discussions which have served to inspire and to inform some of these ideas.

2. An example of a 'futuristic', artefactual, and human-centred vision of nature can be found in *A Moment on Earth* (London, Penguin, 1996) in which Greg Easterbrook makes five claims for a redesigned, or 'Neo-Nature':

   1. New Nature might include the end of predation by animals against animals. Predators could become herbivores with genetic intervention.
   2. It might lead to the end of predation by people against animals.
   3. It might lead to the end of predation by people against people. An initiative to insert a 'no-kill' DNA code into entire human population may correct the worst error of history; the combination of intellect and predation.
   4. Could mean the end of extinctions. Nature has never been able to preserve species.
   5. The end of disease. Perhaps disease is a defect of nature waiting to be corrected.

3. See also Chapter 4 by Andy Goffey and Chapter 15 by Claudia Wegener.

4. For a recent summary of theoretical issues, see Douthwaite, R., *The Growth Illusion*, Dublin, Lilliput Press Ltd, 1992. For a summary of practical issues, see Douthwaite, R., *Short Circuit*, Totnes, Green Books, 1996.

5. Papanek, V., *Design for the Real World; Human Ecology and Social Change*, London, Thames & Hudson, London, [1972] 1992.

6. Who compare total world resources with current population increases.

7. 'Factor 20' is described at: http://www.wmin.ac.uk/media/02/event/desc/factor_20.html.

8. Hutton, W., *The State We're In*, New York, Vintage Books, 1996.

9. For example, its 'farmed' origin.

10. More recently this 'designing' of food products has moved into a more dangerous phase; that of introducing genetically modified bio-material designed to fulfil short-term, narrow consumerist criteria.

11. Wood, J., 'Pay and play; the shopper's continuum', *Design International Magazine*, August 1991.

12. Andrew Benjamin 'Writing, time, and task' in Osborne, P., and Benjamin, A., (eds) *Walter Benjamin's Philosophy; Destruction and Experience*, London and New York, Routledge, 1994, p. 234.

13. German: *Jetztzeit*.

14. For a keener definition of this word, see Illich, I., *Tools for Conviviality*, republished edition, London, Marion Boyars Publishers Ltd, 1990.

15. Wood, J., 'Situated Criticism and the Experiential Present', *Design Issues*, editor Prof. Nigel Whitely, vol. 3 no. 2, Summer 1997.

16. See Andy Goffey, Chapter 4.

17. Naess, A., *Ecology, Community and Lifestyle*, Cambridge, Mass., Cambridge University Press, 1989, p. 15.

18. Bookchin, M., 'Deep Ecology and Anarchism', London, Freedom Press, 1993.

19. Chuang Tzu, quoted by Naess, A., in 'Ecology, Community and Lifestyle', op. cit., p. 41.

20. These claims are either truistic, partial, irrelevant, or misleading when seen in a larger ecological context.

21. 1 kilowatt/hr.

22. A more regimented mode of astronomical time or calendar time.

23. Schön, D., *The Design Studio*, London, RIBA Publications, 1985.

24. This concept was brought to my attention by Paul Taylor of the 'Blowpipes'. It comes from Fuller's 1960 essay of the same name and was reprinted in *The Buckminster Fuller Reader*, ed. Meller, J., London, Cape, 1970, p. 347.

25. This already happens in an elementary way with computer appliances of Energy Star compliance which automatically fall into lower power, or 'sleep', modes when we exceed a preset period of abstinence from the mouse or keyboard.

26. Exhibited in the Scratch Gallery, London, 1982, and at the Anna Bornholt Gallery, London, 1995.

27. And the rest of the universe!

part three

embodying truth

hubble telescope

the artist in the eye of the storm

gustav metzger

When we look at an image from the Hubble Satellite Telescope (HST) what are we seeing? We see a transmission of that which we call information; material sprayed on to another material. In order for us to see something, we must have seen it at some point in the past. When we see, we retrace what has already been seen. How can it be, that an HST image which purports to represent an unfathomable reality, can indeed represent that reality? Let's take the story of Turner lashed to a mast on a ship, whilst painting a storm. Or, indeed, the situation of the artist Turner being influenced by the emergent railways. Let us imagine Turner strapped to the exterior of a spacecraft, or in this case, the Hubble satellite. You might think that this would be the end of Turner. But then *our* Turner would have been protected against the hazards of an inhospitable environment. The new exhausts itself by repetition: a stimulus generated by the onslaught of a new technology can only carry so far. The technology may maintain a momentum whilst its impact on the artist flakes off. You can only beat a horse for so long before it fails to respond.

In time, artists became acclimatised to the idea of travelling in trains. The Shock of the New wore off. Travellers' tales conveyed the excitement until, after a period of decades, the initial surprise mingled with apprehension and the tingling sensation was no longer available as a stimulus to creativity: a potential had been lost, had exhausted itself. The new inevitably exhausts itself by repetition.

The 'new' impacts across the entire society. At first by word of mouth. We recall the horror stories at the birth of the motor car when cattle were disturbed and geese slaughtered on the roads by cars travelling at the then sensational speeds of up to 15 miles per hour. It is not the speed that kills, but the unexpectedness of the encounter. Unpredictability is the fulcrum around which 'Les Chants de Maldoror' [1868] is constructed.[1] In Lautréamont's Tale it is the unexpectedness which is the killer.

We can only go so far. So far at a time – 15 miles an hour, whilst the dust settles. Duchamp's *Dust Breeding* is so sensational because dust has always been regarded as a nuisance or, at best, a preservative of ancient goods. To place dust in the context of art or photography, as Man Ray did with his photograph, is a heroic act because it flies against common sense which tells us to get rid of it.

The principle of 'getting rid of it' is the principle against which artists have put up a united front. One could call it the banner of the avant garde. The world says 'Get rid of it', and the artist says 'No'. Take as an instance the Spanish Civil War. The followers of Franco wanted to get rid of a democratic regime, and artists and intellectuals gathered from all over the world in defence of Madrid. Picasso, with the help of the current girlfriend, found a large studio in the heart of Paris from which to do battle. First he ordered a canvas large enough to sink a battleship. The Spanish government set aside a suitable space in which to place it, and Picasso set to work.

Guernica was a first. It was the first destruction of a town by bombardment from the air. It created the kind of surprise of the first flight of geese killed on a country road by a goggle-wearing automobilist going at 15 miles per hour. Bombs dropped on Guernica. The news came like a bomb. By word of mouth at first, and then by means of all the communication channels of the time, word got out of the massacre. The world was rightly outraged. In our time, a bombing on the scale of Guernica might not reach the front page. It was a first. And because it was first, and because it was horrific, it receives widespread attention.

The first makes such an impact because it literally stretches the imagination. Seeing a head filled with blood for the first time stretches the mind to bursting point, because we begin to imagine *our* head filled with that same volume of blood, and we wonder how we might react. Would we choke on it? Vomit it out? Call for a doctor? The inescapable confrontation with *that* head and ours is the stuff from which Lautréamont created that encounter between the sewing machine and the umbrella.[2]

We 'stretch our head' – that is to say, its innards – around a new phenomenon, twisting in the process of understanding, forcing our capacities. In developing computers, a set of activities is in place. Adding, adding, adding. On and on, that is a summary of our world. And so on with Hubble.

Turner, or his modern-day equivalent, is tied to the outside of the craft. The telescope is in place and constantly taking images, or rather, a complex set of calculations are in process. The telescope does not see – it calculates. Seeing is left to the artist. *But what does the artist see?* The deep expanse of space, and below the earth, our earth.

He or she, sees the sun, the stars, moon and lots more. But there are limits to that which the eye can see, and it is these limits which Hubble is meant to compensate for. Hubble sees into that which passes human understanding. Humans cannot comprehend 45 billion light years, which is what Hubble is in a position to confront. We cannot, by any stretch of the imagination, twist that figure around the confines of our heads. The brain, despite its fantastic capacities, does not have the space to absorb such an immensity of configuration.

The eye cannot see at such distances. What we cannot see, we cannot grasp.

Unlike Turner, our artist lashed to the Hubble craft is in a phase of calm. Despite the immense speed, there is not the violence of a storm to be confronted.

Humanity is engaged in an endeavour to amplify the human capacities. When the limits are reached, mechanisms are put in place. Hubble is about the extending of these limits. Being closer to its objective, it does not have to fight the smog which humans have built up around our globe, and which makes astronomical work so difficult on earth. The other great enemy of astronomers is light flooding the sky from cities around the globe.

We filth up our earth, and that is seized upon as an excuse for space exploration, and the plans for humans to populate space. Filth up the nest, and search for new spaces.

But how does Hubble see? It does not see, it measures. So how do *we* see what it does not see? That is a conundrum which needs to be resolved, because otherwise we are like primitive people confronted by photography for the first time, and who do not understand what they are looking at.

We do not understand the Hubble photographs. We certainly misunderstand them. It cannot be that the exploration of deep space billions of light-years away can result in a flat expanse which we find comprehensible. If our minds cannot figure out the ongoing cosmic configuration, how can it be registered on a piece of plastic 3 x 2 cm in diameter? It does not stand up.

What we have is a mental construct aimed to ease transition to the new. The new in this case would be such a shock, that we are given something that we can latch onto with safety. The Hubble photographs are, for us, what the 'T-in-O' maps were for the Middle Ages. Measures of support for a transitional age.

The 'T-in-O' maps were more statements of faith rather than a description of the world – they anchored faith. They described faith, they produced a feeling of security within the believers. The Hubble photographs support similar functions.

Out there in the indescribable galaxies is a world so inhospitable to humanity that the imagination freezes. The Hubble photographs bring that immensity within our grasp, and so give a measure of comfort; ease a transition towards the new.

Faith is needed to pursue a task as gigantic as the exploration of space. The Hubble photos anchor that faith in icons of this time, carried on the front pages of newspapers like banners at a religious procession of the past.

Maps and globes have always been more than merely descriptive. They are articles of faith, advancing the nation and culture producing them.

They are weapons in a geopolitical endeavour. The Hubble images are fully in line with this. They are used by NASA as well as by its European associate ESA to demonstrate and consolidate Western power.

They are icons of belief and domination in the tradition of crosses and sculptures of Christ, the Virgin and Saints carried in processions. And the more awesome, and to a degree, the more distorted and mystifying, the greater the potential impact on the world.

notes

1. Lautréamont, Comte de, *Lautréamont's Maldoror*, trans. Alexis Lykiard, London, Allison & Busby, 1970.

2. The artist Mark Quinn produced a sculpture based on a cast of his own head, filled with nine pints of his own blood. It is currently part of the Saatchi collection, London.

chapter 8

a more convivial perspective system for artists

peter cresswell

Illusion and art are uneasy bedfellows. This is largely because an illusion short-circuits language while art can only be said to be effective when it manipulates and anticipates language, so illusion tricks the mind while art must persuade the mind. Perspective links the two because it is an idea that seeks to formalise the behaviour of an illusion and in doing so takes on some of the characteristics of language and therefore the potential for being manipulated within the field of art. Perspective organises the apprehension of depth by recognising the shapes which objects adopt when they are described in a theoretical space which is, in reality, a flat, two-dimensional picture plane. Perspective is an agent of picturing and a picture is the product of a relationship forged between the particular and the general – the object and its surroundings. Objects are those things that are identifiable by being named, or recognised, as significant bits of the continuum. We notice them. We also notice their relationship one with another in space because this relationship affects their appearance.

A cube conforms to a set of theoretical determinants: all its angles are right angles, all its edges are equal in length, but when we observe a cube in space none of these theoretical criteria can be seen to apply. Its angles do not appear to be equal and nor do its edges. It has become an irregular shape. Two identical cubes in space appear as two irregular shapes but their irregularity seems to have a common basis theorised as perspective. We expect the more distant cube to appear to be smaller than the nearer one and that the further face of each cube will appear to be smaller than the near face; in fact, the near face might completely obscure the far face so that the idea of a cube is no longer communicated and is replaced by the image of a flat square. These are very simple observations but when we come to examine the exact nature of the shapes adopted by three-dimensional objects when they are pictured within a two-dimensional image, things get much more complicated.

Imagine that you are standing opposite a long, flat, rectilinear wall. It stretches away from you on either side. You look left and you can see that the distant vertical edge of the wall appears to be smaller than the vertical dimension immediately opposite you in the middle of the wall – likewise when you look right. Also, you will notice that the angles formed by each corner of the wall are obtuse – not right angles as you would expect them to be. Therefore, the shape formed by your image of the wall cannot be a rectangle and conflicts directly with the information provided by your tactile experience of the world of objects. In fact, no arrangement of straight lines can correspond to the data assembled in your brain as a consequence of the act of seeing. So, if the wall is to be pictured, it edges must be unstraight. If the wall is endlessly long it will appear to vanish at points on either side of you. As these points are set at infinity and opposite each other, the only way that the visual substance of the wall can appear as an image is for the lines that represent its edges (which you know to be straight) to bend. This is why it is difficult to form pictures of the metropolitan landscape which give the same sense of enclosure that one feels when one is surrounded by tall buildings viewed from the pavement close by. Imagine looking up at two adjacent, tall, rectilinear buildings. Each floor of windows and other features will appear to get smaller as you scan up the building – as will the gap between the buildings. The image formed, therefore, must be of two diminishing structures leaning towards one another. In practice, the eyes will seek out each vertical in turn and observe it to be vertical while at the same time noticing the convergence at the top of the buildings. This is conflicting information and if a picture of the whole is to be formed the brain will be required to negotiate an image that conforms to our particular needs at the time. If we wish to check that the building is rectilinear we will verify that each vertical is vertical by viewing each in turn and ignoring the convergence caused by the top floor being much further away than the ground floor. If we wish to construct a picture of the generality of the two buildings in their relative locations we will have to set aside some of the factors that we have noticed during our detailed observation.

While a pictorial description of an object can take many forms that do not attempt to engage with the experience of seeing (blue-print, map or diagram), those which do will seek to trigger the memory with sufficient conviction to be described as an illusion. Perspective, in whatever form, is a geometric analysis of the effects of the anamorphic changes that occur when we shift our viewpoint when observing known solids in space. If you close one eye and look out of a window from a fixed position and trace on the glass an outline of what you see, you will be drawing an image that conforms to traditional plane projection perspective. If you now look at the same scene in the same way but through a spherical glass dome of equal radius from the eye and make a drawing of what you see on the surface, the image will conform to various theories of curvilinear perspective. If you now overlay both transparent screens in their original positions so that you can view them simultaneously, your two drawings will precisely coincide with one another and with the scene that you have drawn – hardly surprising. Yet when they are viewed separately as pictures, each will demonstrate a surprising divergence from each other and from your memory of the appearance of the real world scene which was the source of your observations. This is because a picture is a material object in the world like all other objects, including those that it is attempting to depict. The picture is both here and not here, in that it will only be communicative if it conveys something beyond its objective self. This will always entail some degree of illusion. If the picture does communicate, it will have engaged with your memory of ordering sensual experience and will be performing in a way that suggests a characteristic of language. Language is learned and communicated through familiarity with its rules; the history of Western painting, now superseded by photography, has trained us to recognise plane projection perspective (the drawing on the flat window pane) as one of its founding regulations. Curvilinear perspective (the drawing on the sphere) has no more status than a novel eccentricity. Likewise, we popularly believe that the pinhole camera is a distortionless instrument and that the fish-eye lens is a distorting instrument. So why is this a problem?

The geometry used to construct an image with simple plane projection perspective is only entirely satisfactory at the very centre of the image. An anamorphic distortion (of the image itself not the objects depicted) radiates from the centre by degrees that are proportionate to the distance from the centre. These can only be 'corrected' by viewing the image with one eye from the precise position demanded by the geometry. (This would require us to squint at a family photograph with one eye from a distance of about 6 inches.) From any position other than dead centre, and at right angles to the plane of the picture, an anamorphic distortion will disturb the image of the frame of the picture so that it no longer appears to be formed of right-angles. Intellectually, we discount this effect because experience tells us that we can anticipate that the shape is probably a real-world rectangle that is only being altered by our oblique viewing position. Nevertheless, in doing so we cannot also accommodate an anamorphic distortion in the picture itself. Similarly, we do not notice the distortion of this text when our eyes are not at right angles to the page, nor do we need to sit precisely in front of the TV to believe that we are seeing a correctly formed picture. A perspective system should be evaluated by the quality of the illusion that it creates. This can be measured by the way in which a shape can represent the anamorphic distortion of the known tactile form of an object when we picture it in space. The shape should encourage belief rather than demand obedience.

Holbein called these ideas into question in his painting *The Ambassadors* (see Figure 8.1). When we view it from a normal position there is this strange disconnected blur slashed over the foreground of the painting. To decode the image contained in the slash we have to move to an extreme angle of view from where it will appear as a skull. (The same effect can be seen when advertising logos are seen to be upright when painted on the surface of a games field and viewed from a fixed camera angle.) However, the interesting thing about the Holbein is that because we correct the automatic anamorphic distortion to the frame as we casually view the picture from a variety of angles, we can hold that correction even at the extreme angle from which we are required to view the skull. The generality of the picture excluding the skull remains the same, held as it is by the 'idea' of the rectilinear frame even though the rectangle, as I have shown with the example of the long wall, cannot be seen, in a diagrammatic sense, from any position. Meanwhile the skull, the receptacle for the sensuary machinery of the brain, remains detached – only visible from a point outside the normal viewing arena for the picture.

Conventional plane projection perspective was given enormous institutional authority by the nineteenth-century academies. The adventurous speculation sparked by the Renaissance had

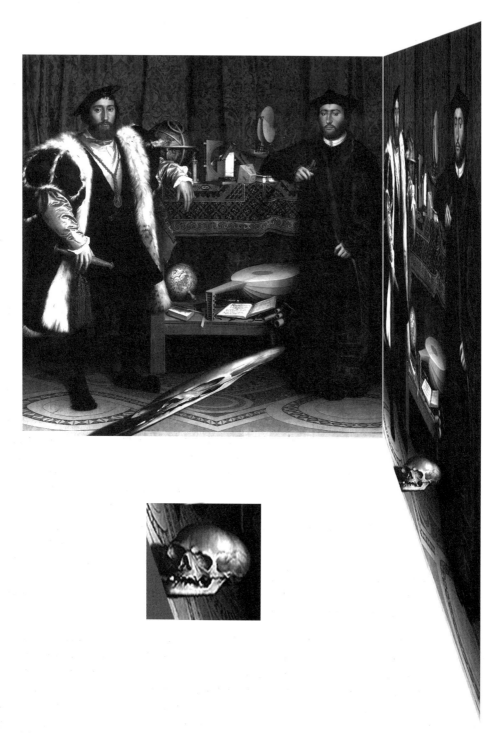

8.1 'the ambassadors' by holbein seen head-on and at the angle necessary to reveal the skull

given way to a mechanistic certainty confirmed by the science of optics. The picture frame belonged to the architecture which housed it and pictorial images were required to reinforce the continuous authority of architectural space. This is a perspective for palaces not for scenes of intimacy and domesticity. Plane projection perspective requires a distant viewpoint and a very constrained angle of view (hence the keyhole character of the modern camera). The larger the subject, the further away it has to be to avoid becoming unacceptably distorted – as opposed to being acceptably distorted, i.e. so little that we are unlikely to notice it. But as the spatial arena for artistic concepts has shifted from grand architectural space to domestic space, or psychological space, plane projection perspective has been largely abandoned by artists as an intellectual concern and its application has been left to the camera. So it is photography that is the present-day standard bearer for a fifteenth-century theory of pictorial representation and, by inference, this suggests that the photograph is as near as we can get to a pictorial representation of the image formed in our minds as a product of the act of seeing. The consequence is that we no longer trust the complex evidence provided by our eyes, preferring instead to defer to the dazzling level of detail seen by the camera, rather than the underlying pictorial structure. The assumption that an image constructed by camera obscura conforms in structure to an image 'seen' in the mind can only be tested against the experience of those (artists) who attempt to reveal what they see. The camera can only describe what it sees and plane projection perspective explains the principles which justify the image produced. However, it does not follow that the same explanation will suffice for the human experience of seeing.

However, there is a history of discomfort with the certainty with which it was assumed that the precise correlation between the results obtained by camera obscura and the geometry of plane projection perspective proved that the images produced must be the same as those formed in the brain as a consequence of the act of seeing. Truth and art are ideas that are difficult to reconcile yet perceived untruthfulness is a barrier to communication. Throughout the history of the development of plane projection perspective, artists have known that they would be open to a charge of untruthfulness if they obeyed the rules of perspective to the letter and in all circumstances. Leonardo da Vinci, Raphael and J.M.W. Turner were all artists who demonstrated considerable skill in the application of the laws of perspective yet, at the same time, they had no doubt that its serious shortcomings would require alternative strategies if their spatial designs were to find satisfactory expression. Each had to find an accommodation between the architectural rigour of perspective and the evidence of their own eyes when drawing from the human model in the studio. They knew that in practice, implausible shapes would emerge if the rules of perspective were strictly applied to spherical or cylindrical forms – no small matter when the human form would be included in this category. So humans had to be drawn freehand and inserted into an environment by reference to their height and little else.

It is instructive to ponder on the meaning of the term 'free-hand'. Until the latter half of this century the European artist was trained by methods that had been institutionalised by the academies and were derived from Renaissance thought. One learned to draw architectural settings (perspective), to invent landscape (from notes and observations made in the field), and to make detailed studies of the human figure by drawing from life in the studio. The first two had a quasi-scientific aspect whilst the third was 'free-hand'. In other words it was, and it had to be, freed from the rules of perspective in order to produce a convincing description of the forms observed. Leonardo's famous diagram[1] explains the problem and torpedoes plane projection perspective as the final solution to the quest for an unproblematic geometry to explain the disposition of shapes that represent three-dimensional forms when seen in space (see Figure 8.2). Leonardo da Vinci wrote about the nature of the mismatch between his observations and the prevailing theory[2] and Panofsky goes so far as to propose that he did formulate a radical alternative, a curvilinear theory of perspective but that this was subsequently lost.[3] If so, he was the first in a long line of non-conformist perspectivists who broadly agree that it is the insistence on portraying the image of a straight line as a straight line which prevents plane projection perspective from addressing itself to objects that are near or to a wide angle of view. The curvilinear systems proposed by Hauck,[4] Barre and Flocon,[5] Hanson,[6] Stark,[7] etc., all agree about the broad strategy and have attracted some critical support but each has been so afflicted with practical objections that they have opened the door to vigorous attack by eminent defenders of the status quo – theoreticians such as Gombrich[8] and Doesschate.[9]

Meanwhile, the adoption of the photograph as an unquestioned image of reality has meant that we have become so familiar with the underlying structure, buried as it is in a wealth of dazzling detail, that any other system of representation is referred to as distorted. Distortion in this case implies a divergence from an accepted cultural norm – plane projection perspective – not a disturbance of a recognised truth. The search for a more truthful (or more persuasive) illusion is still with us. We are impressed, rather than persuaded, by photography. A photographic image looks photographic. Three-dimensional images produced by photographic methods (stereographs, holograms, virtual reality) are still first recognised for what they are. The brain then adjusts and the illusion can take hold. It is perhaps for this reason that artists are so deeply ambiguous about their distrust of illusion and so vigorous in their desire for the evocation of feelings. Although they still use perspective from time to time, it tends to be equated with a cold and distant interest in order. For perspective to become warm, as it were, it needs to address values associated with intimacy, to change *the* cube to *my* cube.

Any picture of an object in space depends upon the recall and application of values that have been perceived when observing our environment. If these values are three-dimensional they will be ordered in an imaginary space, a model in the mind. In order to communicate a picture of this space, a uniform relationship has to be found between our physical experience of the tactile world and our memories of seeing it, and as there is no direct equivalent to the picture in nature, some intellectual basis for communicating ideas about spatial organisation will always need to be adopted or invented. Picturing occurs when a relationship is forged between the particular and the general. In other words, we create an image of our surroundings by noticing things and their relationship to one another in space. The named 'things' can be considered one by one but it is the passage from one to another which generates a structural armature which can be considered as a unifying concept. This armature is a product of an activity, i.e. looking. It is not a characteristic of the 'things'. It is a trace of the continuity of values which occur when any situation is viewed from any particular position. Picturing this armature requires a theoretical proposal for its organisation and while measurable consistency is a primary aim, there remains the question of the character that any system will impose on an image. The effect is not neutral so some further criteria must be introduced to qualify the usefulness of the proposal. Does it look right? Does it feel like real space? Does it suspend belief in the materiality of the object supporting the picture – the paper, the canvas, the screen, etc.?

Drawing is the first primitive step towards pictorial communication; it is the visual equivalent of thinking aloud. A linear outline is an abstract concept which reveals thought rather than sensation. It traces that which we suppose or propose to be there. It is, and always has been, a product of the mind using the resource of the active eye and data gathered from the memory of seeing. Geometry is the mathematical explanation of formalised drawing. Perspective is the application of geometry to the changes that occur in the appearance of objects when they , or we, move. We move so that we can understand what we see. We pan and scan, we range-find and prioritise. The value of a perspective system is that it can reveal elements of these processes. It turns them into language. 'Radial Perspective' is the name that I have given to the procedure that I have devised for generating an image of a known or imagined structure in pictorial space. It is the product of practical experiments and has evolved as a consequence of many years of sporadic enterprise. At each stage, the image produced has had to satisfy specific criteria:

1.   Does a drawing of a simple solid of known dimensions remain convincing when located in a variety of positions within the proposed cone of vision?

2.   Does the procedure still produce satisfactory results when applied to objects in the immediate proximity of the viewer?

3.   Will the image generated produce a satisfying three-dimensional illusion when observed using a Wheatstone-type of stereoscopic viewer?[10]

4.   Does the application of the procedure induce a spatial awareness that feels truthful?

radial perspective: a history of trial and error

I began my quest by literally trying to bend conventional perspective to make it fit my particular needs. At the time, I wanted to draw a tiled floor which I felt I could stand on if it was extended forwards to include me. Observation had already led me to believe that the only satisfactory image would involve bending lines which I knew to be straight in the tactile world. I began by progressively moving the vanishing point for each segment of the picture to reflect the effect of a scan. Intuition did not lead to geometry. A more radical approach was needed. Eventually, I devised a way of drawing the tiled floor with a perspective that I thought was new. The method did not engage my existing knowledge of perspective and gave such a pleasing image that it became the subject of a large painting. However, once I had begun to look for antecedents, I found (to my chagrin) that I had, for all practical purposes, reinvented the system proposed by Guido Hauck in 1875.[11] G. Ten Doesschate had already dismissed Hauck's idea with a devastating proof. (If identical columns are arranged in a circle and viewed from its centre they will, if drawn with Hauck's method, appear as a straight row of identical pillars with no indication whatsoever that they are meant to be situated in a circle.) Yet there was something about Hauck's solitary drawing that suggested to me that he (and I) were on to something. There followed a long period of experiment when I tried endless variations of Hauck's method. The main conclusion of this phase was that while I could obtain a result that looked fairly good, it was not blessed with theoretical rigour. I had sought a compromise between the flat picture plane of conventional perspective and the semi-circular panoramic picture plane proposed by Hauck. My intermediate solution was to reorganise the data provided by a semi-circular picture plane by projecting it on to another arc with a larger radius.

Although I broadly agreed with Hauck that as the predominant axis of the scanning eyes is lateral, one can accept that while in each segment of a lateral pan a vertical would remain vertical, the horizontal axis would be bent. But it is much too prescriptive to limit a proposed pictorial system to a landscape, side-to-side format, so a way had to be found that dealt with the up-and-down. By then I was aware of the system proposed by Barre and Flocon[12] and by Robert Hanson[13] and although I agreed with most of their physiological observations, I found their results unconvincing. (They both work inwards from the periphery of 180° pan.) By then I had exhausted the possibilities of progressive modification and realised that I would have to look for a more radical solution. I knew that I wanted a procedure that radiated from the centre and did not prioritise a particular axis. It would also help if I did not need to locate distant vanishing points. In the end, the answer proved to be very simple. If I had the necessary information to survey a plan and elevation, I had the means of measuring the deflection of the axis proposed by any point in space and its distance from the line of sight or centre of attention. I now had a fluid and theoretically sound procedure which produced very good results but one factor remained a mystery. I was still projecting the image onto a regular arc drawn from a point behind the eye which had been arrived at by trial and error. My instinct has always been that the profile of this arc would be a parabola. (Hanson had developed this argument, Stark had been heading in this direction, Leonardo had set the hare running.) All my experiments had shown me that the optimum picture plane lay somewhere in the space between the flat plane of plane projection perspective and the semi-circular panoramic plane of Hauck. Eventually I found that by simply bisecting the space between these alternatives a surprisingly complex profile is produced which has deliciously appropriate characteristics. I had my answer.

Imagine a three-dimensional conceptual environment which can include all the possible points in the space contained within a cone whose base is at infinity and whose apex is at the eye. The centre line of sight is represented by the intersection of a horizontal and a vertical plane which divide the cone into four equal segments. (The active field of vision is about 90° at the eye but this is not critical.) Any point to be plotted will be found in one of the four spatial segments by projecting a line at right angles from a point on a plan drawn on the horizontal plane and intersecting it with a line drawn from an elevation on the vertical plane. When seen in cross-section (like a clock face) a line then connects this intersection in the space to the central intersection between the two planes (see Figure 8.3). The angle formed at the centre between this line and the line formed by the cross-section of either the vertical or the horizontal is noted (see Figure 8.4). We now know that the point being calculated lies somewhere along a line radiating from the central point at a pre-determined angle from a vertical or horizontal axis. The next step is to measure the precise distance from the centre and thereby locate the image of the point in space. To do this, a picture plane is passed through the cone at a point determined by the scale required of the resulting picture. The profile of this plane will characterise the image which emerges from these procedures. A flat plane produces an image that appears to be

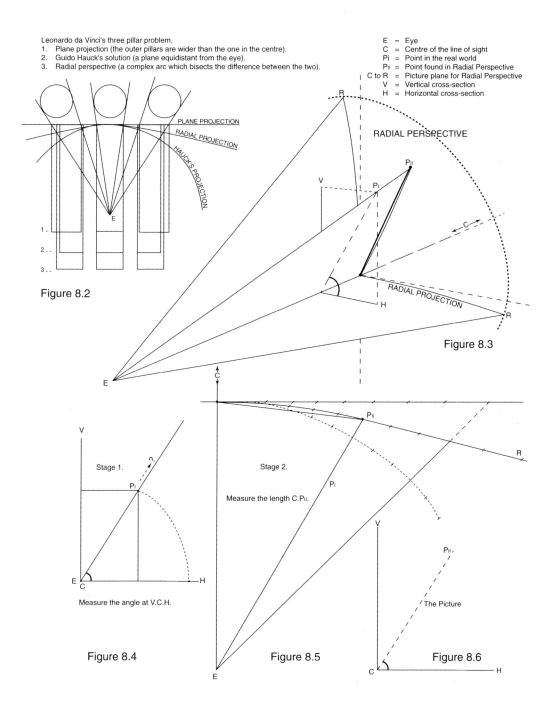

Leonardo da Vinci's three pillar problem.
1.   Plane projection (the outer pillars are wider than the one in the centre).
2.   Guido Hauck's solution (a plane equidistant from the eye).
3.   Radial perspective (a complex arc which bisects the difference between the two).

E   =   Eye
C   =   Centre of the line of sight
Pi   =   Point in the real world
Pᵢᵢ =   Point found in Radial Perspective
C to R = Picture plane for Radial Perspective
V   =   Vertical cross-section
H   =   Horizontal cross-section

PLANE PROJECTION
RADIAL PROJECTION
HAUCK'S PROJECTION

E

1.
2.
3.

Figure 8.2

RADIAL PERSPECTIVE

Pᵢᵢ

V   Pᵢ

C

RADIAL PROJECTION

H

R

Figure 8.3

Pᵢᵢ

Pᵢ

R

V
Stage 1.
Pᵢ

E C
H

Measure the angle at V.C.H.

Stage 2.

Pᵢ

Measure the length C.Pᵢᵢ.

V

Pᵢᵢ

The Picture

C
H

E

Figure 8.4   Figure 8.5   Figure 8.6

concave, i.e., extremities yaw towards you. A semi-circular panoramic plane does the opposite: it produces an image which appears to be convex, i.e., the extremities appear to yaw away from you. Bisecting these extremes with a plane which is produced by halving the section of the space between the flat plane and the semi-circular plane produces a parabola covering about 90° of the cone of vision. It then flattens out again to become a flat plane at infinity on either side of the viewer. When a line is projected from the eye through the point situated in space, its intersection with the parabola is noted and the distance between this intersection and the central point will determine the relative scale of the elements in the emerging picture (see Figures 8.5 and 8.6).

Imagine that you see the world through a taut film of transparent material which stretches to infinity on all sides (the picture plane). You blow and the film flexes away from you forming a circular depression but in the distance there would be little or no effect. You have made a parabolic bulge in the imaginary picture plane which covers the 90° required by the cone of vision.

Radial Perspective can determine the attitude and relative scale of objects in any position within the cone, even when located very near the eye. It creates an image which does not ask the viewers to suspend their normal expectations, i.e., that the periphery can be sensed to be behaving in a subtly different way to the centre of attention. The 90° range of the cone is only notional but it is based on the practical observation that beyond somewhere around 90° there is a marked lack of definition. Although my method can generate a full 180° view, this would represent an unpanned stare which would be an unnatural way of observing this width of view. However, peripheral vision must have a role in contextualising the active central zone. We don't look *at* it because this would move it into the central zone by panning or rotating the head. To take account of the peripheral is to leave it where it is and try to picture it as it is. We can see that the periphery is vague and unfocused but we can still recognise the relative scale of objects so it is in this region that the extreme can become pictorially effective.

When two drawings, one for each eye, are constructed in this way (see figures 8.7 and 8.8) and viewed through two mirrors set at 90° (the Wheatstone arrangement, illustrated in figure 8.9), the resulting stereoscopic image demonstrates the capacity of the system to maintain the illusion of undistorted solids throughout the apparent space, even when these are located very close to the eyes. The brain is able, on the basis of the information provided by the drawings, to negotiate virtual objects set in a virtual space of infinite depth. My previous versions, using a plane arc drawn around a centre set behind the eye, had only been exposed as deficient when viewed through the stereoscope and it was the objective clarity of the stereoscopic image which developed the critique which has eventually led me to my present conclusions.

At present, Radial Perspective is hand-made and very laborious, requiring a considerable working area to produce an image. For me, however, the results are deeply satisfying so the man-hours are justified. I am not a mathematician but I do know that the mathematics are relatively simple so a predictive computer program is at least a sporting possibility. There are also obvious implications for the photographic image. If, as I maintain, there is a natural or undistorted attitude for the plane which gathers together the relative measurements which

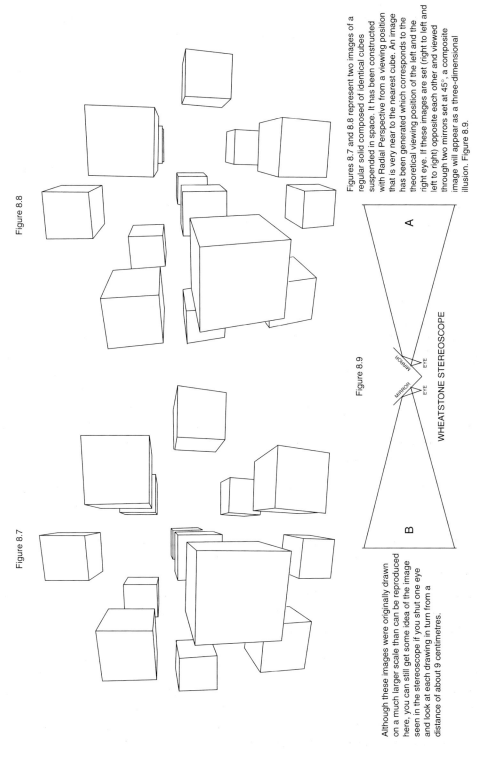

Figure 8.8

Figure 8.7

Figure 8.9

Figures 8.7 and 8.8 represent two images of a regular solid composed of identical cubes suspended in space. It has been constructed with Radial Perspective from a viewing position that is very near to the nearest cube. An image has been generated which corresponds to the theoretical viewing position of the left and the right eye. If these images are set (right to left and left to right) opposite each other and viewed through two mirrors set at 45°, a composite image will appear as a three-dimensional illusion. Figure 8.9.

WHEATSTONE STEREOSCOPE

A

B

MIRROR

MIRROR

EYE

EYE

Although these images were originally drawn on a much larger scale than can be reproduced here, you can still get some idea of the image seen in the stereoscope if you shut one eye and look at each drawing in turn from a distance of about 9 centimetres.

8.7 to 8.8 two images of a regular solid constructed with radial perspective

8.9 the wheatstone stereoscopic viewer

determine the appearance of objects in space, this would have implications for the lens manufacturer. The present benchmark is the pinhole but as I am suggesting that the pinhole is at one end of the spectrum of distortion and the fisheye at the other, a plane arc between the two will not suffice. A lens manufactured to conform to the profile proposed by my Radial Perspective would be a joy indeed.

notes

1. Kemp M., and Walker, M., *Leonardo da Vinci on Painting*, New Haven, Yale University Press, 1989, p. 60.

2. Ibid. p. 63.

3. Panofsky., E., *The Codex Huygens and Leonardo da Vinci's Art Theory*, London, Warburg Institute, 1940.

4. Hauck, G., *Die Subjektive Perspektive und die Horizontalen Curvaturen des Dorischen Styls*, Stuttgart, Verlag von Konrad Wittwer, 1879

5. Barre, A., and Flocon, A., *La Perspective Curvaligne*, Paris, Flammarion, 1968.

6. Hanson, R., 'This Curving World; Hyperbolic Linear Perspective', *Journal of Aesthetics and Art Criticism*, 32, 1973–1974

7. Stark, F., *Netzhautbild-Perspective*, 1928, cited by Doesschate, G., *Perspective*, Nieuwkoop, Nieuwkoop B. de Graaf, 1964, pp. 52–53.

8. Gombrich, E.H., *Art and Illusion*, Oxford, Phaidon, 1960, p. 218.

9. Ten Doesschate, G., *Perspective*, Nieuwkoop, Nieuwkoop B. de Graaf, 1964, p. 59.

10. Wheatstone, C. *The Bakerian Lecture – Contributions to the Physiology of Vision*, London, Philosophical Transactions of the Royal Society of London, 1852, Part 11, p. 2.

11. Hauck, op. cit.

12. Barre and Flocon, op. cit.

13. Hanson, op. cit.

bibliography

Alberti, L.B., 'De Pictura and De Statua', ed. Grayson C. London, Phaidon, 1972.
Barre, A., and Flocon, A., *La Perspective Curvaligne*, Paris, Flammarion, 1968.
Carter, B.A.R., 'Perspective' entry in *An Oxford Companion to Art*, edited by Harold Osborne, Oxford, Clarendon Press, 1970.
Crary, J., *Techniques of the Observer*, MIT Press, October Books, 1992.
Davies, M., *Turner as Professor*, London, Tate Gallery, 1992.
Gombrich, E.H., *Art and Illusion*, Oxford, Phaidon, 1960.
Gombrich, E.H., Hochberg, J., and Black, M., *Art Perception and Reality*, Baltimore, The Johns Hopkins University Press, 1972.
Hanson, R., 'This curving world: Hyperbolic linear perspective', *Journal of Aesthetics and Art Criticism*, 32, 1973–1974, pp. 147–161.
Hauck, G., *Die Subjektive Perspektive und die Horizontalen Curvaturen des Dorischen Styls*, Stuttgart, Verlag von Konrad Wittwer,1879.

Irvins, W.M., *Art and Geometry*, New York, Dover, 1964.

Kemp, M., and Walker, M., *Leonardo on Painting*, New Haven, Yale University Press, 1989.

Pirenne, M.H., *Optics, Painting and Photography*, Cambridge, Cambridge University Press, 1970.

Panofsky, E., *The Codex Huygens and Leonardo da Vinci's Art Theory*, London, Warburg Institute, 1940.

Panofsky, E., *Perspective as Symbolic Form*, New York, Zone Books, 1991.

Ten Doesschate, G., *Perspective*, Nieuwkoop, Nieuwkoop B. de Graaf, 1964.

White, J., *The Birth and Rebirth of Pictorial Space*, London, Faber and Faber, 1957.

Wheatstone, C., *The Bakerian Lecture – Contributions to the Physiology of Vision*, London, Philosophical Transactions of the Royal Society of London, 1852.

chapter 9

ancient oaks

a one-act play

garth rennie[1] and ronald fraser-munro[2]

CHARACTERS

OSCAR: A senior member of staff at the Academy

DICK: A rising academic star and untenured lecturer at the Academy

The location is the Dean's chambers at a prestigious academy. The room is large and spacious with a high ceiling and windows draped in heavy velvet curtains. It has the air of a Victorian patriarch's study. A large, leather-topped desk divides the far end of the room in two. The desk is minimally furnished with an old-fashioned desk lamp, a foolscap leather binder, a small metal globe of the world, and a small leather picture frame. It is early afternoon and the curtains are open, yet the room is somehow gloomy and austere. The middle-aged, sour-complexioned academic Oscar is dressed in black and white.

ACT I The Interview

Scene I An Introduction

Oscar is standing behind the desk, his hands clasped behind his back. There is a knock on the door and Oscar removes his pocket watch from his waistcoat, looks at it and purses his lips before replacing it.

OSCAR: [*moving from the window and sitting at the desk. He opens the binder as he bellows*] Come! [*Dick enters and closes the door behind him. He is taller than Oscar and much younger. His dress sense is postmodern bohemian and he wears two wrist-watches on his left wrist*] Hello Dick, take a seat . . . [*Oscar offers his hand to Dick who stretches over the desk to shake it. Oscar gestures to the chair in front of the desk*] I have your file here and I must say that I find the work you're doing very . . . interesting . . . !

DICK: [*pulling the chair towards him and then sitting. He places a small file of papers upon the desk*] Thank you.

OSCAR: [*looking at Dick who sits upright in his chair throughout Oscar's address*] However, there are several things we need to discuss; in particular, the university's new self-appraisal form you have submitted. Given the nature of your work on academic politics, I know you have given considerable thought to the complex 'realpolitik' within which we must operate. [*Oscar puts his hands on to the desk in  front of him and crosses his fingers which he occasionally twiddles*] Now I probably don't need to spell this out to you but, in my view, this new form of assessment is perhaps not so much about staff development as it is about the college administration demanding that department heads assume responsibility for the productivity of their staff, so that a more explicit system of responsibility for monitoring productivity is established. Clearly, the outlook is that self-assessment at individual, departmental and collegiate levels will become more important, since appraisal will be increasingly tied to funding. So I intend to be as clear as possible about what we are dealing with here, since you are only on a temporary contract. [*Oscar averts his eyes from Dick*] On that note, I have to say that the budget for next year is still uncertain, and given the Rector's targeting of temporary and sessional staff, we cannot guarantee that your position will be renewed next year, despite the fact that we would, ahem . . . miss your teaching in the department. We're in the invidious position of 'wait and see', therefore we cannot yet discuss a permanent contract for you . . . and although there is some strong support amongst senior staff there is, as I expect you're aware, some noteworthy dissent. Personally, I think the nature of your work is very ambitious and challenges many assumptions within the discipline. But the picture of your research from your vitae and self-assessment document needs to be much, much clearer. [*Oscar leans back*] If you had to summarise your research in one or two sentences what would you say?

Scene II Two Short Answers

DICK: [*relaxing a little and taking his time with his thoughts*] Well, broadly speaking I would say my work falls within the domain of sociology of science, since it is about the role of academic politics in the production of knowledge, especially those categories of knowledge in the human sciences which in some way claim to be 'critical'. My aim has been to develop a means for investigating the  constitution of authority, particularly that surrounding the evaluation of academic practice and the forms of comportment these practices promote.

OSCAR: [*glancing down at the top sheet in his binder on the desk*] And how would you say this materialises into academic research? [*Oscar picks up his pen and starts to make short notes on the paper in front of him, glancing up occasionally as if doodling*]

DICK: Well, this is where it becomes more complicated, obviously, since it involves trying to address a range of interrelated issues, not the least of which is what it might mean to attempt to do such work given our current circumstances . . . whereby the concept of 'the embodied present' comes to take particular importance. For instance, what are the costs associated with a person's refusal to participate? What are the boundaries of entitlement? I would like to draw attention to the ethical —

Scene III Practices and Points of Research (Dick's Sales Pitch)

OSCAR: [*with minute excitement*] But this is exactly the point I'm trying to make . . .

DICK: [*agreeing as he interrupts Oscar*] All right, well, firstly I've attempted to identify divisions of thought in the human sciences; for instance, the struggle over the term 'discourse'. Secondly, to locate this struggle within a particular discipline of knowledge, such as psychology. [*Dick is getting into his thoughts and starts to use his hands to elucidate his thoughts. As the meeting continues noises and visions manifest themselves within the environment of the room. These are audio-visual incarnations of Dick's psyche and although Oscar cannot see or hear them clearly, he is aware of the occasional odour or blur of spirit manifestation and becomes increasingly unsettled by these disembodied familiars.*] These could be researched genealogically, by tracing a system of practices and truths through seemingly discontinuous events leading to the emergence of an identifiable field of knowledge such as 'critical' psychology. This would investigate the use of particular materials as evidence of the emergence of fields of expertise populated by individuals and legitimised by relevant institutions. [*Oscar clasps his fingers*] For instance, 'discursive psychology', 'qualitative research' and 'critical psychology' are some of the terms coming into legitimacy in the academy. This is an important dimension of the research since it focuses on relations of power in the production of knowledge, especially when it incorporates the constitution of the 'critical' psychologist as subject acting upon him or herself. So, there is a need to open up this space and to focus on the negotiations of this rather unusual human subject in its environment.

At the same time though, I'm very interested in what I see as some of the limitations posed to the examination of pedagogic institution from a post-structural framework and this has led me to develop comparative methods in research between post-structuralism and more traditional empirical approaches. Subsequently, I've tried to produce discourse which focuses on subjective experience and, like the productive kernel of genealogical research, produces a contradiction rendering 'the epochal present' problematic; a solitude from which, discourse seemingly cannot continue. Subsequently, the empirical work takes the form of conversational monologues with academics about the subjective experience of being qualitative researchers in psychology. This practice involves producing non-argumentative, testimonial discourse – or what I see as a particular form of 'truth-telling', the representation of which is ultimately 'undecidable'. These are some of the components I feel are of importance when attempting a history of the present, focusing specifically on the politics of truth in academic knowledge production.

OSCAR: [*nods briefly, but looks a little unsure of his surroundings, clears his throat and reasserts himself*] I think I understand a bit more the unresolvableness of the conflict for you in representing what was said . . . which, in a sense, is a measure of the productiveness of the space you have opened up by your interviewing strategy.

DICK: Yes, and by so doing, to bring the question of normativity to the forefront of a 'mutually embedded' form of knowledge. For instance, the divisions in linguistics presently dividing the human sciences need to be viewed simultaneously, as in Jean-Luc Nancy's idea of 'being-with' rather than being reduced, or put in contradistinction with one another, a form of aesthetics which is able to accommodate and to appreciate similarity and difference in the movement across forms of thought and being. Part of the task is to articulate and to illustrate these different forms as co-existent, rather than having to choose or to interpret, and I think that is a truer representation of what it means to aspire to a critical positioning in the academy . . . but it requires a tremendous amount of work.

OSCAR: [*trying to appear sympathetic*] Certainly, but . . . I'm not sure that is something which the academy has the mechanism and the wherewithal to do.

DICK: [*in a calm relaxed manner*] No, I think it's antithetical to the climate within which we're being asked to produce ourselves and our work. It's about scholarship really: the academy as it is presently constituted is opposed to that, the academy asks us to construct, not deconstruct ourselves. [*The room becomes still and Oscar makes a note on his papers. He looks up*]

Scene IV Oscar's Beloved Ancients (A Convergence of Ideas)

OSCAR: [*leans back in his chair and looks directly at Dick*] What about the form of the book . . . because I always see the book as almost an inextricable part of the academy, the form of the book in its role and significance. Does the book have the propensity to allow us to deconstruct ourselves? [*leaning forward in anticipation of talking on one of his favoured subjects*] This is perhaps my own critique of the book culture since Plato at least. Parmenides put the world in a timeless frame, there is the assumption that the truth [*Dick has floated off into his own thoughts, and although facing Oscar, is conferring with a stern, middle-aged* VICTORIAN GENTLEMAN *in a frock coat and large whiskers standing to his right and clearly bemused by Dick's attitude towards him*] in discourse can only be found momentarily: it has a freeze-frame mentality which has made a substantial impact on the way we lead our lives . . . it has produced a form of [*Dick returns to Oscar's monologue and the Victorian gentleman stops his assault on Dick and vanishes, obviously disgruntled*] rationality which makes us feel uncomfortable in believing two things at once . . . when in fact, the whole metaphor of believing two things at once is not necessarily inconsistent. In speech we can only make one axiomatic proposition at a time; yet, as Heraclitus showed, everything has multivalent attributes . . . and where I find your work challenging, [*Oscar's face lights up*] and inspiring, actually. In your reference to people like John Shotter, rather than just sticking *to* the adversarial model you talk about speaking *into* the discourse. The discourse is not this classic alternating exchange mode, from A to B and back again, which is what the information theorists often presume: it is a kind of being-with and speaking-with [*a* ROYAL CANADIAN MOUNTED POLICEMAN *stands at the door observing Dick and Oscar suspiciously*] and, arguably, the Internet is a writing-with or even an 'indexical signing'-with, and that is a novel proposition. I think one of the things I've been trying to write about in the original title to my book collection refers to the virtual and, in looking at the Latin word from whence it comes, there seems to be a much closer relationship between virtue and truth, between the semantic and the ethical notions of virtue, and . . . er, I take it you are referring to specific academic discourses and seeing a lack of rapport?

DICK: [*moving his chair to face slightly outwards, as if expecting someone to enter the room. This is seen by Oscar who looks at the door before composing himself and focusing upon Dick's words*] I think that is an important point which is another facet of academic conduct as an ethical issue, that it is about what form of rela-tionship to oneself and one another that each of the forms of being necessary for survival should have. Since what is foremost at issue is not the question of the content of academic research but the more foundational question of the form of academic practice. For

instance, what does it mean to oppose? To what extent can one refuse to participate in, for instance self-assessment? Because, as people like Foucault suggest, it is not so much that such a thing as being critical is denied or refused, but rather the way being critical is transformed into discourses which are normative and politically conservative. Confessional technologies of evaluation such as self-assessment are integral to opposition becoming normative discourse, hence the institutional need to make them obligatory. This motivates my interest, on the empirical side, in exploring the testimonial as a mode of expression and different from the confessional. Is the bourgeois institution willing and able to accommodate practices potentially antithetical to its established system of power maintenance? Pecuniary advancement, prestige, privilege, career . . . ? Is such a creature as the intellectual, the critical scholar able to survive, and indeed not only survive but flourish and grow in the bourgeois model of knowledge production upon which the university institution is based? Are such an institution's ethics capable of addressing the multiplicity and complexity of the positions of enunciation – of 'the real' complex negotiations? I think engaging the issue of the politics of intellectual authority demands an attempt to address some of these issues. It is about truth in the present, which leads one to the division in thought between form's aesthetics derived from a minimal and relational conception of the subject . . . [*A sharp gust of wind is heard and the curtain behind Oscar flaps. Oscar stiffens but does not look behind him*]

Scene V *The Dean Reclaims the Meeting's Purpose (Appraisal)*

OSCAR: [*enjoying a small sinister smile*] Is there any way you can put a more ambiguous spin on the title of your article [*glancing down*] . . . er . . . 'Self Assessment: Confess the Truth about Oneself or be Damned' . . . so that it might be more suitable for inclusion in the department's next performance review by self-assessment?

DICK: [*manages a sickly grin*]

OSCAR: [*in a warm but official voice*] Participation is mandatory, Dick; you cannot *not* participate. The department needs to get its most successful members on the inside; obscurity is disadvantaged, despite all the flannel about deregulation, the government believes that academic institutions have gained too much autonomy, they need to be cut down to size. We are all aware that publication is a major part of the criteria for assessment. The requirement is for succinct statements of identifiable objectives and evidence of our attaining these objectives. Models of best practice include being counted 'research active', perhaps through several small, shortish projects . . . but increasingly these must also be funded projects. Your articles are interesting scholarship, not funded research.

Scene VI Dick's Theory of Academic Reality

DICK: What one is not, or seemingly cannot be, within the academic framework . . . um, the academy has been modelled on bourgeois individualism, on providing a safe seclusion, hidden away and removed from society. The discourse was always false, and is now being both affirmed and challenged in complex ways. Self-appraisal is working to make oneself transparent, or perhaps identifiable according to arbitrary prescriptions . . . the inevitability of self-renunciation in such a context, of me having to find the right balance of the positive outweighing the negative within an overall focus on the negative . . . how we come to understand ourselves, our sense of possibilities and limitations in such an environment is of great concern to me. I mean, the idea that I'm to appraise myself according to my own standards is just such a joke, as if there wasn't an existing gold standard from which to evaluate myself!

OSCAR: But the appraisal asks you to evaluate according to your own standards!

DICK: [flushes and looks straight at Oscar] Sorry, but nothing could be more ridiculous, as a-contextual, as a statement such as that. If I were to do this task honestly, really and truly evaluate myself according to my own standards of objectives for my life and my work, it might be impossible to identify what the outer limit might be. What space is there for speaking the truth? What would it mean to speak of desire – to [with a hollow chuckle to himself] want to become the most influential scholar of my generation, to want to destabilise the system of knowledge and power, to want to destroy the system of authority? What opportunity is there for that? It is just outside of the system of discourse available. So what does it mean to tell the truth about oneself in such a context? Since success would mean realisation of the refusal to serve. [Dick pauses] So far our discipline, and human sciences in general, have largely failed to respond to these 'developments' in the university. Consequently, there is a huge despondency amongst academics with critical aspirations. Witness the emergence of cynical reason, of so-called enlightened false consciousness amongst feminists, post-colonial theorists, critical psychologists, gender theorists and so on, where one has a profound sense of hiddenness . . . an incompatibility of objectives whereby career aspirations are pitted against personal aspirations. The only position in this context is to continuously identify oneself as not knowing, of being incapable, of forever failing to meet the competing demands. These cynical positions of enunciation are important, but there can be the evasion of value when there is the presumption and celebration of choice between competing desires, something Steven Connor has referred to as 'retrolepsis', whereby critical knowledges come to reproduce their own authoritative antecedents. There often is no clear choice or delineation between positions one has to occupy as critical academic and normative academic, that position of opposition recedes indefinitely through the depth and continuous practices to affirm legitimacy, the infinite regress of conduct confirming standards so as to demonstrate legitimacy, especially in the practice of evaluating the work of others. As Nietzsche asked, 'Who has the right to speak of rank?' For junior academics like myself, there increasingly appears to be hardly any official accreditation other than that which operates on a system of short-term, identifiable objects such as the fixed-term research project, preferably funded by mainstream funding bodies. These diverse objects and materials must be grouped together into a fictitious unity of procedures so as to demonstrate truth and legitimacy . . . which Foucault referred to as bio-power; or when power/knowledge assumes responsibility for life processes.

EPILOGUE

OSCAR: Yes . . . well, returning to your self-appraisal, I appreciate what you have said, but what we need is the statement in your self-assessment of clear objectives for the upcoming year and evidence of the completion of the objectives identified last year. In other words, looking at your self-assessment from last year as your first objective. Do you understand?

DICK: [*de-energised*] Yes, I believe I do . . . [*Dick stands wearily and pushes the chair towards the desk before turning and leaving the room. Oscar makes a single note before standing and returning to the window, looking out of it and clasping his hands behind his back*]

notes

1. Garth Rennie would like to thank Nick Couldry for insightful comments, some of which found their way into the text.

2. The authors would like to thank John Wood for his support in the preparation of the manuscript.

chapter 10

culture, technology and subjectivity

an 'ethical' analysis

lisa m. blackman

programming freedom

Virtual space – and here I shall refer specifically to virtual reality – has been understood as either providing the means to enable greater freedom and autonomy (a place where one can choose an identity and play away from the material constraints of repressive society) or, in a more dystopian fashion, as dissolving and fragmenting the 'whole person', leading to greater alienation and estrangement from the self and others. These parameters have set the limits or boundaries through which virtual space has been theorised in wider sociological, philosophical and psychological perspectives, and has also entered everyday discourse surrounding the fears and fascinations attached to new communication technologies. Within contemporary 'consumer-led' marketing of technology, virtual space is offered as the site for enabling and maximising freedom and autonomy seen as both desirable and beneficial to humankind. Spanning mainstream representations such as the recent Microsoft commercials to more counter-cultural forms, such as the journal *Wired*, virtual space is the place where the digital revolution is happening, and technology is the new tool of transformation. The lure of freedom and power is seen to be in the hands of the consumer who need only be concerned with making the right 'product choice'. In a utopian fashion, technology and its allied virtual space, are seen as providing liberation for the individual no longer chained by the shackles of everyday space and time. These are familiar arguments and it is not the purpose of this chapter to debate either the utopian or dystopian merits of virtual space, but rather to examine how particular notions of freedom and autonomy have come to define virtual space, and what relation those meanings attached to new technologies circulating within popular culture can tell us about the way we conceive of ourselves and the world in which we live.

beyond the cyber-utopia

One of the most popularised academic discourses surrounding the role of new technologies and their relation to subjectivity is one which Cubitt[1] terms the 'antinatural'. This discourse presumes that new technologies have transformative potential and are credited with the capability to alter 'what it means to be human'. Its transformative ability is usually linked to its interactive potential, enabling it to break down traditional distinctions within the communication process, between the sender and the receiver.[2] The user then takes up a position where they are 'free to choose' from the range of cultural options on offer.[3] Despite the obvious criticism that the choices on offer are themselves highly regulated, the user is seen to take up a position of choice, fluidity and flexibility. This choice gives the user a feeling of control whereby they are able to choose an identity and play away from the material constraints of society. Cubitt[4] terms this a 'cybernatural' discourse, where virtual space is viewed as a 'third space' – a space existing beyond those divisions and limits that currently position subjects in the social world. Virtual identities are those that are fluid, flexible and multiple, heralded by many as a consequence or effect of the greater freedom and autonomy created within the virtual world. It is argued that technology is forcing us to re-evaluate and reconsider the very ways we are formed as human subjects. Gender, race, class and age are now positionings that we are free to choose, play with and discard at will. Play within these accounts is seen to have radical consequences, allowing the user to engage in a non-hierarchical space, where women can be men, men can be women, where anything is possible. Choice, fluidity and flexibility are viewed as part of the process of subject reconstitution, which shows up the constructedness of all those categories and terms through which we are defined.

Both the antinatural and cybernatural discourses view new technology's interactive potential in relation to the *agency* credited to the user within these changing forms of communication. The human subject is seen to be more active, responsible for giving their lives meaning in relation to a more fluid and diverse set of cultural resources inscribed within the virtual space. The subject is capable of forging new and novel connections from the resources or knowledges embedded within these spaces no longer 'territorialised',[5] or governed by particular sets of discursive relations. However, there have been many critiques of the supposed radical potential of the space created for the user in the virtual world. Rather than creating agency and autonomy, they are instead seen to produce subject positions that are organised around fantasies of control, omnipotence and mastery.[6] Virtual space is seen to reproduce a Cartesian space, one where we see from a unique, fixed, monocular viewpoint. At a design level, Penny argues that words such as 'natural', 'simulation' and 'mimesis' enter discussions on how to make virtual reality as 'real' as possible. This viewpoint or 'tacit knowledge' has been criticised as culturally specific, based upon Western art practices which privilege the viewer as the bearer and locus of meaning. As Penny argues, they assume an 'objective' observer, who when placed in an unhindered position can take up an 'ideologically neutral' relation to the images. This creates a subject position or point of identification where the eye of the viewer is in a position of command, entering into a 'world of unhindered voyeuristic desire'.

Woodward[7] has drawn on Freudian psychoanalytic concepts to account for the pleasure and seduction offered through these constructions of virtual space. Freud suggested that one of our deepest-rooted wishes or desires was to become immortal, thus denying the inevitable vulnerability and materiality of the body.[8] He suggested that the way we deal with terrifying feelings of lack and loss attached to these fears is through fantasy. Fantasy thus acts as a defence against the fear, in this case of mortality, and becomes the 'reality' through which we 'live' the social world. Woodward[9] suggests that the desire for immortality inscribed both within the virtual space, and also within those popular stories told about virtual space (such as within the film *The Lawnmower Man*) is one of the biggest fantasies or illusions. In this sense knowledge about the self embodied within the virtual space locks into and reproduces one of our deepest psychic wishes.

This account of virtual space presumes an intimate relation between the 'geography' of the virtual world and a set of psychological wishes or desires which are re-enacted and played out within this world. Play within these accounts is not necessarily radical, reproducing rather than transforming the ways we understand ourselves and others as human subjects. This may be a plausible account of the seductiveness and pleasure afforded to the user within virtual space, but as Woodward[10] warns, it is also important to analyse the way the body is discursively constructed within the virtual world. She locates her argument within the writings of both Donna Haraway[11] and Michel Foucault, suggesting that the virtual world also reproduces power relations. She argues that an 'ideology of difference' is inscribed within the virtual world where particular bodies are despised and abjected. The virtual world merely naturalises divisions that operate in the social world, defining, dividing and positioning the individual in specific ways. One such division which is given attention is the relation of 'age' to the body. She analyses those practices of the self within contemporary Western culture which mark out 'youthfulness' as an aspect of being, to be worked upon and transformed. She asks the question: 'Does our discourse about technology conceal an ideology of age?'

This opens up the debate to consider those other divisions which are inscribed into and reproduced within the virtual world. Many writers and practitioners have focused more on the reproduction rather than the resistance of these ubiquitous images of virtual life to those inequalities and oppressions which epitomise twentieth-century society i.e. gender, class, age, sexuality and sanity.[12] I also want to problematise those fantasies of liberation and transformation attached to technologies, and offer a way of understanding them which not only considers their reproduction of inequality, but also their seductiveness as cultural forms.

foucault's ethics

Foucault in his later writings on 'ethics' and 'techniques of the self' suggested that we are both made, and make ourselves, into particular types of human subject. Rejecting any notion of a pre-given human nature, defined by Cartesian rationality, he analysed instead the way in different spaces and places we are defined and define ourselves in relation to particular knowledges. Knowledge, for Foucault, as for many contemporary writers stemming from post-structuralist and postmodern ideas, does not objectively describe or capture any pre-given reality. With specific regard to the 'self', knowledge does not represent the 'truth' of our being, rather it plays a part in constructing the very terms through which we come to understand and act upon ourselves. Foucault referred to this process as 'subjectification'; the way we are turned and turn ourselves into subjects through particular discourses.

Within contemporary society Foucault suggested that the human sciences play a central role in this process, providing the knowledges through which we come to understand ourselves. Integral to the human sciences, and especially to the 'psy' disciplines (psychology and psychiatry), is an image of personhood which is defined as autonomous, self-regulating, independent and choosing; a clearly bounded entity separate from others. It is this notion of freedom as independence which is viewed as natural to modern forms of sociality and operates as a regulatory ideal. Rose[13] terms this image an 'ethic of autonomous self-hood' where we are required to experience our lives and the decisions we make as reflections of our capacity to choose. Freedom and autonomy are naturalised as goals which enter into the very ways people think about themselves and others. From the sensationalised spaces of talk-shows to adverts for banking services, we are urged and incited to relate to ourselves as selves who are autonomous and independent. As Pini in this collection cogently argues (Chapter 13) this desire for freedom and autonomy also underpins those practices of the self centred upon raving as the ultimate form of freedom and self-expression.

obliged to be free

Many critical psychologists[14] have argued that the 'psy' disciplines play a central role in these processes of subject formation, creating our very desires to be free, autonomous and independent. Rose[15] argues, 'we have come to define and act towards ourselves in terms of a certain notion of freedom'. This notion of freedom is not merely construed as autonomy and independence, but as Rose goes on to argue, as subjects 'who wish to exercise choice in all aspects of their existence, to steer themselves through the world by calculating how to better themselves and their families, striving to increase their quality of life'. It is the linking together of choice, freedom and autonomy which, I shall argue, marks the limits of those tacit knowledges embodied within many virtual worlds. The seductiveness or potency of these virtualities may be the way they reproduce or lock into our very desires for freedom and autonomy, bound up with our very production as human subjects.

interactive art

In a recent exhibition in Helsinki of interactive art,[16] where I presented an abridged version of this chapter,[17] I became excited by the commonality between the theoretical critique I was attempting to mount and similar critiques being made by designers and artists working with interactive art forms. One of the principal strategies employed by many of the artists in the exhibition was to disturb the *choice* offered to the user. The user's expectations were deliberately played around with by introducing into the electronic art works 'bugs' and 'malfunctions'. In this way the works not only offer comments upon mainstream views of interactivity, but also attempt to force the user to reflect upon their own preconceived expectations and desires within virtual space. The purpose of these works is to make strange the familiar, so that the user may begin to 'think differently' about interactivity.

An interesting work in the exhibition by Jim Campbell was entitled, *Untitled (For Heisenberg)*, which attempts to make the spectator aware of his or her own impact and presence in relation to the art work. The work responds to the spectator: as the observer moves through a darkened hallway a life-size image of a couple is projected on to salt from above. As the observer moves towards the image, the image gets smaller and smaller. The viewer's position affects the image in a continuous and gradual way, where no viewer will ever see the same image. The work is based upon the 'Heisenberg Uncertainty Principle' from Quantum Physics, which states that one can never observe an object 'objectively' because the process of observation has an impact upon the object. The more accurately one tries to observe an object, the more that object will be affected and transformed. Campbell uses this principle as a strategy for questioning those concepts, namely control and choice, which are central to mainstream interactive arts. As he states: 'The more you want to see it, the less you see it.'

A similar strategy has been utilised by Tessa Elliot at Middlesex University, where within the context of computer-generated imagery/sound, she moves away from virtual spaces defined in relation to the user's choice to one of reciprocity. This is a notion which forces us to consider how we are affected by, as well as affect, our environments. The concepts of reciprocity, interdependence and contingency which enter into the design and structure of these alternative virtual spaces are radically different and, indeed, provide a meta-commentary upon those concepts such as choice inscribed within traditional virtual forms. Rather than reconfirming those images and terms central to our subjectification, the user's relations are deliberately thwarted and possibly transformed. This is achieved by the use of formulistic devices, sound and imagery which create a very different 'point of identification' or spectating position for the user. The user is not 'free to choose', and indeed any attempt to do so will result in failure.

These examples highlight the need for cultural theorists to develop new and innovative ways of understanding the relation between new technology and wider social and cultural processes. Predominantly within the literature, either utopian or dystopian discourses surround the theorisation of the role of new technology. We have already explored the more utopian discourses, where technology is accorded liberationist potential. The reverse of these are more dystopian discourses that view technology as being bound up with increasing surveillance within society. Technology has become a metaphor for the Panopticon,[18] for the increasing involvement of the state in the personal and private realm. Notably these arguments extend theories of social control, arguing that power relations are now diffuse and multiple, existing within networks of surveillance apparatus throughout the cultural sphere. Although these accounts are seductive and certainly seem to account for the use of digitised information in crime, e.g. the Bulger case,[19] they rely upon a particular conception of power as repressive and dominating, pushing down on us from above. New technology can also be used to challenge the legal and police apparatus, as has been seen with the use of camcorders by activist groups. These discourses entirely disregard Foucault's argument that power is productive and not repressive, actually creating the possible ways that people understand themselves, and restructuring those resistances against them.[20] Power does not act by force or violence: indeed Foucault suggested that if the relationship is one of force, it is not a power relation.[21] Power works on and through free subjects, subjects who are able actively to invest themselves within certain ways of making sense available within the cultural sphere. The question is not so much how power constrains, but why people continually invest themselves in certain ways of understanding their social worlds. What therefore is the link between power as a discursive force, knowledge and people's own desires and investments?[22] This would require going beyond utopian/dystopian arguments to consider the role that new technology may play in processes of subject formation or subjectification.

I suggest that this would involve approaching new technology as a 'culturally embedded phenomenon'. By this I mean that technology is 'more than the sum of its parts'; it is traversed by, and has inscribed within it, culturally embedded values, beliefs and 'ways of making sense'. It is a discursive and signifying practice like any other form of media. One therefore needs to explore the discursive relations inscribed within specific examples of new technology in order to theorise the link these relations may have to a person's own subjectivity. This would involve seeing neither the human subject as pre-given, nor the technology and its effects as predetermined. Both are historical and discursive phenomena and need an analysis that can explore the contingency and specificity of their possible transformative and reproductive potential(s). In order to illustrate these theoretical arguments, I shall focus on a specific example in order to contextualise my claims. Graham Harwood's CD Rom, *Rehearsal of Memory* is pertinent, as it does not fit into new modes of techno-criticism. It is attempting to transform the way people understand so-called insanity and mental distress by resignifying the dominant ways that insanity is constituted as 'other'. It does this, I shall argue, at a psychic, social and discursive level. The work shows not only the failure of the current mental health system, but also the failure of current discourses of technology to address the technologies of subjectification through which we are governed and regulated as human subjects.

mad, bad and dangerous to know

> If you can't show someone how things really are, then it's not worth showing them at all.
> (Inmate, Ashworth Maximum Security Hospital)

> Until now, it seems to me that historians of our own society, of our own civilisation, have sought especially to get at the inner secret of our own civilisation, its spirit, the way it establishes its identity, the things it values. On the other hand, there has been much less study of what has been rejected from our own civilisation in terms of its systems of exclusion, of rejection, of refusal, in terms of what it does not want, its limits, the way its is obliged to suppress a certain number of things, people, processes, what it must let fall into oblivion, its repression–suppression system.
> (Foucault 1989, p. 65)

The above two quotes aptly situate Graham Harwood's CD Rom, *Rehearsal of Memory*, within the context of what modern societies ignore, silence and would rather forget, namely the costs or consequences of modern forms of subjectification. *Rehearsal of Memory* aims to problematise and critique modern psychiatric and cultural understandings of mental distress. In its aim it follows a range of practitioners, theorists and activists who have claimed, since the early 1960s, that psychiatry is less a clinical discipline and more a form of custodial management. *Rehearsal of Memory* re-presents the voices and stories of six maximum security prisoners at Ashworth Maximum Security Hospital. It is an interactive CD Rom which allows the user to engage with the lives of those involved in the work. Those involved in the work, whom Harwood closely collaborated with, are classed as 'mentally disordered offenders', namely those who in the popular imagination, and cultural landscape, are viewed as 'other' to those values most exalted and celebrated at the present moment – rationality, self-development and self-control/ regulation. It is these concepts which many writers following Foucault suggest are central to the modern ethical formation of the self.[23]

The work, recently shown in an exhibition in Helsinki, was described as challenging preconceived views of insanity and the exclusions and divisions operated in relation to this normative image. Usually within psychiatric practice those who experience mental distress are condemned to silence and thrust into oblivion – their stories and voices merely signs of their disease and illness. This is even more common if their distress is manifested in outward displays of hostility and violence. For many of those who have taken part in the work have killed or maimed; the horror or atrocity of their crimes silencing their own stories which act as traces to their own private suffering and humiliation. We have to believe these are acts of irrationality, of those who have lost the capacity to be human. Harwood confronts us with this filth and forces us to consider the significance of their lives: lives that are full of ritual abuse, humiliation, violence and torture; stories that are rarely told and forced to exist and be coped with through the inmate's own private suffering.

the return of the repressed

> This was the worse I'd ever cut up before. I cut open my old appendix wound, stuck pins on the inside of the wound and swallowed a broken light bulb.

The user is confronted with a body that is an embodiment of the skins, the physical traces of the six inmates involved. The traces are scanned into the computer to produce a composite image with the purpose of retaining the anonymity of those involved. An intended or perhaps unintended effect of this enforced institutional limit is the creation of a disquieting and disturbing body. The face resembles a mug shot, reminiscent of the photo-fits used to identify the criminal. The body is written on, connoting perhaps both signs of its supposed degeneration, and the psychic traces of those lives reduced to their bodies and denied a voice. This effect parallels the way historically 'the body' has come to be seen as the visible marker of criminality and insanity – a body without brain. The scars and tattoos – normally indisputable signs of their wearer's illness, sickness and corruption – can be clicked on by the user who will be confronted with a suppressed signification, or with a contradiction that acts as a jolt to consciousness. A tattoo of a coffin with RIP emblazoned across it connotes a body marked by death. A reptile clicked on reveals a video scene of a man fighting, not just violence or aggression as one might expect, but perhaps a body fighting for survival. Other tattoos such as 'evil', 'man's work', 'giro' and 'shark' reveal the voice of a man repeatedly telling us how hard he finds it to relate to people; or we hear the sound of beautiful piano music.

As the user navigates around the body, at any moment they can 'click on' and be confronted with text – with a hidden story – relating to one of the inmate's lives. These are stories of sexual abuse, emotional abuse, torture, humiliation and accompanying feelings of hate, anger, frustration, guilt and depression. This I think is where the filth one is confronted with converts to shock when one is exposed to those stories usually silenced and reinterpreted by the experts – the doctor, social worker, psychiatrist and psychologist – as signs of pathology. These stories that usually function as ciphers for illness, disease, and deviancy embody the burden of pain that has accompanied these lives. As one man says:

> When I was younger I didn't like myself and I still don't. The reasons for this were because in some way I blamed myself for what had happened to me and my sister. My Father was, and is, a monster.
>
> My Dad's always been handy with his fists . . . And if he couldn't get his own way by talking, the fists start coming.

The living-out of pain and the struggle that has ensued for all those voices embodied within this piece is startling. Although they are marked in the public imagination by outward acts of hostility and violence, there is also a return to their own bodies through self-harm and 'cutting up', as a means of expressing lives and emotions that have no space within a culture organised around a fantasy of control. For cutting oneself and ingesting objects is a violation against the commonly held definition of our essence – the capacity for autonomy, to be responsible for oneself and others. The experts, also embodied within the piece, speak from the position of the 'guardians of truth', continually asking 'Why do you cut up?', confirming the inmate's position as irresponsible and irrational. Self-harm is not an acceptable response to pain in Western culture. Louise Pembroke from 'Survivors Speak Out'[24] argues in response to common responses to self-harm, that we would rather someone fade away quietly or cry than tear himself apart. What is interesting about psychiatric responses to self-harm is that it is seen as immature, deviant, manipulative, maladaptive and even passive. Again, these responses to suffering are constituted as 'other', mirroring what we as a society do not want to acknowledge.

We are reminded of this when we linger 'too long' on the personal stories and are confronted with those tabloid headlines reserved for those who expose the fragility of those divisions that define us. These narratives organised around risk and danger remind us of how we choose to recognise them, as 'Patients Who Kill' or 'Insane Killers'. They are rapists: evil, dirty, dangerous, sick and immoral, and always 'other'. The headlines that flash up may be comforting but they also function as resignifications, challenging these assured wisdoms and locating them within our own fears and fascinations connected with those behaviours and experiences that are excluded from so-called civilised societies and which function to delimit the fantasy of control through which the social world is organised.

What this piece alerts us to is the impossibility of living out this fiction, this illusion or fantasy of control. It may be reassuring to believe that there is a 'them' and 'us': that there are simply those that cannot and can cope and function in society. We may wish to draw limits around what we are willing to accept as normal and natural – but these words themselves become part of the problem. What happens when guilt, anger, frustration, conflict, etc. are lived in relation to this impossible fiction? I think this piece shows the costs and consequences of modern forms of subjectification or ethical relations. The way conflict, for example, becomes not only individualised and pathologised, but also experienced as personal inadequacy or violence against others. As one man says: 'If we learn violence we grow up hard and we express ourselves in a violent way. But the human heart can change given time with love, care and attention. A jab of medication isn't the answer.'

On many levels Harwood's piece challenges the current response to insanity, its segregation and institutionalisation. It takes us to another place – a place of pain and suffering which has no space in our culture other than as pathology. It takes us to an unknown place – a place shrouded by fear and fascination – a place usually contained within a secure unit policed by experts. This virtual space, which is dream-like, haunting, slow and fluid forces us to confront those things, people and experiences we exclude, in relation to a regulatory ideal we hold up to ourselves. This space may not only mirror our hopes and fears but force us to rethink how we see and relate to ourselves and others in our everyday lives. It may force us to recognise what we fail to acknowledge in our bid to draw limits around society and protect its so-called innocence.

Harwood's piece achieves this through a combination of sound, dialogue, text and imagery, where at any one moment the user may be unsure of their navigational position. The user travels across the surface of the body accompanied by the sound of a heartbeat and running water. These sounds are indicative of a body that is very much alive, its surface revealing as Harwood describes the filth which it acts as a container for. Computers and especially new technologies are often described as being beyond or after the body. As Cubitt[25] has cogently argued, discourses surrounding the new digital media are beyond the natural, superseding the flesh or meat which is viewed as redundant in the cybernetic future. Many stories of the cyborg future within popular culture reproduce these discourses where, as in *The Lawnmower Man*, the gateway to the new order is through the computer mainframe where the body is literally left behind. Computers are juxtaposed to the flesh of the body, which is disavowed in these new virtualities. In the virtual space that Harwood has constructed, the body or flesh is central, literally scanned into the technology contaminating and disturbing those discourses that delimit what we take virtuality to be.

Rehearsal of Memory is a rehearsal not so much of memory, but of forgetting. We could invoke here the idea of a 'collective memory', which would take the concept of memory away from the property of individuals. This shifts the concern from memory as a representational process to one that views remembering and forgetting as inherently social activities. In this sense it is important to consider why we construct the past and indeed the present in a particular way at a specific point in time and space. We can then consider representations for the way they shape what can and can't be said or thought, and the relation these representations have to wider social, cultural and governmental processes. Harwood reconfigures those collective acts of forgetting into a record or storehouse of cultural silences, transforming their cultural significance. In this sense the rehearsal that is undertaken contests and challenges the way those stories central to modernity function to legitimate a particular form of personhood which modern society relies upon for its reproduction. Harwood shows us the contradictions that lie at the heart of this modernist dream and the way they function as limits to the ways we imagine ourselves and others in our ethical relations.

the shock of the old

Rehearsal of Memory as an interactive artwork does not fit with the discourses surrounding technology so pervasive within techno-criticism. It is not structured around choice or play; it is more an exploratory journey which takes the user into a territory of filth, dirt, pain, suffering and sickness. It shocks and I think it is the idea of shock which is most fruitfully utilised when discussing its interactive potential. Susan Buck-Morss[26] in a reconsideration of Walter Benjamin's Artwork Essay, discusses the role of art or aesthetics within the modern experience. Benjamin argued that shock was the correlate of contemporary experience; an experience which shielded the human subject from 'excessive energies' or those experiences that threaten what Buck-Morss terms the 'myth of modern man'. This myth is similar to the image of personhood embedded within the 'psy' knowledges – an 'autonomous, autotelic subject' – the warrior. The warrior is self-contained and in control, taming those forces that threaten its existence. These fantasies of control have their 'Other': those fears created in relation to those things we cannot control. Buck-Morss constructs an interesting history of the emergence of (an)aesthetics within the nineteenth century and its association with a discursive field of phenomenon organised around the concept of shock. Within the psychiatric nosography there were a range of diseases seen to be related to 'excessive energies' or overstimulation. Interestingly, with the exception of shell-shock, a form of male hysteria linked with the shock of war combat, most of these diseases were peculiarly feminine. Neurasthenia was a form of female exhaustion seen to be brought about by excessive study or overstimulation of the mind. The mind was shocked from its habitual paths, making novel connections and literally 'going off the track'.

The resultant shock was seen to function as a way of paralysing the mind, numbing it so as to protect it from further disintegration. This deadening would result in 'eyes that have lost their ability to look'.[27] (An)aesthetics was, she argues, developed as a technique for relieving the individual of pain and overstimulation; a compensation for physical and psychic shocks. She says in relation to this technique,

> It was not only the patient who was relieved from pain by anaesthesia. The effect was as profound upon the surgeon. A deliberate effort to de-sensitise oneself from the experience of the pain of another was no longer necessary. Whereas earlier surgeons had to train themselves to repress empathic identification with the suffering patient, now they had only to confront an inert, insensate mass that they could tinker with without emotional involvement.[28]

She argues that being 'insensate to pain' is part of the social imaginary, which as we have seen emerges in relation to a very specific way of constructing the human subject.

If the technique for compensating for shock or even defending against shock in the nineteenth century was anaesthetics, then what is its modern counterpart? Buck-Morss argues that new technology extends the fantasy of control so central to modern forms of subjectification, and functions as a defence against the fragility of the human body. This fragility, I would argue, is not only a physical or psychic fragility, but a fragility in the very concepts and terms we use to make sense of ourselves. In other words, technology may operate as a defence against the difficulty of 'living' modern forms of subjectification, i.e. the way conflict, frustration, guilt, shame, etc. are experienced as personal inadequacy or pathology. Buck-Morss describes the virtual body as one 'that can endure the shocks of modernity without pain'.[29] If this argument is persuasive then the 'psy' conception of personhood has merely become embedded within and reproduced within many virtual spaces. Images of freedom, choice and autonomy have their 'other' side, those experiences against which they are defined, relegated to a space of pathology and personal acts of suffering.

Rehearsal of Memory shocks, but it shocks in a way that forces us from our complacency and the banality of the way in which we currently view insanity. The idea of shock is an interesting metaphor for thinking about its interactive potential. The concept links together the many interwoven elements within this work which function at a psychic and social level. It shocks because it disturbs the hygienist principles which function within the modern conception of the subject, thrusting 'others' into oblivion. It shocks because it confronts us with pain and suffering, not merely disease and degeneration. It shocks because it forces us to confront vulnerability, both in ourselves and others. It shocks primarily because it takes us to a place which most are usually protected from through the segregating actions of modern psychiatric practice. The gaze constructed within Harwood's virtual world is not one that allows the user disinterested pleasure. The elements within it act upon our very social and psychic defences, perhaps producing affects not usually articulated within discourses surrounding new technology. Sadness, hostility, disbelief, anger, pain, hurt, etc. are not the usual emotional economy structuring virtual worlds.

Rehearsal of Memory has transformative potential. It forces us to confront the way we draw limits around what we take so-called normality to be. It resignifies those terms, images and languages central to our subjectification and shows how they function to maintain and reproduce a particular regulatory ideal we hold up to ourselves. It shows the contingency of these terms by exploring the gaps, silences and contradictions created through these regulatory images, i.e. the way that certain people, behaviours and experiences are simply thrust into oblivion, signifying as 'other' within the cultural landscape. It produces a range of affects – not pleasure – but difficult emotions that lock into our deepest psychic and social defences.

Foucault's later work on 'ethics' and techniques of the self provides us with a set of theoretical tools to explore those terms, images, etc. central to our formation. We can then explore how these are inscribed into new technology and virtualities – whether they are reproduced or resisted and transformed in specific ways. The implications of this argument are that we can no longer make general claims about the role of new technology. We must avoid either/or arguments – utopian and dystopian – and approach technologies as historical and cultural phenomena. The human subject is entirely constituted through signs and discursive relations; technology is articulated and organised through particular discursive relations. It is the relations between these two which are the key to exploring the possible transformative and reproductive potentials of new technologies. Technology may then become a useful tool for transforming subjectivity and achieve the radical potential it claims.

consequences

If virtual space is going to achieve its radical potential for transforming subjectivity, 'who we take ourselves to be', then this needs to be built in at both a design and discursive level. The argument I have developed has sought to demonstrate that virtual space is already embedded within a cultural matrix, both in terms of its geometry and symbolic aspects. There have already been discussions touching upon what an alternative 'feminine' virtual space might look like: a space not playing on what are seen as masculinist desires for control, mastery and omnipotence. The question I want to pose is what a virtual space might look like, if it is to produce an alternative ethics; an alternative way of relating to the self and others. I shall discuss some of my ideas at a discursive and symbolic level, unaware of the design implications that would enable this to be a possibility. One metaphor that may provide a fruitful starting point is to think of virtual space less as a mirror and more as a looking-glass. By this I mean that current constructions of virtual space, based upon the Cartesian knower position, place the user at the centre of the virtual world. It acts much like a mirror, offering images and identities to the person to play around with at will; playing upon our desires for freedom, choice and autonomy bound up with our production as human subjects.

I would propose the construction of a virtual space that acts like a looking-glass, moving to a world beyond dichotomies, beyond those very divisions through which we are defined as human subjects. One aim of this virtual world could be to show up the embeddedness of subjectivity in different spaces and places. This would not only emphasise the fluid and contextual nature of identity, but also expose the mechanisms of those power/discursive relations through which we are constructed and construct ourselves. I shall attempt now to give a more concrete example to these rather abstract ideas in relation to gender.

Walkerdine[30] gives a good example of how our subjectivities are constituted differently in different spaces in relation to different discourses at different times. She cites the example of a female schoolteacher who, despite being accorded a particular status through her positioning as a teacher, becomes through an interaction with her pupils positioned as an object of sexual desire. Her subjectivity becomes 'read' or constituted as a woman rather than as a teacher. The following transcript of her interaction with a group of children aged 3 to 4 will illustrate the argument.

SEAN: Get out of it Miss Baxter Paxter.
TERRY: Get out of it knickers Miss Baxter.
SEAN: Get out of it Miss Baxter Paxter.
TERRY: Get out of it Miss Baxter the knickers paxter knickers, bum.
SEAN: Knickers, shit, bum.
MISS B: Sean, that's enough, you're being silly.
SEAN: Miss Baxter, knickers, show your knickers.
TERRY: Miss Baxter, show your bum off.
MISS B: I think you're being very silly.
TERRY: Shit Miss Baxter, Shit Miss Baxter.
SEAN: Miss Baxter, show your knickers your bum off.

SEAN: Take all your clothes off, your bra off.

TERRY: Yeah, and take your bum off, take your wee-wee off, take your clothes and your mouth off.

SEAN: Take your teeth out, take your head off, take your hair off, take your bum off. Miss Baxter the paxter knickers taxter.

MISS B: Sean, go and find something else to do please.

Walkerdine argues in relation to the above interaction that the boys, through the position of men in language, refuse to be constituted as powerless objects in her discourse and recast her as the powerless object of theirs. She has ceased to signify as a teacher and becomes signified as a woman in relation to terms and categories that define women as passive sexual objects. As Walkerdine[31] argues, 'Individuals, constituted as subjects and objects within a particular framework, are produced by that process into relations of power. An individual can become powerful or powerless depending on the terms in which her/his subjectivity is constituted.' Thus, subjectivity or identity is not merely a shifting, mutable process based upon choice, but a complex process whereby subjectivities shift and are constituted differently in different spaces and places.

Perhaps to produce a virtual space that takes into account not only how we might position ourselves, but also how we can be positioned, although showing up the power relations which produce the human subject, may not be as pleasurable. However, these positionings are based upon the supposed 'truth' of who we are, and if we are going to construct a space which is *open, inventive* and *questioning*, part of the process must be to attend to these issues. Perhaps the image of the looking-glass could be incorporated into this world where once the relations are exposed, one can move into a land beyond dichotomies; a carnival space of play where we may become something 'other'.

notes

1. Cubitt 1996.

2. Cf. Poster 1996.

3. Cf. Blackman 1995.

4. Cubitt 1996.

5. Deleuze and Guattari 1988.

6. Penny 1994; Woodward 1994.

7. Woodward 1994.

8. Freud 1963.

9. Woodward 1994.

10. Ibid.

11. Haraway 1991.

12. Brook and Boal 1995; Fuller 1994; Harwood 1995; Spender 1995.

13. Rose 1996.

14. Blackman 1994; Rose 1996; Walkerdine 1995.

15. Rose 1990.

16. MuuMedia Festival 1995.

17. Blackman 1995.

18. Kember 1996.

19. Cf. Kemper 1996.

20. Cf. Halperin 1995.

21. Foucault 1980.

22. Cf. Henriques *et al.* 1984.

23. Blackman 1996; Dean 1994; Rose 1995.

24. A self-help user group; see Pembroke 1994.

25. Cubitt 1996.

26. Buck-Morss 1993.

27. Buck-Morss 1993, p. 131.

28. Ibid., p. 136.

29. Ibid., p. 139.

30. Walkerdine 1990, p. 4.

31. Ibid., p. 9.

bibliography

Bender, G., and Druckrey, T., *Culture on the Brink: Ideologies of Technology*, Seattle, Bay Press, 1994.

Blackman, L., 'What is doing History: The use of history to understand the constitution of contemporary psychological objects', *Theory and Psychology* 4(4) 1994, pp. 485–504.

Blackman, L., 'Programming Freedom; New Technology and the Production of the Modern Human Subject'. Paper given at the MuuMedia Festival, Helsinki, Finland, October 1995.

Blackman, L., 'The dangerous classes: Re-telling the psychiatric story', *Feminism and Psychology* 6(3), August 1996.

Brook, J., and Boal, I., *Resisting the Virtual Life. The Culture and Politics of Informations*, San Francisco, City Lights Books, 1995.

Buck-Morss, S., 'Aesthetics and anaesthetics: Walter Benjamin's Artwork Essay reconsidered', *New Formulations* 20, Summer 1993.

Cubitt, S., 'Supernatural futures. Theses on digital aesthetics', in Robertson, G., Mash, M., Tickner, L., Bird, J., Curtis, B., and Putnam, T., *Future Natural. Nature, Science, Culture*, London and New York, Routledge, 1996.

Dean, M., *Critical and Effective Histories: Foucault's Methods and Historical Sociology*, London and New York, Routledge, 1994

Deleuze, G., and Guattari, F., *A Thousand Plateaus: Capitalism and Schizophrenia*, London, Athlone Press, 1988.

Foucault, M., *The History of Sexuality. Volume 1*, London, Allen Lane, 1979.

Foucault, M., *Power/Knowledge: Selected Interviews and Other Writings 1972–1977*, ed. Gordan, C. Brighton and New York, Harvester Wheatsheaf, 1980.

Foucault, M., *The History of Sexuality. Volume 2: The Use of Pleasure*, Harmondsworth, Penguin, 1987.

Foucault, M., 'Technologies of the self', in Martin, L.H., Gutman, H., and Hutton, R.H. (eds) *Technologies of the Self*, London, Tavistock, 1988.

Foucault, M., *Foucault Live*, New York, Semiotext(e), 1989.

Foucault, M., *The History of Sexuality. Volume 3: The Care of the Self*, Harmondsworth, Penguin, 1990.

Freud, S. *Civilization and Its Discontents*, London, Hogarth Press, 1963.

Fuller, M., *Unnatural: Techno-theory for a Contaminated Culture*, London, Underground, 1994.

Halperin, D., *Saint = Foucault. Towards a Gay Hagiography*, New York and Oxford, Oxford University Press, 1995.

Haraway, D., *Simians, Cyborgs and Women: The Reinvention of Nature*, London, Free Association Books, 1991.

Harwood, G., Exhibition of *Rehearsal of Memory* at the MuuMedia Festival, Helsinki, Finland, 1995.

Henriques, J., Holloway, W., Irwin, C., Venn, C., and Walkerdine, V., *Changing the Subject. Psychology, Subjectivity and Social Regulation*, London, Methuen, 1984.

Kember, S., 'Feminist figuration and the question of origin', in G. Robertson *et al.*, *FutureNatural*, London and New York, Routledge, 1996.

Miller, P., and Rose, N., 'Political power beyond the state: Problematics of government', *British Journal of Sociology*, 43(2), 1992, pp. 173–205.

Pembroke, L., *Self-Harm: Perspectives from Personal Experience*, London, Survivors Speak Out, 1994.

Penny, S.; 'Virtual reality as the completion of the Enlightenment project', in Bender, G., and Druckney, T. (eds), *Culture on the Brink: Ideologies of Technology*, Seattle, Bay Press, 1994.

Poster, M., 'Postmodern virtualities', in Robertson, G. *et al.*, *FutureNatural*, London and New York, Routledge, 1996.

Rose, N., *The Psychological Complex: Psychology, Politics and Society in England, 1869–1939*, London, Routledge & Kegan Paul, 1985.

Rose, N., *Psychology, Power and Personhood*, London, Routledge, 1996.

Spender, D., *Nattering on the Net. Women, Power and Cyberspace*, Melbourne, Spinifex Press, 1995.

Walkerdine, V., *Schoolgirl Fictions*, London, Verso, 1990.

Walkerdine, V., 'Subject to change without notice. Psychology, postmodernity and the popular', in Pile, S., and Thrift, N. (eds), *Mapping the Subject*, London and New York, Routledge, 1995.

Woodward, K., 'From virtual cyborgs to biological timebombs: technocriticism and the material body', in Bender, G., and Druckrey, T. (eds), *Culture on the Brink: Ideologies of Technology*, Seattle, Bay Press, 1994.

part four

when becoming meets becoming

CHAPTER 11

THE DREAM GARDEN

Notes on a Virtual Idyll

ROBERT WELLS

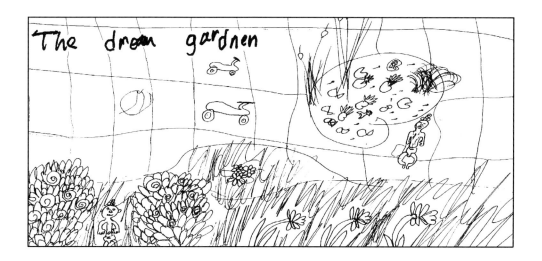

The ideal garden is a place with neither
toil, pain, anger, nor discomfort;
a perfected Nature; safe and under control.

Gardens can reveal the perceived relationships between individuals and Nature. These relationships may also be symptomatic of the sort of buildings and cities we make, and how we behave towards each other.[1]

Once, in order to settle and become 'civilised', a degree of control over a locality would have been essential.

Today, in prosperous lands where security and comfort are seen as human rights, and where we are unlikely to be devoured by wild animals, we may need to find new ways for Nature to be revealed and understood.

'Eternal Spring' and 'abundance' are key concepts in the garden, as in many visions of Eden. Whenever a place is 'unproductive', or has not been subject to human will, we call it a wilderness.

BOTANICAL NOMENCLATURE

Linnaean classification formalises and fossilises plant names in science. It is indispensable to the botanist, but does it increase our wonderment or sense of connectedness to our surroundings?

We may assume that even before formal classification became widespread, people related to plants in many sophisticated ways:

- as food
- to identify a system/region/place/home
- for their magical/symbolic properties
- as reminders/indicators of seasonal time
- for their scent.

THE LAWN

'For generations it has been an accepted fact that the lawn is the foundation and the special characteristic of the English garden.'[2]

The lawn has been the subject of very little serious scholarship. For grass to be perceived as lawn it is generally expected to be:

- even, flat and level
- uniformly (bright) green
- free of 'alien' species
- cut very short and carpet-like.

Increasingly, the lawn is seen as a 'backdrop' for events regarded as centre-stage.[3]

Pesticides, herbicides, fungicides are used routinely to reduce the number of species in a given area.

Growth enhancers, growth inhibitors and colorants are used routinely for cosmetic purposes.

Extreme manifestations of the garden lawn can be found on the greens of North American golf courses, where the grass may be treated with a green dye in order to heighten the colour for television companies.

An evergreen type of grass has recently been genetically engineered to resist fading or tanning. Even in conditions of drought, it will retain its brilliance.

In golf course design the agrochemical companies are beginning to have more influence than that of landscape designers.

A POTTED HISTORY OF THE ENGLISH GARDEN

A history of the garden, and the way that plants, tools, and products are marketed, may help us to understand what we have become.

Plants, products, and tools

Plants have been an important marketable commodity since the Middle Ages.

The variety and availability of plant species increased slowly from the Middle Ages to the eighteenth century.

Novelty in plant species has been valued for many hundreds of years.

Their association with the exotic emerged from stories and fables.

In the twentieth century a greater diversity of plants became available, with many new varieties created specifically for the mass market.

The industrialisation of horticultural techniques has introduced mass production methods to plant propagation and cultivation.

All tasks in the garden can be accomplished with hand tools.

There were few significant changes in tool design between Roman times and the nineteenth century.

Tools adapted to local conditions have been replaced by standardised tools.

The increasing popularity of gardening has led to a market-led uniformity of garden products and tools.

Gardening has become big business.

WHAT IS IN THE GARDEN

Plants

We like certain plants[4] to be:

- abundant
- quick and easy to grow
- neat, compact, tidy
- interesting all the year round
- exotic
- new (novel varieties)
- large, brightly coloured, everlasting.

Seed catalogues[5] help us to choose plants:

'This is one of those prolific little plants that can cover your garden in wall-to-wall colour.'

'A completely new type of junior Petunia! These busy little plants furiously envelop themselves in myriads of small trumpet-like flowers.'

'Comet blazes its trail through beds and borders in a riot of colour.'

'The big, exotic blooms flaunt their rich gold and bronze plumage.'

'They'll bury borders and rockeries in a mass of vibrant, long-lasting colour.'

'It will explode into a free-flowering mass of colour.'

We like to remind ourselves that plants are alive, that they are our friends and companions.

Products, tools and machines

Popular magazines often present a picture of gardens under siege. Here, some plants may fail to attain perfection. Insects, moulds and viruses are shown to be unwelcome alongside cultivated plants.

The heightened and 'perfected' state of the modern garden can only be sustained with the aid of science and technology.

Today, activities such as grass cutting are unthinkable without the help of machines. Tools for gardening and DIY are increasingly similar, with many machines for the garden now sold alongside other household appliances. Conceptually, gardening is a domestic chore; the house has been extended to enclose the garden.

The garden – Nature perfected

'Silk and other artificial flowers are so good these days, it's hard to tell them from the real thing! I have to admit I looked twice when Unwins' new double-flowered petunia "Heavenly Lavender" started to reveal its inner glories.'[6]

The garden is a human paradise. It is a natural wilderness brought under control, dominated and improved.

It offers a space which represents a virtual Eden.

Within this space we daydream and remake Nature.

It is a space for individual freedom.

It tells us how to be human and how to relate to the living world.

It constructs human presence outside and above the organic world.

Our plants are increasingly colourful, abundant, everlasting, perfect.

The perfected Nature garden is guarded and defended. Enemies, aliens and wilderness are repelled at the boundaries.

Nature

Popular gardening media encourage the popular view that:

- Nature can, and should, be under our full control.
- Some parts of Nature – bugs, moulds, mutations etc., are out of place.

- Dirt, mud and mess are undesirable.
- Nature should be bright, colourful and exotic.
- Nature should be static or predictable.
- Other forms of Nature – the rainforest, for example – are acceptable at a distance.

Space

Genres of private spaces are sustained in the popular gardening media.

Garden space is privatised and carefully delineated by borders.

Garden space is domestic and personal. Its geographical and historical provenance is not usually acknowledged.

This space is constituted by mass-produced, fetishised products.

Ideal spaces are neat, tidy and meticulously structured.

Ideal spaces are colourful, friendly, animated.

We want these attributes to endure. We fear becoming changed, lost or confused in these spaces.

Space is described not by interaction but by domination.

If we analyse modern gardens, we may find ideas of Nature that correspond to the modern animated cartoon or electronic game.

YOSHI'S ISLAND™

This refers to a Nintendo[7] game, popular in the mid-1990s, which portrays an image of paradise. The game provides the setting for an epic adventure, but my interest is in the graphics rather than the narrative threads. There is a close correspondence between these images and the idealised gardens of popular culture. Yoshi's Island is indebted to landscape genres deriving from animated cartoons and advertising. It offers a secluded 'other world' to the player.

During a typical adventure the player will encounter stereotypical landscape styles. In the graphics there are alpine mountain scenes, waterfalls, meadows, flower gardens, subterranean caverns, grottoes, and forests, as well as the paradise island itself. The game is designed to encourage a pleasant interaction with each setting and to encourage the player to seek further fantastic worlds and new spaces.

Playing Yoshi's Island is a way to explore, enjoy and 'possess' desirable places without getting your hands dirty.

Brief visual analysis of the 'worlds' in Yoshi's Island

My research was undertaken with the help of an 8-year-old child. I have tried to summarise his accounts of what he liked:

- There is a lot of nice scenery.
- There are mountains and blue sky with puffy white clouds.
- The scenes do not have as much difference as compared to the street outside.
- The scenes are flowery (with cartoon-like flowers).
- They are bright and colourful.
- The places are cheerful.
- It was the sort of place he would like to visit if there were no baddies present.

In addition to the above points I would suggest that where some of the worlds are intended to represent an idea of paradise, others relate to the kind of mythical and magical places associated with fairy tales. The cartoon-like quality of the 'worlds' appealed to my helper. The fact that mountains, plants, machines and animals are all presented as friends, and that everything is equally animate, is vital to the whole notion of the game and the appearance of the 'worlds'.

There are no towns, cities or roads in any of the worlds that we visited.

VIRTUAL EDENS

Our 'picture' of Eden is a proposition about an ideal world. Technocratic culture constructs Nature as external to ourselves – i.e. 'out there' – as an abundant, highly coloured and always-in-flower world. It is a world of visual effects and spectacle, defined by products.

Our post-Disney Eden incorporates an appeal to the state of being new-born or unborn. It evokes a sense of nostalgia, longing and loss. It is always spring time, so we will never grow older. It is eternally abundant, so we will not starve. It is non-confrontational and static; there is no need to work or to feel pain or anger. It is a sort of comfortable, warm, lazy place where everything is friendly.

It is a naïve, childlike vision, but one that evolved when a fear of predators, hunger, disease and early death were ever-present anxieties. Eden, or paradise, is an exotic land of peace and plenty to provide an escape from the 'real'.

This type of Eden no longer soothes life-and-death fears and immediate concerns. Today we struggle with problems of identity, loss of self-respect, alienation, uniformity (of products and places). We cope with a loss of meaning brought about by a systematic pursuit of passive comforts which distances us from the biological world.

The Virtual Eden	A Non-Utopian Eden
Excess and abundance	Seasonal difference
Emphasises visual spectacle	Encourages convivial interplay
Commodified	Self-seeded/collected
Designed for export anywhere	Always local and particular

Self-centred	Co-operative
Scientific / technological rationale	Enhanced not dominated
Instant gratification	Pleasures at the pace of growth and nurture

A new, non-utopian Eden

This could:

- celebrate the seasons and daily changes
- acknowledge emptiness (as opposed to conative abundance)
- celebrate locality and acknowledge its situated meaningfulness
- celebrate flux and difference
- imply interaction and involvement
- encourage more interplay between 'civilisation' and 'wildness'.

THE MUDDY PATH[8] MANIFESTO

A muddy path is worn by animal feet. It is wet and slippery, dry and cracked. It becomes rutted when heavily used and vanishes when forgotten.

It reveals, and is revealed by, patterns of behaviour.

The Muddy Path exposes habits of human interaction.

It is shaped by expediency and co-operation.

It unselfconsciously brings together Nature and cultivation.

The Muddy Path recoils from the motorway, the paved path and the domination of place. It witnesses animal activity and renews a Nature rooted in convivial actions and observations.

It reconciles human and non-human values as a way to invent Nature.

NOTES

1. My ideas about the garden have evolved over twenty years of working with the landscape as a gardener, painter and designer. These notes were knocked into shape on the MA Design Futures programme at Goldsmiths College, University of London, with the help of John Wood, Sam Deeks, Richard Stock and Chi Roberts.

2. Lucas Philips, C.E., *The New Small Garden*, London, Pan Books, 1979.

3. See Olu Taiwo's Chapter 12.

4. Conclusions elicited from *Garden Answers* journal, February 1996.

5. From a seed company advertisement: Dobie's 'Easy-to-Grow Plants' by post, 1996.

6. *Amateur Gardening*, 3 February 1996.

7. The Nintendo company was established a hundred years ago in Japan. Originally a playing card manufacturer, it entered the American interactive electronic games market. One in three homes in the United States owned a Nintendo system by the end of 1990. See Fuller, M. and Jenkins, H., 'Nintendo and New World travel writing: a dialogue in CyberSociety', in Jones, S.G., *Cybersociety: Computer-Mediated Communication and Community*, London, Sage 1994.

8. I am grateful to Elise Liversedge for permission to use the term 'muddy path', which is taken from an unpublished essay (1996) on urban planning.

BIBLIOGRAPHY

Bunce, M., *The Countryside Ideal*, London, Routledge,1994.

Dickens, P., *Society and Nature: Towards a Green Social Theory*, Hemel Hempstead, Harvester Wheatsheaf, 1992.

Fuller, M., and Jenkins, H., 'Nintendo and New World travel writing: a dialogue in CyberSociety', in Jones, S.G., *Cybersociety: Computer-Mediated Communication and Community*, London, Sage, 1994.

Guignon, C.B. (ed.), *The Cambridge Companion to Heidegger*, Cambridge, Cambridge University Press, 1993.

Harris, J. (ed.) *The Garden: A Celebration of 1000 Years of British Gardening*, London, New Perspectives Publishing Ltd, 1979.

Harvey, D., 'From space to place and back again', in Bird, J., Curtis, B., Putnam, T., Robertson, G., and Tickner, L., *Mapping the Futures*, London and New York, Routledge, 1993.

Illich, I., *Tools for Conviviality*, London, Marion Boyars Publishers Ltd, 1990.

Lefebvre, H., *The Production of Space*, trans. D. Nicholson-Smith, Oxford, Basil Blackwell, 1991.

Lucas Philips, C.E., *The New Small Garden*, London, Pan Books, 1979.

Prest, John M., *The Garden of Eden*, London, Yale University Press, 1981.

Wilbert, C., 'The apple falls from grace', in Bookchin, M., *Deep Ecology & Anarchism*, London, Freedom Press, 1993.

Williams, R., *The Country and the City*, London, Chatto & Windus, 1973.

chapter 12

the 'return-beat'

'curved perceptions' in music and dance

olu taiwo

introduction

This chapter uses a performance-centred approach[1] to look at some implications of rhythm. It draws attention to a particular mode of rhythmic perception which we shall call the 'return-beat', and uses it to highlight certain shared experiences in a group. These practices are then cited as a way to discuss individual and cultural practices of 'becoming'. It includes practical instructions for conducting a situated and embodied experiment. This exploration synthesises theory and practice and uses techniques that I have developed from my experiences as a performer, dancer and teacher, following the traditions of Rudolf Laban,[2] the pioneering choreographer, practitioner and academic. In Laban's approach, knowledge is derived from, and is understood to be located in, the dancer's active 'centre' of the body. In exploring the way we share the experience of physical movement, rhythm is used as an organisational focus for what the group shares in space–time.[3]

Loosely speaking, we could polarise our received approaches to rhythm and space–time in the following approaches:

- empirical data-gathering by a 'detached' observer

- phenomenological and subjective observation with direct participation.

This chapter takes a phenomenological perspective in exploring the problem of action and its observation.[4] It looks for protophenomena as a way to theorise actual subjective experiences whilst maintaining a concern for the subjective and phenomenological.

The first study looks at a linear approach to movement which is probably best characterised by a strictly regular pace and metre. This mode usually summons mental images of distracted and strenuous walking in a straight line. This image will become the background figure against which we can compare the second mode – the 'return-beat' – which, when enacted either by dancers, whether professional or not, usually gives rise to a more 'centred' and richly 'embodied' experience. In our reference to the first, 'linear' mode this experience is not inevitably brought about by a reliance on, for example, the artificial beat of a metronome or digital pulse. Rather, it is dependent upon the user's active compliance in the illusion of undertaking an evenly paced journey whilst maintaining a rather 'blinkered' approach. As we shall see, whereas such a simple 'metric' experience of rhythm and movement is focused on the idea of linear travel, the 'return-beat' prompts a more 'curved' and reciprocating sensation of rhythm. It should be noted that, although the proposition emphasises the difference between these two models, in practice all music and rhythm promotes a balance of both sensations. The boundaries between the two modes are crossed and recrossed in the profusion of rich cultural histories expressed in the art of many peoples.

embodying the 'return-beat'

How can we characterise the experience of the 'return-beat'? This is difficult to achieve in a conventional, static book because there are certain types of knowledge which text cannot easily declare without reference to experiences of a differently embodied nature. One way of describing the 'return-beat' in narrative form is to consider a musical conductor who, when rehearsing with the orchestra, invites them to close their eyes and to trace out imaginary shapes with their hands. Western military music has a weak 'return-beat' and, in tracing virtual lines for a military march,[5] the players may find it helpful to imagine themselves marching inexorably fowards in a line that extends outwards from their bodily centres and towards the horizon. By contrast, they may find themselves tracing out the petals of a large flower when imagining music with a strong 'return-beat'. In this imaginary 'petal drawing', the line repeatedly curves back to the (dancer's) centre and serves to reinforce a sense of 'return' to (her)self. As this individual experience is often felt to be shared with those of the rest of the group, it makes the experience more shareable. In other words, it helps to transform an 'I' into a 'we'. This has obvious social and cultural implications which we shall discuss later. The models can be visualised (for music in four-four time) in Figs 12.1 and 12.2.

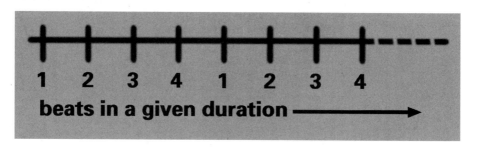

12.1 the 'linear–beat' time graph

'linear' model

Imagine that the 'spaces' between the handclaps are taking you in a straight line through static and finite points in space and time. The space is perceived to be motionless, and therefore you move into it, or through it. When clapping with this model, imagine tracing a straight line between each handclap, so that it will lead sequentially to the next clap, and so on.

'return-beat' model

In between each handclap, imagine tracing a curved line which goes out from your 'centre' and returns to you for the next clap. Think of this space–time as a dynamic whole. Imagine each next clap as augmenting the previous clap rather than the next one in the sequence.

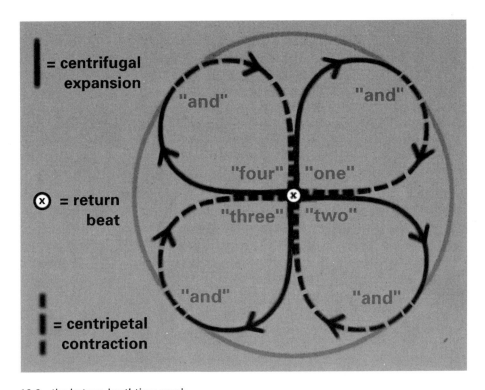

12.2   the 'return-beat' time graph

Whereas in Figure 12.1 we tend to project ourselves on to the next beat, in Figure 12.2. we constantly come 'home' to the centre by following the pattern: '1 and 2 and 3 and 4, etc.' Here, the beats take place in the centre and the 'ands' are on the perimeter of the circle. The particular shapes are offered here merely as a prototype, and would be different for specific rhythms which may emphasise a particular sense of the beat. The precise profile of the petals is important in conveying the fluid nature of bodily presence and movement between beats. Likewise, the word 'and'[6] would probably be voiced in such a way as to slide us from one beat to the next. Solid lines are used here to suggest a feeling of centrifugal expansion, and dotted lines to convey a centripetal feeling of contraction. Textual descriptions of movements are always problematic, and in trying to 'feel' the two modes of rhythm it may be helpful to follow the flow-diagram in Figure 12.2 and to ask ourselves – or, in more dualistic terms, to ask our 'active bodies' – some questions:

- How are we experiencing the intervals between the beats?
- How are we experiencing the moments at which the beats occur?

One way to contrast these differences is as follows:

Linear–beat	Return–beat
Dualistic	Holistic
Often perceived as external	More phenomenologically apparent
Often perceived as objective	Often perceived as subjective
More deterministic	Self-reflexively experienced

12.3 comparisons between the two modes

guidelines for the experiment

You can begin to 'embody' some of the many implications raised here, by conducting a practical hand-clapping exercise intended for a group of three or more. This exercise is a comparative study, first for 'linear-beat' and then for the 'return-beat'. Each experiment uses a single pulse beat. In both cases the pulse is provided by everyone clapping their hands in unison, in a regular, metronomic way.

Take time to read the guidelines in Figures 12.4 and 12.5 carefully. Reflect upon what they entail and then follow the flow-chart as illustrated in Figure 12.6.

1 Find a calm, reasonably uncluttered space.
2 Find at least two other willing participants.
3 Settle everyone with some relaxation exercises (Figure 12.5).
4 Get everyone to read, and to understand the two descriptions in the boxes below.
5 Make sure that everyone closes their eyes.
6 Tell everyone to listen to the others.

12.4 preparations for the clapping experiment

1   Sit in a comfortable position with your spine upright and relaxed – more like a straightened string of pearls than an iron rod.

2   Close your eyes and focus the eyeballs up into the centre of the forehead.

3   Breathe from the stomach area, expanding the abdomen as you inhale, contracting it as you exhale.

4   Repeat points 1–3 a few times until you feel relaxed.

12.5   relaxation exercise

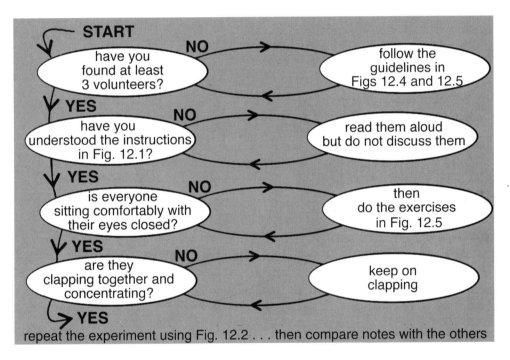

12.6   flow chart for the clapping experiment

cultural implications of the 'return-beat'

The 'return-beat' is a term that I have also used to describe the West African's socio-cultural distinctive experience of rhythm. The above rhythmic experiences (facilitated by the 'return-beat') start primarily with the body, with the heartbeat. This experience is echoed throughout Africa and the African Diaspora. The Blues, Jazz, Rock, Funk, Soul, Hip Hop, Juju, Samba, Reggae and the Groove, Back Beat and Swing Beat are all socio-cultural forms and terms that emphasise the 'return-beat'. It can also be found in the folk traditions of the British Isles as in England, where there is Morris dancing as well as the dancing derived from the Celtic peoples of Scotland,

Wales and Ireland. In Nigel Williamson's article on Womad,[7] he explores the musical relationship between African and Celtic cultures:

> Most intriguing of all is Afro-Celt Sound System, whose producer Simon Emmerson believes that the Celts migrated from the Middle East through Africa into Western Europe. He notes that: 'The Kora and the Celtic Harp, The African Talking drum and the Bodhran essentially seem to talk the same language' . . .

However, for me, the term 'return-beat' defines more than just musical and dance experiences. It can also be argued for West African, if not for all the above-mentioned cultural practices, that they are both informed and created by a particular perception of space–time that emerges from these varieties of the 'return-beat'. In this discussion I shall look at the significance of this perception and how it influences personal and social artistic practices.

In contemporary urban cultures it is important to note the mode and level of 'situatedness' associated with the 'return-beat' in contemporary culture. This invokes the question of the mediating role of technology in human cultural experiences. As we all know, where some rhythms are produced 'live', other forms use some type of prerecorded sound. In either case digital tracks are quite likely to have been laid down, often before 'live' musicians add their own tracks. It is clear that such differences may affect the perceived rhythms but, whilst digital modes are often synonymous, in many people's minds, with creative revolution, some critics see 'digitised' rave culture as a symptom of alienation exacerbated by the above technologies. In this chapter, I take one or two strands of the cultural and historical roots of the 'return-beat', to sketch out its possible role in today's technological culture.

During the Renaissance in the West, sequential linear codes, probably underpinned by the alphabetical form, found their expression in almost all aspects of the cultural, educational and political life of the bourgeoisie. In the European theatre, for example, the proscenium arch tended to fix roles by creating an invisible fourth wall to separate the spectator from the performer. From the viewpoint of the spectator, a particular illusion of space was sustained around this 'straight', linear code of perspective. Lefebvre notes:

> Tuscan painters, architects and theorists developed a representation of space – perspective – on the basis of social practice which was itself, as we shall see, the result of a historic change in the relationship between town and country. Common sense meanwhile, though more or less reduced to silence, was still preserving virtually intact a representational space, inherited from the Etruscans, which had survived all the centuries of Roman and Christian domination. The vanishing line, the vanishing-point and the meeting of parallel lines 'at infinity' were the determinants of a representation, at once intellectual and visual, which promoted the primacy of the gaze in a kind of 'logic of visualisation'. This representation, which had been in the making for centuries, now became enshrined in architectural and urbanistic practice as the code of linear perspective.[8]

The code of linear, or 'plane projection perspective'[9] imposed a lasting, and geo-historically specific ideology of power on to the popular conception of space as we perceive it in daily life. This 'embodied' ideology is in sharp contrast to West African traditional 'perspectives', because these are inclined to bring out spatio-temporal sensibilities which are more circular than rectilinear. West African cosmology emphasises non-teleological, organic and rhythmic forces, which emerge from a primordial state of becoming. This is seen as the essential material of all manifestations, both physical and psychological. Wole Soyinka claims that: 'Continuity for the Yoruba operates both through the cyclic concept of time and the animist interfusion of all matter and consciousness.'[10] He also suggests through his explorations into the nature of Yoruba tragedy, that the principles of illusion, which seek to represent ideas and inspirations that have been structured, through a structure, are vastly different from the Yoruba principles of tragedy in theatrical expression:

> In our journey to the heart of Yoruba tragic art which indeed belongs to the mysteries of Ogun and the choric ecstasy of revellers, we do not find that the Yoruba, as the Greek did, 'built for his chorus the scaffolding of a fictive chthonic realm and placed thereon fictive nature spirit . . . ' on which foundation, claims Nietzsche, Greek tragedy developed: in short, the principle of illusion. Yoruba tragedy plunges straight into the 'chthonic realm' the seething cauldron of the dark world will and psyche, the transitional yet inchoate matrix of death and becoming.

Soyinka's 'cyclic concept of time' and 'matrix of death and becoming', can be seen as essential ideas for understanding the 'return-beat' model. When we become physically and psycho- logically aware by embodying the paradox of simultaneous centripetal and centrifugal impulses leading to movements, then we can become aware and have a direct experience of the cyclical matrix and partake in 'the dance of the primordial realm'. These ideas are processes which are manifested, in various ways and with varying degrees, at all aspects of Yoruba social life, from language and meta-communication to traditional, i.e. pre-colonised society. Within the traditional theatrical context, a manifestation which is frequently seen throughout West Africa is the dance of a performer(s) in the sacred or social circle, as s(he) 'plunges straight into the chthonic realm'. The sacred circle or 'Agbo' is an arena where all the temporal forces meet. It is where the whole group – and each individual – suspends disbelief and where, through improvisation, the performer(s) communicate the many mythopoetic muses in the active present, to an active audience. This may serve to illustrate how our perceptions of social values are embodied within particular spatio-temporal forms in dance and empathetic observation. Conversely, it would be almost impossible to transpose the linear and non-linear models of rhythm without compromising the attendant myths and ethics of the culture that produced it.

the nature of perception within the 'return-beat'

We can say that seeing and perception encompass more than just the use of our eyes. They embrace all five senses including, arguably, many more, such as our body's self-reflexive ability to perceive itself, i.e. proprioception. Perceived features occur in the extended and active mode of seeing which occurs when, for example, one person's *becoming* meets with another's. The changes in the act of acknowledging a particular perceived feature (or, in other words, a change in perception) depend largely on the phenomenological attributes of that individual's personal 'becoming' as it interacts with the other's, or with other objects and presences. The changes in phenomenological attributes derive from both interior and exterior conditions:

1.   internal influences (e.g. metabolic, emotional, psychological)

2.   external influences (e.g. environmental, social, cultural).

If our experience of space–time is subjective, then it is likely to be affected by a range of conditions such as our alertness, mood, general health, bodily co-ordination, or focal awareness for things with which we have a particular desire, attachment or antipathy.

I would characterise West African manifestations of the 'return-beat' as tending to promote a *shared* individual experience of dynamic balance. Here, the participant's response to the 'return-beat' is perceived as a kind of focal aggregate of the rhythm. Perceptually, this feels like the timeless 'centre' of the rhythmic return, and I call it the 'root pulse'. The root pulse differs from the 'return-beat' by a small *perceived* difference in phase. Curiously, it accentuates our awareness of an *outward-going* sensation of a given beat . . . yet this is simultaneous to an *inward-going* beat. The illusion of co-existent and yet opposite forces seems to confound our rational understanding! In the 'return-beat' model, this root pulse would be located at the centre of our diagrammatic circle (see Fig. 12.2). The 'return-beat' can then be described as the body's internal experience of a perpetual return to the place from where we can feel the root pulse. It constructs a situated, active present. Where the 'return-beat' is strong, – as in, for example, Latin American dance music – it may create a subjective sense of curvature within the rhythm. This curvature seems to have magnetic properties which draw the body into the 'return' zone. Each participant may find slightly different 'routes' to the root pulses of a given rhythm, and this creates an individual dance for that particular rhythm. This is useful in that it permits everyone, almost irrespective of their physical size, mobility and weight, to dance to the same music whilst occupying their own spatio-temporal zone. It offers an interplay between different cultural, social, emotional and aesthetic values.

maintaining internal and external balance

The active, autonomous and situated 'return-beat' offers an organic framework which facilitates embodied communication between participants. It also maintains a balance between what we generally understand to be 'interior' and 'exterior' to us. This balance serves to confirm and renew relational values between people in a convivial setting. In rural, or traditional West African traditions, the literal and poetic domains are seen as twins from the same womb, implying an inextricable fusion of the two modes of truth. Micky Hart in his book *Drumming at the Edge of Magic* says:

> The master drummer of a West African ensemble is like the senior percussionist in a Western orchestra. His position depends as much on mastery of drum lore as on technical skill; in Africa it's hard to separate the two. Knowing the right rhythm to play on an occasion is as important as being able to execute that rhythm. When the chief gets up from his stool and begins strolling, the master drummer must be able to switch rhythms effortlessly. He might, to borrow an example from ethnomusicologist J. H. Kwabena Nketia, play a rhythm that repeats the message: 'The chief walks. He is not in a hurry.' Besides

calling attention to the fact that the chief is up and moving, this little rhythm also impresses upon the chief that he should walk carefully and consciously; stumbling would be a bad omen.[11]

In the above example, the processes of communication and the maintaining of internal and external balance occur within and throughout the body, to communicate complex ideas with balance, dignity and perhaps a feeling of bliss. This process aims to renew the active present/presence that exists within the vast plethora of human emotions and situations. It is tempting to argue that the more harmonious the relationship between ourselves and our orbit around the 'return-beat' of a rhythm, the greater will be our subjective flow and experience of bliss. If our sense of flow and bliss is strong, we will feel more balanced, both internally and externally. This balance can be seen to be both simple and complex. It is simple, because the mechanisms are homoeostatic[12] and use rudimentary processes of 'feedback' and adaptation. It is complex, because an overwhelming array of simultaneous physical and psychological phenomena are involved.

In describing this process in more detail we can refer to the heart, which plays a prominent (mythical and metabolic) role in sustaining internal and external balance physically. Here, an imagined möbius strip comprising two beats of the heart ('lub-dub') is responsible for pumping out, and receiving blood. The rhythm this creates can be argued to be an originary motif for the sensibilities of the organic 'return-beat'. External rhythms that are made visible by dance and music seem to emulate the 'return-beat' produced by the internal rhythms of the heart beat.

digitising the 'return-beat'

There is an important distinction to be made between a digital root pulse and an organic root pulse. If we create a rhythmic form using the most basic, digitally generated pulses, its shape is likely to be homogenised, especially if the cycles on the individual tracks have been shaped to fit the 'return-beat' of each digital rhythm pulse. Digital 'return-beat' genres include certain Hip Hop, Pop, House, Acid House, Techno, Trance, Progressive and Jungle. Each has a distinct rhythmic style which relies heavily on the repetitious form of the (often digitised) figures. The DJ often 'curves' the more rectilinear structures by scratching and mixing the different styles, weaving these wave forms into a single, perhaps more 'human' tapestry. This tapestry constitutes a major part of the Rave or club event with the DJ creating and changing the moods around the digital root pulse subtlety, seeking to orchestrate the collective emotions while everyone orbits the digital 'return-beat'.

The Rave scene raises important questions about many issues, and reflects, to some extent, popular preconceptions and fantasies. In the 1970s and early 1980s, dancing in clubs used to be assumed to be part of the mating game before it was afforded a particular association with 'minorities' (i.e. 'women', 'gay' or 'black men'). More recently it has been taken to be a less cultish celebration of human presence in a shared sense of bliss. We could also interpret Rave culture as a form of escapism, or as a celebration of consumerism, technocentrism, or utopianism. As Josephine Leask says:

> For club culture reveals a new focus on the body, one that constructs the body as an object of consumption, that dehumanises the body, that provides pleasure that can be bought and used for private entertainment, that is about the vanishing of self-identity and communication through artificial devices (technology and drugs). It is a journey and an arrival at a spiritual void. The act of clubbing is one in which the individual partakes in the ecstasy of disappearance.[13]

The mythology of the Rave culture promises individual euphoria for those who manage to merge with the many hundreds or thousands in the collective body of dancers. The ecstasy is often heightened by the use of drugs as well as the digital pulse itself. The popular Western mindset perceives a dilemma here. In Rave, do we find our 'authentic selves' in an ethical, embodied sense, or are we trapped in a false, consumerist image of community? Baudrillard describes a disembodied mode of sovereignty similar to Josephine Leask's 'ecstasy of disappearance'. This reminds us of the distinction between an 'organic' return-beat which must, of necessity, correspond to the 'live' emotions of its makers, and the digital 'return-beat' which may not.

> Each individual sees himself promoted to the control of a hypothetical machine, isolated in a position of perfect sovereignty, at an infinite distance from his original universe; that is to say, in the same position as the astronaut in his bubble, existing in a state of weightlessness which compels the individual to remain in perpetual orbital flight and to maintain sufficient speed in zero to avoid crashing into his planet of origin.[14]

a personal reflection

My work with the 'return-beat' has provided a cross-disciplinary, artistic–academic context where I can analyse and enact models of difference, similarity and mutual co-existence. Although I had originally sought to polarise the 'linear' and the 'return' models of creative presence, in retrospect, it occurs to me that the 'good' can be located in an active fusion of the organic and the technological, the actual and the virtual, the practical and the theoretical.

notes

1. 'Choreology' is the accepted term used to describe the study and description of the movements of dancing.

2. Rudolf Laban (1879–1958), Hungarian-born choreographer, invented a system of dance notation (Labanotation).

3. See John Wood's Chapter 6, 'Redesigning the Present', for distinctions between Western concepts of time.

4. See Taiwo, O., and Wood, J., 'Some proprioceptive observations of "being-with"'. Paper given at the 'Problems of Action and Observation' Conference, University of Amsterdam, April 1997.

5. The action of marching; the regular forward movement together and in time of a body of troops (OED).

6. Pronounced more like: '..aaaaand'.

7. Williamson, N., 'On the global village green', *The Times*, July 1996.

8. Lefebvre, H., *The Production of Space*, Oxford, UK/Cambridge, Mass., Blackwell, 1994.

9. See Peter Cresswell's Chapter 8, above.

10. Soyinka, W., *The Fourth Stage – Art, Dialogue and Outrage: Essays on Literature and Culture*, London, Methuen, 1993, p. 28.

11. Hart, M., *Drumming at the Edge of Magic*, New York, Harper, San Francisco, 1990.

12. Cybernetics has proposed that the physical process that sustains metabolic balance is a homeostatic one.

13. Leask, J., 'Club culture: the body in the bubble', *Dance Theatre Journal*, 12(4) Spring, 1996.

14. Baudrillard, J., *The Ecstasy of Communication*, New York, Semiotext, Foreign Agents series, Automedia, 1988, quoted in Leask, op. cit., pp. 15–16.

bibliography

Bachelard, G., *The Poetics of Space*, Boston, Beacon Press, 1969.
Barba, Eugenio/Savarese: *A Dictionary of Theatre Anthropology – The Secret Art of the Performer*, London, Routledge, 1991.
Ch'Ing, Cheng Man, *Cheng Tzu's Thirteen Treatises on T'ai Chi Ch'uan*, Berkeley, Ca., North Atlantic Books, California 1985.
Diallo, Y., and Hall, M. *The Healing Drum*, Vermont, Destiny Books, 1989.
Elam, K., *The Semiotics of Theatre and Drama*, London and New York, Routledge, 1994.
Gilroy, P., *The Black Atlantic*, London and New York, Verso, 1993.
Laban, R., *The Mastery of Movement*, London, Macdonald Evans, 1971.
Lefebvre, H., *The Production of Space*, Oxford (UK) Cambridge, Mass., Blackwell, 1994.
Soyllka, W., *Art, Dialogue and Outrage*, London, Methuen, 1993.
Wilson, S.G. *The Drummer's Path*, Vermont, Destiny Books, 1992.

chapter 13

'peak practices'

the production and regulation of ecstatic bodies

maria pini

Raving is about the time you spend doing things that are about freedom . . . It's the time when you can really be yourself. (Jane)

[Raving] just gives you a personal freedom. It's like self-expression, isn't it? . . . It's like a total expression. (Teresa)

It's when you let it all go and just become yourself. You let go of all your inhibitions and feel much freer to be yourself. (Kate)

You feel really free . . . It felt like you were yourself. (Miriam)

As has historically been the case in interpreting youth cultural practices, a familiar association between the practices of raving and notions of freedom has emerged, and the British rave scene has, since the late 1980s, generated its own particular version of what this freedom entails.[1] The main aim of this chapter is to challenge certain (arguably) oversimplistic readings of rave culture by indicating some of the complexities and contradictions involved in the experiences of raving. In particular, I want to contrast claims for 'freedom' made on behalf of rave with the strenuous efforts which can be seen to go into its production. I therefore emphasise how much self-regulation and management is required to produce what many ravers and academics valorise as a form of unregulated being.

Lisa Blackman in Chapter 10 highlights the tendency to polarise the new technologies into liberatory or repressive modes; invested either with some radical transformative potential or feared as an extension of repressive state control and surveillance. There are many parallels between current techno-criticism and the discursive interplay that surrounds contemporary rave culture. First, there is the association between raving and freedom. Just as virtual space is often ascribed celebratory readings, so the rave space is commonly seen to transform the socialised self into a 'freer', less regulated state of being; one that reveals a basic human core within its socialised exterior.[2] Somehow, the use of drugs, the effects of music, the practice of communal social dance, and the collective nature of rave events are seen to dissolve this exterior leaving participants in a more 'natural' state. Some academic readings of rave events thus make claim to a pre-Oedipal nature of being,[3] whilst others invoke the primitivist language of shamanism and tribalism.[4]

The second parallel between rave and techno-critical debate is the established dualism which casts rave culture as signalling either a form of progressive, postmodern youth politics or a form of escapism on the part of youth attempting to 'avoid' the realities of wider economic and social hardship.[5] Hesmondhalgh correctly notes that the discussion of rave tends to divide into categories of either celebration or lamentation.[6] Where some commentators see it constituting a form of 'unregulated' space reminiscent of Hakim Bey's 'Temporary Autonomous Zone' (TAZ),[7] others, such as Richard Sutcliffe, emphasise autonomy, suggesting that 'rave is about free corporeal expression in relation to music'.[8] Sutcliffe attributes individual experiences of autonomy to the collective autonomy of rave organisation which he likens to Deleuze and Guattari's notion of a war machine, i.e. rhizomatic in form and resistant to fixture. Here, the evasion of police surveillance and control, and the erratic way that fliers are disseminated can be seen as a sign of rave's rhizomatic form. Some researchers read rave in terms of Deleuze and Guattari's figuration of a Body without Organs (BWO), arguing that rave dance-floor movement can best be captured through the concept of Lines of Flight. However, the above arguments are difficult to support. For example, Bey has recently claimed[9] that the freedom from state interference described within the TAZ is no longer possible, and this may also be true for other forms of public meeting. Sutcliffe makes an automatic connection between practices that may fall outside of state bureaucratic control and a 'free' form of subjectivity. Equally dubious is the (academic) theory[10] that rave is a culture of 'disappearance' that somehow resists meaning, and therefore cannot be classified and appropriated by the academy.

Where rave culture is likened to a TAZ or to a BWO, with the implication that it is somehow less rule-bound and hierarchically structured than other forms of collective organisation, ravers are commonly read as embodiments of 'freedom'. Their subjective 'freedom' is assumed to stem from the absence of classificatory devices and 'masterful' gazes which apparently characterise other, more 'rational' forms of subjectivity. For example, Rietveld argues that the raver experiences 'an undoing of the constructed self'[11] and Jordan writes that: 'In these vast celebrations usually called raves, participants gradually lose subjective belief in their self and merge into a collective body whose nature is best captured by Deleuze and Guattari's concept of the Body without Organs'[12] Whilst I do not deny the genuine sense of freedom which can be involved in raving, nor the 'loss' of rationality which can emerge from the particular technology/body/chemical assemblage which constitutes an event, I also believe that a more cogent interrogation of the precise nature of this perceived freedom is overdue. Conversely, whilst many of the more celebratory readings of rave imply some kind of essential, unregulated and basic human state, others imply that ravers are 'duped', 'mistaken' or 'confused'. A common argument about contemporary social dancing is that it empowers girls and women. Sarah Thornton, by contrast, dismisses experiences of freedom felt by female ravers by referring to the 'reality' of their subordinate social situation. She also criticises certain studies which, she claims: 'conflate the feeling of freedom fostered by the discotheque environment with substantive political rights and freedoms'.[13] Admittedly, her concern is not with the study of experience, but with the accumulation, within club culture, of an influential mindset which she calls 'subcultural capital'.

I believe it to be inadequate to dismiss experiences of 'freedom' simply because it is possible to counter these by pointing to a more visible 'reality'. Donna Haraway states that 'experience is a semiosis, an embodying of meaning'[14] and in this sense, experience is no less a cultural signifier than are the more concrete signs of 'rights and freedoms'. Experience is therefore just as worthy of serious treatment as are the more formal traces of culture. What is needed, however, is for references to 'freedom' and 'liberation' to be explored more closely. To argue that an experiential moment of 'freedom' might be produced whilst being monitored and otherwise constructed is not to argue that it is not real. It is merely to reiterate the arguments of social constructionism. Seeing experiences of 'freedom' as simply the product of rave's supposed lack of regulation is insufficient. It seems to rest upon an essentialism which posits a pre-socialised human core which is somehow uncovered through the practices of raving.

In short, just because raving can provide a freedom from certain wider day-to-day regulatory practices (including perhaps, the self-practices involved in maintaining the more coherent and rational subjectivity required for say, working, going to school, or conducting a conversation), this does not mean that it constitutes an essentially unregulated space. There is, I am arguing, no such thing as an entirely unregulated space or an essentially unregulated subject, and even the experience of freedom may involve its own regulatory and self-governmental mechanisms. This view is not shared by the 'postmodernist' perspective taken in *Rave Off*,[15] whose authors seem to see rave culture as belonging in an almost post-apocalyptic 'beyond', in which both 'meaning' and the constructed 'self' are dead. One of the problems with this interpretation is that little or no consideration is given to the various operations which work towards the production of what may come to be experienced as a state of meaninglessness, freedom or 'undone' selfhood and the work which goes into maintaining such a state. Instead, the impression given by many of these writers is that the raver enters this state of 'freedom' simply and automatically, as a result of being within the rave environment. Attending to these operations would necessarily involve acknowledging the extent to which selves are 'done' as much as 'undone'[16] within the context of the rave event. Further, the lack of specificity which commonly characterises this work makes for a denial of the numerous differences that exist between different individuals' and groups' experiences of raving, and indeed, their different notions of what constitutes 'freedom' or 'autonomy'.[17] In much of this commentary therefore, one is far more likely to encounter the raver as a non-specified general; as a 'techno-shaman' or a 'cyber-hippie' rather than as a raced, sexed and otherwise inscribed and embodied subject.

The tendency to present ravers as non-specific abstracts is centrally related to the 'semiotic totalitarianism'[18] which marks a lot of work on rave; work that makes strong claims to the 'truth' about rave. Concentrating too hard on specific negotiations of the possibilities opened up by rave would clearly disturb such a tendency. This however, is precisely what is needed in order that the 'freedom' which an individual raver might experience does not become 'Freedom' as an abstract concept.

the constitution of a 'peak' moment

Writing almost a decade ago, Simon Reynolds made the following observation:

> Our culture has long since ceased to demand deferment of gratification or sublimation of energy: it insists on enjoyment, incites us to develop our capacity for pleasure. 'Youth' – because coterminous with sex, style, hedonism, fitness – has become the supreme value in our society, almost a definition of health . . . Pop has always been body-music, but the body is now the prime locus of power's operation, where power solicits us. Being a success in life involves a maximisation of your body's potential for health and pleasure.[19]

If Reynolds sees, within popular cultural practices of the mid-1980s, a growing incitement to the heightening of bodily pleasures, then rave can be seen to have taken this to an extreme in the 1990s. Although it is important to recognise the growing fragmentation of 'rave culture', what unites the various modifications of this culture is the (often relentless) pursuit of the 'peak' or 'limit' experience. As I have argued elsewhere, within rave it is the individual mind/body/soul which becomes the primary target to be worked on in pursuit of this limit.[20]

The analysis that follows seeks to trouble any oversimplistic attribution of 'freeing' potential to the practices of raving whilst simultaneously acknowledging the reality of this potential and the pleasurable sensations that its pursuit and achievement can effect. Drawing from interview material I simply want to illustrate how, in several specific situations, the ecstatic peak comes to be achieved. One thing that emerges from this unfortunately brief discussion is the need to look to the specificity of subject's situated realisations of these peaks. The following examples – which illustrate some of the various self-operations involved in achieving and maintaining a desired raving state – are intended to raise questions about claims such as Sutcliffe's that 'autonomy is inherent to raving' and 'rave is about free corporeal expression in relation to music'. They also highlight some of the contradictions that are part of the ravers' own discourses.

Foucault writes that:

> Technologies of the self . . . permit individuals to effect by their own means with the help of others a number of operations on their bodies and souls, thought, conduct and way of being, so as to transform themselves in order to attain a certain state of happiness, purity, wisdom, perfection or immortality.[21]

●   ●   ●

Sally and Jean are two 19-year-old, unemployed single mothers. The following excerpts are taken from a group interview conducted in 1996. When asked initially what they got out of raving, they agreed that it was the freedom which it afforded them – what Jean calls 'complete self-expression'. Within the wider contexts of their lives, where the demands of single motherhood and financial constraints limit how and where they can 'express' themselves, it is easy to see how the rave environment comes to signal this moment of 'freedom'. Paradoxically however, their moment of 'freedom' and 'self-expression' – which both agree constitutes their 'happiest' times (in both cases, as important to them as becoming mothers) can cost them the equivalent of four weeks' house-keeping money, which means that they have to make major sacrifices during their non-raving time. Similarly, both repeatedly return to detailing the growing intensities of their 'come-downs' from drugs: Jean describes these as 'pure hell' and points out that she 'just knows' that she's always going to have a bad come-down, and 'just knows' that it's going to be 'hell'.

What is immediately apparent from these accounts is the rigorous management of time, energy, money and pain which goes into the production of their moment of 'freedom'. The following extracts indicate how the 'wrong' music; the 'wrong' drugs; the 'wrong' look or word from a fellow raver; attacks of cramp, drug-use, all pose threats to the achievement of the desired state. As a result of the constant potential threats posed to 'peak', aspects such as paranoia and interpersonal relationships are all worked out in terms of a specific set of 'management' strategies devised to deal with them. This clearly brings into question any suggestion that the 'peak' or ecstatic state is a necessary or straightforward effect of any one aspect of raving – such as drugs. What Sally and Jean's accounts make clear is the amount of sheer hard work which goes into making rave function in the correct way for them. On many occasions the women stress having to 'push it' in order to achieve desired drug effects – again, something which challenges simplistic 'pharmaceutically determinist' arguments:

> I find that on a lot of Es though, to begin with you have got to push it. And then like, I'd done the three Es and was feeling nothing and I thought, fucking hell, I've just borrowed all this money to come up to London and I'm sitting down and I've got to push this. So I was like 'push it. Push it.' (Jean)

'Rushing' on particular drugs; 'peaking' with particular people; staying 'on one' in particular crowds clearly involve much effort. The fragility of this state becomes clear as Jean and Sally gradually describe more and more potentially disturbing forces. For example, Julie speaks of a 'bad' night where her high-heeled boots stopped her dancing, and made her feel that people were looking at her, which in turn made her feel self-conscious for the whole night. For Jean, a particular threat to her enjoyment is embodied by her boyfriend Peter. Jean's 'peak' experiences are therefore very much structured around what he does, and doesn't, 'allow' her to do:

> I mean, say if I am talking to a geezer, I've always got that constant fear of Peter wandering by and seeing me. Cause he's so jealous. I have to be careful. So what I tend to do is dance until I come down. I've always got people coming up to me saying 'Pete's looking for you'. I'm 'yeah, yeah. Alright. I mean, don't tell him you've seen me' kind of thing. Then, when I come down, I go and find him. I didn't go out for a long time. That was only because my boyfriend didn't let me.

Where women such as Sally and Jean have devised certain techniques for recognising, handling and coping with the paranoia, Andy's account exemplifies how men have to deal with the perceived need to 'cope' with the pressures within rave. In this case, Andy's ability to control and manage is articulated in 'fighting' terms; as an internal battle; a test of personal strength. Andy says of his E-use:

> I suppose it's whether you can control it . . . some people can't take it. Some people's personality can't cope – they can't control the rush. I've been close to it but I've stopped it. It's the paranoia at the back of your head. It always gets to you. Sometimes you do a pill and think 'fucking hell, I wonder if I'll be alright on this one?' You can be scared, but at the end of the day, you just got to put it aside and say 'bollocks' to it.

The theme of paranoia is also something which, in Jean and Sally's accounts, is clearly tied up with more general preoccupations with seeing and being seen. Jean, for example, says that nothing is quite as good for her as realising that she is being watched by a 'horny' man. She dances where the 'horny' men are and claims that being looked at by an 'ugly' man simply does not give her the same intense pleasures. Sally agrees. Realising that she is being looked at by the 'right' kind of man intensifies Jean's peak: 'It's like whoosh, you're up there'. And she says that 'horny men make you rush'. It is not surprising that one of the things that cause both women most discomfort is the thought of being seen in the 'wrong' light. Discussing the possibilities for 'pick up' in a club, Jean says: 'Imagine if it's still dark and then you left. You know, you're *alright* in the dark. You don't look too bad. It's when, after a few hours . . . all your oils start coming out.' She reiterates this later: 'I was fine at that point – until people started looking at me . . . Did my head in. I hate that feeling.' Sally makes a similar point: 'I'd never let the kids see me like that. It's not fair.' The pure 'self' expression which both women claim they get from raving is clearly brought into question by the emphasis placed on remaining in a certain light. As Sally puts it, 'you're not yourself in a rave are you?'

I have suggested some of the ways in which the self is worked, managed and otherwise produced within a rave context. This troubles any easy reading of such selves as 'free'. Jean and Sally make clear the extent to which coming to recognise and 'know' the different potential disturbances to their 'peaking', and the best ways to combat such disturbance, is an integral part of raving. Self-knowledge can be seen to be constituted here, in terms of a clear classificatory system wherein experience comes to be known in terms of 'coming up', 'peaking', 'handling it', 'losing it' and so forth. What is also made clear is that such knowledge does not simply 'reveal' itself upon entry to an event. It is gradually negotiated. For example, the 'knowledge' of certain drug effects develops, which arguably *constructs* as much as it can be said to 'describe' such effects. This is indicated on several occasions when the women express a sense of uncertainty over precisely what they are feeling. This uncertainty is then dissipated once they come to 'know' what they are supposed to expect and experience. Hence, drug effects – which are commonly viewed as unmediated physiological responses to particular chemicals – are clearly experienced in accordance with their discursive construction. In the following extract, Sally is describing not knowing what is going on after she has taken an 'E'. This frightens her and clearly stands in the way of what she wants – enjoyment. Reaching her 'peak', rather than being about embracing such ambiguity and lack of certainty, is only achieved after recalling what Jean had told her to expect:

> And I started feeling a bit sick and it was like 'phew, get to grips'. But I just kept telling myself what Jean had told me beforehand when we've talked about stuff. When she told me

the first time she really came-up on an E, how it shocked her. So I kept telling myself this. In the end, I came out of it and I just enjoyed it. I just went with it. But it was scary.

Although it is clearly important to recognise the links between paranoia and the physiological effects of drugs like Speed, it is equally clear that such effects are as much the product of a wider discursive and material assemblage as are experiences and understandings of dance, interpersonal relations and so on. One thing that is clear is the extent to which Sally and Jean have to develop a particular 'knowledge' of what to expect in order to 'peak'. In the following extract, Jean is feeling 'bad' until she comes to know that this is in fact 'good':

> And I thought I was losing it. Yeah, that's why. I hadn't been raving for two years and I went for my birthday to 'World Dance'. I was only in there about an hour and a half 'cause I walked in, first of all and the beat was different . . . It was faster and instead of walking into the rave and thinking, 'cor, yeah', I thought 'shit'. I started coming up on the 'E' and it was a totally different feeling to Speed, see. So I wasn't expecting all that . . . I didn't like it, you know. And I went outside and I was . . . right off my head and I thought I was losing it. But now, I know that it was just a good E you know. I mean, it frightened me. I didn't know the feeling and it frightened me.

Drug effects are therefore subject to particular ways of knowing. Here, Jean describes a specific instance of how drug effects are experienced in terms of being able to know and classify these:

> I did the rest before we went in like I always had done, but I should have known that these were really strong – stronger than we'd ever had, you know. And I lost it. Like, you can lose it on Speed. But like, when I first went in there, I thought you know, this Speed's not working. Because I didn't have the confidence that Speed gives you. I thought, this ain't working, so what is it? That's when me and Mel had an E each. So, I did my E thinking that I hadn't come up. So I was coming up on eight Speed pills and the E and then, Mel was on a good one 'cause she'd only done four Speed pills. So I was like 'let me have your half E. Give me half of your E' kind of thing. So I had that as well. Then I realised you know, this isn't that I haven't come up. This is really strong – and I'm too off my head.

Experience is heavily classified in terms of the stages of 'coming up', 'coming down' and so forth. These women have also come to recognise what type of trip and what stage in a trip the other is experiencing. They have also come to know what particular types of music, drugs, crowds, venues and so forth 'work' for them. Consequently these women have devised what is almost a set of 'rules' about these features. These include those relating to the management and risk assessment of drug intake:

> JEAN: Never do a whole E. Not at first . . . My first E was a whole one and it was a 'Dove'. So I'd say never do a whole E.
> SALLY: No . . .
> JEAN: I'd even do it in quarters I think.

Drugs, like experiential 'stages', types of people, music and towns, are all shown to be rigidly classified. Distinctions are made between E-ravers and Speed-ravers; black men and white men: 'horny' men and 'ugly' men; 'happy' ravers and 'smack-ravers'; Dover (as a Speed town) and London (as an E town).

A further aspect of these women's self-management in relation to drug use becomes clear in their descriptions of how their time (their weekends) is organised so as to allow an appropriate period during which to 'come-down'. The management of 'come-down' is most clearly manifest in their negotiations of the cross-overs between raving and motherhood. Both organise childcare in advance and stress the importance of not having their children around during 'come-down':

JEAN: Absolutely. I wouldn't be on drugs around them 'cause, nah. For a start I couldn't have (son) back on, like, a come-down. I wouldn't have him back because . . . 'mum can I have this. Can I have that' and I would lose my patience. I couldn't do it.

SALLY: Yeah, it's not fair on them.

JEAN: No, 'cause they're at that early age now . . . I wouldn't like them to see me like that.

All of these points indicate the extent to which, rather than being about a necessarily 'freer' or less regulated time and space, raving for Jean and Sally is – at least partly – about regulation and management. To reiterate, pointing this out is not about denying the clear pleasures they get from raving. Indeed, the amount these women sacrifice, in terms of both time and money, evidences how very important raving is to them.

That one has to know – to possess some pre-existent knowledge – in order for rave to 'work' challenges any oversimplistic claim that rave is somehow disconnected from its wider cultural context; that it is independent, autonomous and self-contained. For example, Sally and Jean's construction on 'black attitude'[22] as a disturbing force indicates too clearly how the rave 'world' continues and reinforces the categories of the wider cultural 'world'. So too do their remarks on their fears of being labelled a 'slag' if they seem to be talking too much to a particular man.

Knowledge is therefore central to Jean and Sally's accounts. These women's fears are shown to be intricately tied up with notions of not 'knowing'; not being familiar with what's going on:

> It was scary 'cause it was my first time at a rave and I was with Nick who'd been to a rave before. They knew what to expect. I just couldn't handle the main room. (Jean)

> Like I hadn't been raving for two years and I'd got into the club and [the music] had really picked up – really fast and I couldn't handle it. My first rave in two years I did not enjoy. (Jean)

In discussing bad 'attitude' from fellow ravers, Jean says of Sally (who began raving later than her):

> So she's seeing it now whereas she had never seen it so she didn't know. She didn't look out for it 'cause she didn't know what to expect but I'd tried to say it happens.

ecstatic freedom reconsidered

In this chapter I have tried to indicate how what is commonly thought of as a moment of 'freedom' and 'self-expression' is far more complex than is usually acknowledged by academic commentators on rave. I have indicated how, for Sally and Jean, their 'free' moment is in actuality one that is carefully managed, regulated and monitored. Far from being about the 'loss' or 'undoing' of the self, this moment is clearly about the production of a particular ecstatic self. It is about a rigorous working on the self rather than a relaxation of self-consciousness. For these women, their moment of 'pure' self-expression is not about presenting some naked essence (as self-expression implies), but about projecting a very particular image of themselves. Indeed, both agree that in rave you do not see people as they 'really' are. On the one hand then, the 'ecstatic' or 'peak' state is experienced as a moment within which one simply 'lets go' and by implication, somehow returns to some more 'natural' state. On the other it is seen as a moment of not being oneself; a moment wherein one is 'hidden' by drugs, dark lighting and the general 'unreality' of an event. I have also indicated the strict classifications that mark and inform the production of particular sought-after experiential states for Sally and Jean which underlie these women's experiences. To reiterate, it is by no means my intention to dismiss or undermine the pleasures of raving: the real sense of release it can be seen to afford, the often incomparably pleasurable intensities it can produce, or the central importance it can have in one's life. Instead, I would suggest that interpretations of these experiences and pleasures be dislodged from the language of the 'natural' and the essential which so commonly frames them and reconsidered as particular and embodied manifestations of the wider technology/chemical/physical assemblage that constitutes rave.

notes

1. Pini, M., 'Women and the early British Rave scene', in McRobbie, A. (ed.), *Back to Reality? Social Experience and Cultural Studies*, Manchester, Manchester University Press, 1997.

2. The polar opposite of this argument is most usually found in early 'panic' press reportage of rave, which stressed its ability to numb and hypnotise youth. See Redhead, S. (ed.), *Rave Off: Politics and Deviance in Contemporary Youth Culture*, Hampshire, Avebury, 1993.

3. Rietveld, H., 'Living the Dream', in Redhead, S., op. cit.

4. Sutcliffe, R., 'Rave and Techno-Shamanism', paper given at Goldsmiths College, University of London, November 1996.

5. See McRobbie, A., 'Shut up and dance: Changing modes of femininity', in *Postmodernism and Popular Culture*, London, Routledge, 1994.

6. Hesmondhalgh, D., 'The cultural politics of dance music', in *Soundings* (5), Spring 1997.

7. Bey, H., *T.A.Z. The Temporary Autonomous Zone: Ontological Anarchy, Poetic Terrorism*, Brooklyn, NY, Autonomedia, [1985], 1991.

8. Sutcliffe, R., 'Rave and Techno-Shamanism', paper given at Goldsmiths College, University of London, November 1996.

 9. Hakkim Bey (Peter Lambourn Wilson) Lecture to MA Design Futures students and MA Creative Curating students at Goldsmiths College, University of London, 24 February 1997.

10. Steve Redhead, op. cit.

11. Rietveld, H., in Redhead, S., op. cit.

12. Jordan, T., 'Collective bodies: raving and the politics of Gilles Deleuze and Felix Guattari', in *Body and Society* (1), March 1995.

13. Thornton, S., *Club Cultures: Music, Media and Subcultural Capital*, Cambridge, Polity Press, 1995, p. 21.

14. Haraway, D., *Simians, Cyborgs and Women*, London, Free Association Books, 1991.

15. Redhead S., op. cit.

16. Rietveld, H., in Redhead, S., op. cit.

17. My own ethnographic work shows, for example, how in several cases, young white ravers' achievement of a state of 'freedom' is dependent upon the absence of what they call 'black attitude'. PhD thesis, Goldsmiths College, 1997.

18. A term commonly used in discussing the work of Bakhtin.

19. Reynolds, Simon, *Blissed Out: The raptures of rock*, London, Serpent's Tail, 1990.

20. Pini, M., op. cit.

21. Foucault, M., 'Technologies of the Self', in Martin, L.H., Gutman, H., and Hutton, R.H. (eds), *Technologies of the Self. Seminar with Michel Foucault*, London, Tavistock, 1988.

22. See Pini, M., 'Other traces: a cultural study of clubbing and new modes of femininity', PhD thesis, Goldsmiths College, University of London, 1997.

part five

between saying and showing

[saɪt]

The self is a cloister full of remembered sounds
And of sounds so far forgotten, like her voice,
That they return unrecognised . . . [1]

Let me begin by counting sides. And perhaps, let me speak, in the beginning, of what might remain – by what necessity – unspoken, or unheard, later. I shall summon and count, and attempt to account for sites *and* for counting, until infinite counting may lead to some end, summon, or perform its limit.

If I were summoned to name 'my project', perhaps I would have to respond by saying that it is to hold on to that end, attempt to face it and wait. Tempt time. There is need to remain 'there', where – perhaps – nothing remains, near a limit, for that short, that perhaps impossible moment. And speak it in writing it, or, as Celan says, 'let some words go in that direction'.

There is narration, an itinerary. There are also questions of litigation. We shall leave them aside, on one side. Litigation concerns, what goes from 'what is/ was there?' to 'who did what?' in order to perform and, in this performance, witness an apparently inevitable link of these questions (usually via a motive, 'why?'). This is how a limit is traced *and* avoided. Everything begins again in yet another re-turn, around familiar circles.

Still, something returns. As if from elsewhere. But it is not a matter of questions. It counts.

A drama in the passages of the visual, the proper and the evidential, a play of visual and aural traces, a tragedy on one, two, three (or more) sites and the inescapable (cross)determinations *and* slippings which can be traced 'there':

sight	the visual, seeing
site	the place, placing
cite	repeat, summon, serve, count, list, litigate, sue (*cito*, Latin: to repeat fast, again and again, as in religious ceremonies)
[saɪt]	sign of a sound, spelling without meaning, writing acoustics of/without voice
side	[saɪd] perhaps also that site: *the right side and the reverse side* . . . neither one nor two
sait	don't listen, just read without knowing, 'he knows' . . . *savoir, sais, sait* . . .

Another play, another tragedy, the analytical theatre of theory. Here, writing offers itself to explore the general domination of the visual or the specular, and how, on what path this domination becomes the very movement of theorisation (specularisation). The interferences of aural contingents alternate and return: potent tele-instrument, insight extension, stick of the blind. A kind of telepathy, a passion also, which placeless and without an alternative route, takes its way right through us. The aural trace seduces and contests the sites of the visual and of knowledge, the stability of same and different, where theorisation takes place, with the insistence almost, of a repulsive, a blasphemous rhyme. Origin *and* destination of this play on interferences are a dispersal of *property*, of thinking, of language and of images as possible and *proper sites* of habitation, unique residencies of concentration.

A play on homophones. There is no more (or more fundamental) truth in sound, speech or voice, nor a possibility of 'rectifying' the inadequacies of seeing, language, writing. This would be no more than the domination of the visual in reverse (which is however precisely how 'the voice' is traditionally appropriated). The aural trace cites a flight of tension, a passage of attention. Conventions of seeing *and* placing, origin *and* fiction may subside. It bears the spark to diffuse a mechanics of theorisation. Attention, a passion of the unknown.

Response of experience and of representation. Citing responsibility. The photograph can become the site where a lack in experience, a wounding incompleteness of experience doubles, where it is cited, where it is (re)experienced as if the photograph were its origin and its proper site, as if it were the photograph 'itself' that were marked by a 'difficulty in existing'. Here, the drama coincides with photography, and perhaps, technology at large. Somewhere near the sites where writing encounters experience, where the inescapable necessity of representation coincides with its breakdown, where theories dissolve themselves and perhaps not only themselves: sites of doubling, of repetition, entropy of exteriorisations (of mourning, as some might say).

Reading aloud, underestimated and dismissed as it may be in Western culture, may allow another insight to writing, perhaps the strange, unheard-of experience of another, a siteless citing, while at once exposing it to its final dissolution.

11th April 1996

German state prosecutors are to press charges of criminal negligence and manslaughter against a Dortmund maintenance company and its sub-contractor after the Düsseldorf airport fire in which 16 people, including a British soldier, died and more than 60 were injured.

(The Times, 13.04.1996)

A photograph of footprints has been published accompanying press reports on a fire at Düsseldorf Airport in the afternoon of 11 April 1996. The following lists its publications, dates and places:

Daily Telegraph (London)	13.04.1996
Guardian (London and Manchester)	13.04.1996
The Independent (London)	13.04.1996
The Times (London)	13.04.1996
Der Tagesspiegel (Berlin)	13.04.1996 (*detail of the photograph*)
Die Welt (Berlin)	15.04.1996
Welt am Sonntag (Berlin)	14.04.1996
Bild Düsseldorf (Düsseldorf)	13.04.1996 (*detail, horizontal format*)
Der Kölner Stadtanzeiger (Cologne)	13./14.04.1996
Die Rheinische Post (Düsseldorf)	13.04.1996
Die Rheinische Post (Düsseldorf)	06.06.1996
Westfälische Allgemeine Zeitung (Essen)	13.04.1996

The photograph caught my attention. A visual document about a disaster, a blaze in a crowded public space, this photograph comes as surprise. Indeed, it might rather give the impression of belonging to the genre of 'interesting images' (offering some kind of visual, often graphic delight, sometimes grotesque, funny or confusing) printed by some papers, typically with no more than a brief caption underneath: the category of *image-without-text*.

Soldier died in airport fire
(*Daily Telegraph*)

Airport staff may face charges over fire
(*Guardian*)

Sixteen die in blaze at German airport
(*The Times*)

For quite some time I had the photograph on my desk, uncertain what to do with it, unable to determine what nonetheless, caught my attention. The photograph shows part of the arrival/departure hall of the airport. What it shows seems to be a look into the depth of the building with the exit somewhere behind the camera's view point. A Lufthansa sign over one counter. Nobody is around. The electrical lighting is on, so are some display screens, and daylight comes in from windows above a mezzanine floor. There is nothing which unequivocally designates '*this*' as the sight of a site where destruction and panic have taken place only a short while before this photograph has been taken. Even a metal ashtray and a notice-board near a column seem to be in their proper place. The camera focuses on the ground, two-thirds of the image in fact show the floor. A strange staring at the ground. Perhaps it is the obvious thing to do at this scene that is so unlike a scene, no dramatic movements and gestures, nothing in fact, nothing but the unsettling presence of an incommensurable absence and emptiness. Why all this light if nobody is around? The reason (for staring) at the ground: white footprints on a dark carpet? – was my first thought. Perhaps the fire brigade used foam to fight the blaze? But in this case there would be stronger and weaker prints, since the imprints would become weaker with every step. Yet what is so surprising, is the sight of perfect footprints; without fading or disturbances, each single print is perfectly recognisable. The captions account for it:

> Footprints of fire fighters and fleeing passengers left on the soot-stained floor of the airport terminal at Düsseldorf where 16 died after smoke and poisonous fumes filled the packed hall.
>
> (*Guardian*)

> The footprints of fleeing passengers left in the soot at the main terminal of Düsseldorf airport.
>
> (*The Times*)

> Footprints of fleeing passengers and of rescue service workers mark the soot-stained terminal floor.
>
> (*Daily Telegraph*)

> Footprints from fleeing passengers, staff and fire fighters on the soot-covered terminal floor at Düsseldorf after the fire that killed 16.
>
> (*Independent*)

Moving back and forth between image and text, I begin to decipher: a floor of white polished tiles is covered with black dust, soot, ash, sedimentation of the fire, of the poisonous smoke that had filled the hall. It evenly covers the floor. At the lower edge of the photograph, the grid of the tiled floor can just about be traced underneath the soot. The ash has stuck on the soles of shoes. 'Footprints in the soot', the captions rush in to name. Negative prints in a surface of dust. Yet a 'surface' which is not surface but its apparent disappearance, the *effacement of surface*, its very dissimulation. I am reminded for a moment of Man Ray's photograph *Elevage de poussière* (Dust Breeding) from 1920, layers of dust on Duchamp's *Large Glass*. Dust, almost veil-like, simulating what it covers without finally covering or simulating it. An insufficient presence on/in itself – dust even more than veil – brings about an improbable unity with whatever it merely and only momentarily adjoins.

Barthes talks about the photograph in terms of the *this*, the photograph as locked in the mute experience of a mute showing. He recognises that the photograph denies transcendence. 'In the Photograph, the event is never transcended for the sake of something else.'[2] But when and

where is *there* an event? Where is its site? Denial of transcendence does in no way warrant immanence, neither of 'the event' nor of 'the photograph'. What strikes me, looking at this photograph, is perhaps the expansive play, the disastrous, the mute eloquence of a double disavowal. The photograph disavows transcendence *and* immanence, as Blanchot might say.[3] The photograph does not involve a transcendence of what it shows *and* it is at once nothing but photograph *of*, image *of* something. There is, with the photograph: event as non-event *and* the utter strangeness of the image. *This* is the site of confrontation that 'is' the photograph: it confronts us as the very mechanics *and* the excessive reality of a sight of disavowal which it apparently merely cites.

> At least 16 people were killed and 150 injured when a fire broke out in a flower shop at the Düsseldorf international airport yesterday, causing planes to be diverted to Cologne. Police said many of the deaths were caused by inhaling poisonous fumes from burning plastic.
>
> (*The Times*, 12.04.1996)

Looking at photographs may resemble reading, yet there is no code to be deciphered. What 'there is' is not given to language, nor to speech, nor to immediate apprehension. A sight where seeing is opened to a white interval between transcendence *and* immanence, a frightful gap, but a gap always and already *transfigured* into a space, a happy delay, the very pleasure of resemblance, sight-seeing. What on the right side promises *and* misses, figuration, destination, breathing space, on the reverse side, exposes and exposes us to the burning of an early, an immemorial disaster. Fire without light, still *and* again ablaze in language, in images, in dates, in names.[4]

> (the photograph) . . . recalling the event more or less clearly, like the undisturbed ashes of an object consumed by flames . . . [5]

There is death involved, when looking at a photograph: death, time – ever lacking, ever missing 'itself', returning in rhythms and rituals of desire – and a seeing that does not see, and a forgetting beyond 'its' sound limits. There is figured in the photograph the space of a breakdown of representation, an avoided site, in sight of the unavoidable – possibly only received when one encounters, like Barthes, 'the only photograph' – a sight furiously oscillating between the end of representation and representation without end.

The disaster ruins everything while leaving everything intact[6]

One of my first considerations regarding this photograph was, that if the preferred 'image' of the photograph is that of an 'imprint off the real' – referring to the things in the world '*in a manner parallel to that of fingerprints or footprints*'[7] – then what about photographs of imprints? A structure of doubling (i.e. more than a simple duplication) is set into play.

The love of the step for its imprint[8]

There is *nothing* that unites the step and 'its' imprint, *nothing* that may join one lover to the other – or almost. If there is nothing, there were to be pure love. Love still, in the absence of love. *Nothing* will have been joined, ever. An impossible coincidence, an encounter, that is, none the less unaccountable. Forgetting has become the site of a relationship. A relation which is more *and* less than relation, separation, infidelity (Blanchot's 'relation without relation'). A marked disappearance erasing 'itself'. The reflection of a fire burning the mirror, the system of mirrors. 'I', sleep-walking and dreaming footprints in the light of the day.

If you desired it, for you I would be nothing, or merely a footprint[9]

Traditionally, the undecidability regarding the question of truth and *mimesis* has been put to rest at the site of a coinage, in sight of an imprint. Traditionally, that is since Plato, the imprint has been cited and confined to education, *paidea*, *Bildung*. The imprint is not an ontological problem, since it has been kept away from the ontological question. While reflection has come to stand for the possibility of a decision on mimesis in terms of deceit, the imprint has been reserved as a site (a turnstile rather than a site) of the (dis)appearance of indecision, the freezing of an interminable undecidability in the very image of the imprint. The imprint cites the attachment of a thing and 'its' double, cause and effect, in a flawless continuity of time, *step by step*. The thing and 'its' imprint are detached, there is nothing which can test their coincidence in time and space, nothing to testify to their origin. There is however the ideology of their temporal and spatial coincidence in a present now passed. This demand for continuity is often confused with *the real* and appears in its name. Citing that extensive chain linking every thing to *another* thing – whilst foreclosing otherness all at once – according to a law of causality whose working can be traced in the newspaper reports:[10]

> A group of welders were working above a flower shop in terminal A when they inadvertently melted a bitumen sealant. The sealant dripped on to a false floor containing electrical wiring. The PVC-covered cables began to smoulder, giving off cyanide, chloride, carbon monoxide and possibly dioxin. The fumes were funnelled down ventilation shafts to both the arrival and the departure areas and the railway station underneath the terminal.
>
> (*The Guardian*, 13.04.96)

What are we supposed to understand when under the ruling order of cause and effect something 'happens' *inadvertently*? *Ad-vertere* designates a turning towards, a destination, an attending to, attention. If something occurs *in-ad-vertently*, it happens without having been attended to, it occurs as if *elsewhere, in another time*. Yet the gap which opens here – as if inadvertently – remains (within) causality *as* its very exception. It is included *as* the system's margin, as accident. *Inadvertently* is understood in terms of unintendedly, i.e. the welders intended to weld metal, but the heat of the welding *also* melted *something else* – inadvertently, unintentionally. It is *another thing* – rather than *another time*, a lapse in continuity's time/space – which got in the way, which was not in order, not in its place, its proper site. The 'human factor' [*menschliches Versagen*] is cited, as in a commentary in *Die Welt*, which is presumed to interfere in terms of intention or lack of intention but without threatening the law of causality as such. Instead, it seems to become necessary to attend to, to (con)serve the stability of a separation of subject and object – traditionally established in/as the order of sight, the order of order – and to affirm the distance and direction from a subject to an object as if from cause to effect. Time threatens to run backwards.

> **16.02** Frank Kühlborn draws a ticket at the entrance of the car park. Although the terminal is already ablaze, the gate opens, as if nothing had happened . . . they are looking for the lift to the arrival hall. **16.07** Frank and Christian Kühlborn are waiting in front of the lift, while downstairs the first vehicle of the Düsseldorf fire brigade arrives . . . Maria-Anna Albanese and Antonio Raschella join them. Also the policeman Christian Heidrich. **16.10** The orange coloured doors of the lift open. Five unsuspecting people enter the lift. One presses the button next to the sign 'arrival hall'.
>
> (*Der Stern*, 17/96)[11]

Die Welt laments today's inflation of the term 'catastrophe' which, the commentator says, serves only to withdraw what has happened from reason and from human responsibility, while in this case, cause and effect, defects and faults were perfectly intelligible. He continues – in an ironic manner (whilst the direction of this irony remains unclear) – to define '*menschliches Versagen*' as usually asserting nothing but that some perfectly functioning machines were being used in a non-professional, in a *non-proper* way. Concluding with two remarks which run like this:

> Even if it might at first have appeared thus, the event [yes, he says '*Ereignis*'] was not unforeseen [the German idiom is, 'to come as if from a merry sky'] . . . *it did not come out of the blue. It only came unexpectedly.* But it is the unexpected, above all an unexpected death, which is disquieting, and which suddenly deprives human beings of the self-certitude of having everything under control.'[12]

The commentator in *Die Welt* is fighting two different worlds, but since he does not desert his belief in a unitary one, it is his argument that falters.

> **Das Ereignis kam – auch wenn es zuerst so scheinen mochte – nicht aus heiterm Himmel. Es kam nur unerwartet.**

> In the Hegelian system (that is in all systems), death is constantly in operation, and nothing can die.[13]

The law of causality and of the unitary system is in fact not followed in all its consequences. It is silently abandoned at the very point where rationality threatens to turn irrational; where we could not but conclude, that in Düsseldorf Airport, built in 1975, certain cables and sealants, the design of the floors and suspended ceilings, cable shafts and air conditioning system were all chosen in order to gas people in the arrival and departure halls. This, for obvious reasons, appears an unacceptable claim, and the argument aborts well before reaching there, it interrupts itself, turns and begins to rotate in what almost sounds like a counting-out rhyme and may yet be the only attestation we can rightly give in a situation where testimony precipitates.

A *situation*[14] – given to the presupposition of homogeneity – should allow for some degree of siting, of locating in time/space, a reasoning which precisely seems to run into difficulties here: '*It did not come unexpectedly. It only came unexpectedly.*' The commentary began with a criticism of the resignation from reason as bound to sensationalism and what Barthes might call an ideology of naturalisation. Here, the lapse is structural and the text itself is its site. It is the appearance of a sudden loss, an evaporation, an unappropriable heterogeneity of time and place. *It did not come unexpectedly. It only came unexpectedly.* A turning and over-turning, the very threat of the *catastrophic.* The appearance of a void which can pass almost unnoticed. A site of disappearance re-turning in, and turning on text. A text may falter, but it is also never far from a possible return to chronology and continuity. The photograph may leave a space, be it only a pause, in which an insufficiency of chronology and topology can transpire.

> The encounter designates a new relation. At the point of juncture – a unique point – what comes into relation remains without relation, and the unity that thus comes to the fore is but the surprising manifestation (a manifestation by surprise) of the un-unifiable, the simultaneity of what cannot be together; from which we have to conclude, even should this

ruin logic, that where the junction takes place it is disjunction that rules over unitary structure and causes it to shatter.[15]

The repetition in reverse '*not unexpected/unexpected*' does not annul itself, nor does it submit to a proper exchange of oppositions, where finally accounts are settled profitably. It marks and it substitutes for a shift in time/space that remains unappropriated, unappropriable – at least under the given rule of continuity and causality. It can only be forgotten, pass as if unnoticed in a flow of language experienced as continuous. The phrase almost turns back to logic, when we allow for a radical disjunction between these two sentences of an apparently inverse identity, separated by nothing – so it may seem – but a full stop. What appears *here* like a strain on logic, is *there* the hiatus that holds apart *and* holds 'together' two irreconcilable worlds, two times, 'non-coincidence intervening at the very point of coincidence'.[16] *It did not come unexpectedly. It only came unexpectedly.* Death escapes into another name. It is how death has entered the scene, before and without a beginning or a scene: a distortion of time and place, an insufficiency of 'the event', as (its) name, signifying rather than 'occurring', signifying always too much. Already an effacement of the other, the absent other, and the (non)event a play of death and 'its' supplements.

> What introduces the thought of chance is this hiatus wherein is lodged, through recurrence, and for the sake of filling it in, the mortal possibility called the stroke of fate. So in this case, in order to kill there must be: (a) a determining cause; (b) the absence of a determinate cause – and it is the absence of cause that always causes death, this lack that signifies a rupture of continuity.[17]

Obviously, one should refrain from reintroducing the *rupture of continuity* back into the world, since it is already and always the demand for continuity which attempts – for the sake of *filling in* the gap – to reintroduce, to reunite what cannot be united. We cannot but discontinue this demand for continuity. In a unitary world whose language we speak and write, what on the one hand, makes us stare in horror into an abyss of time and logic, on the other hand, adapts and melds back silently into the system, naturalised as super-catastrophe which – everything out of control/ everything the same – finally and always again reaffirms causality by means of inclusive exclusion.

> The encounter pierces the world, pierces the self; and in this opening, everything that happens, not happening (coming about with the status of what has not arrived) is *the reverse side* that cannot be lived of what *on the right side* cannot be written: a double impossibility that by a supplementary act – a fraud, a kind of falsehood, also a madness – must be transformed in order to adapt it to living and writing 'reality'.[18]

It is not as a problem of representation, coming in from elsewhere and as if after the event, as an inevitable and necessary translation, that the event escapes from itself, from us, from a supposedly natural condition of immediacy. In Blanchot, experience is always already withdrawn as *what happens not happening* and what cannot arrive, cannot be lived. Experience is always and already this interval: '*the reverse side that cannot be lived of what on the right side cannot be written*'. And this is precisely the wound, the trauma that *is* experience.

The photograph can become (it is invented to become) the place where the wounding incompleteness of experience doubles, where it is (re)experienced (and here, an inversion occurs) as if the photograph were its origin and its proper site, as if it were the photograph 'itself' that were marked by a 'difficulty in existing'. This is what appears at the very centre of *Camera Lucida*, when Barthes writes, 'is it not the very weakness of Photography, this *difficulty in existing* which we call banality?', and when he finally states (and this takes place in parentheses): 'I cannot reproduce the Winter Garden Photograph. It exists only for me . . . at most it would interest your *studium*: period, clothes, photogeny; but in it, for you, no wound.'[19] As if the desire for the imprint, for the double, the spiralling fascination of reproduction and technology were a substitute mourning, and the infinite desire for such a substitute, relieving ourselves as if in advance from the burden of all too great a mourning. A mourning which were to be infinite, without end and without measure, continuously raking the fire in which an insurmountable loss burns itself under my skin (*der Verlust 'geht mir unter die Haut'*, it goes under my skin, is the German idiom). Yet a mourning which has established itself in its double, sited in a substitute, a certain and finite thing, has at least, as far as it has achieved enclosing itself in this kind of horizon, reached some finitude, some reference, some measure, and, one might even say, 'objectivity'.

What we have been naming above as 'two worlds, two sides, two times', in fact all too easily denotes two separate, facing entities, whilst it is rather more *and* less than two, 'the right side and the reverse side'. The hiatus that holds apart, at once, holds together what cannot be together: an impossible coincidence. What Blanchot calls 'derangement' and what we have been trying to trace through his writing is not a disorder showing itself in some *form* or perceivable representation. 'Derangement is at work, but it produces no work. It is not outside what can be attested, but its attestation is always an attestation of default'.[20] 'Derangement' appears – appearance of a disappearing – as a movement continuously supplementing 'itself' in an always again original recurrence.

A narcissistic investment, 'my' obsession with the origin, has left its trace, its imprint, in the common identification of shoes, feet and what is supposed to be their trail. '*Footprints*', '*Fußabdrücke*' – we are so certain what we speak. What we see in the photograph of 'footprints' – if one can indeed ever be certain about (seeing) imprints – are imprints of shoes, prints of variously patterned soles.[21] 'Narcissism': a footprint of Western metaphysics. Photography has been invented as a late descendant of this old love (the 'oldest' love, according to some sources). It has been invented as the infant (i.e. the one who does not – not yet? – speak) of a family organised under the authority of light's relation to knowledge, speech's relation to sight, where continuity is nature, and thus is the family and the family-story itself. 'We say "to develop a photograph"; but what the chemical action develops is undevelopable, an essence (of a wound), what cannot be transformed but only repeated under the instances of insistence (of the insistent gaze).'[22] Photography practises a metaphysics in/as a fiction of development, *in sight* of the development of the very touch 'off the real'. Yet it also stands in as the essential supplement of what cannot (only) be 'developed', sight as trauma.

In a photograph of footprints, the very structure of photography, its *libidinal* structure, becomes doubled as/in the image 'it is'. It *becomes* the disturbing site of an impossible photographic self-reference. Just as the photographer at the site of the fire might have been staring at the footprints as the improbable sight of the passing of a disaster, so is the viewer of the photograph

left to stare – in amazement and horror – at the *sight of the invisible*: the very invisibility of derangement, the invisible structure of photography. An interminable oscillation of sites whose very 'structure' cites dislocation. The *sight of the invisible* resides in/as a system of excessive doubling which unworks the double yet without ever arriving beyond. The disaster consumes site.

> What haunts us is something inaccessible from which we cannot extricate ourselves. It is that which cannot be found and therefore cannot be avoided. What no one can grasp is the inescapable. The fixed image knows no repose, and this is above all because it poses nothing, establishes nothing. Its fixity, like that of the corpse, is the position of what stays with us because it has no place.[23]

The photograph does not reveal anything. It is the experimental proof of the emptiness of revelation. Revelation reveals only 'itself'. *This*, Barthes talks about, is the unanswerable *what* – seeing what, desiring what – turned to affirmative exclamation, affirming always in advance, yet, unable to fill the gap, sinking into muteness. The certainty of the exclamation reveals only its own certainty, an echo of a call – 'my' call – of desire, the precarious, the glittering presence of a wish. The photograph does not give any answer to the great questions of Being, it responds with/in a great silence. It is an exclamation of surprise and recognition which subsides in the silence of waiting and anticipation. That is to say, not an exclamation at all but a *subsiding. This*, a little, surprised sound by which the verticality of memory and (its) desire gently subsides and dissolves into horizontality, citing a flatness without surface which never arrives, never yet passed. *This* –

> recalling the event more or less clearly, like the
> undisturbed ashes of an object consumed by flames

It has perhaps never been put more strikingly: the 'object' – if there ever was one, and who could say for certain when talking of ashes and cinders – is *consumed in the event*, the *event* of/as photography, as in a flash of light, consumed by flames. The event is incineration and incinerating, it can only be *re-called* – more or less clearly. But *called* again and again none the less. The event is also object-like, in so far as this object will already have been consumed: *what/this* will have been. *This* is the 'evidential' importance of the event, of the 'now'. Photography mimes once more the inescapable consummation, the immediate incineration of a 'now'; and in this play, this tragedy, we are offered (we have come to offer ourselves) a *final* memory. 'Life/Death: the paradigm is reduced into a simple click'.[24] An ultimate forgetting that we cannot but repeat. The unrepresentable has already slipped away.

As if in passing, elegantly careless and blasphemous, such a statement (on ashes, like cinders) sets ablaze immediately all footprints, sedimentation of dust and shrouds of Turin which have been gathered around the site of photography.[25] *This* is as far as the 'evidential' goes. An appearance of *what* has been lost, an appearance of the other as lost – already withdrawn in another loss.

This – as far as it is always and already filled by meaning, a thing, a name, by a particular relation, holds photography in analogy to language. Yet, as far as *this* may remain empty – that perspective and impossible emptiness it initially stands for, the gap, 'the shifter' – it diverts the photograph elsewhere. *This* is the space of a frightening mobility, the very in-between, the passing between madness and certainty, desire and death, experience and *Darstellung*, opening photography always in advance to desiring hope *and* abyss. 'It is this kind of question that Photography raises for me: questions which derive from a "stupid", a simple metaphysics . . . probably the true metaphysics'.[26] *This* retains, as if in a watchword, the inescapable question of Being – always risking the slippage toward mute affirmation. '*Il y a la cendre.*' Yet it also retains in a strange but typical forgetting only the one side of the *fort – da*.

The 'essence of photography' Barthes is searching for comes to him, and not only to him, inadvertently, on the way from 'only photography' to 'the only photograph'. It is a site that can indeed never be *discovered*, never, but in a boundless forgetting, the abandonment of waiting, an infinite passion for the other. It is a last way, a terminal space, where seeing looks at its limits: sight a photograph, and photography a *staring at the unknown*.[27] And in staring, still *the desire, the pure impure desire*, for the one, the singular one, the last look back. The excessive 'end' of Barthes' (re)search: he desires the sight of his mother, one last return of his gaze.[28] The desire to encounter the other – only once more – in her inaccessible otherness, myself nothing but a footstep, an echo of what has disappeared still listening for her step.

Niemand zeugt für den Zeugen.[29]

Where the weight of the visual, an obsession with Being as question, suddenly lifts (without falling into the trap of an anti-mimetic argument), where the analogy of seeing and language subsides, when repetition, possibility of meaning, turns and multiplies without end, 'there', the photograph may come to cite a third site, a third sight. A siteless site, uninhabitable, outside reciprocity. The blank infinity in between mirrors. My sight the eye of the other, the non-present other. Left with nothing but an immemorial token of loss. An inverse memorial, outside and before any beginning. Yet the I as if suddenly relieved, absolved, from meaning, memory, time, the lukewarm fascination of dates and names ... *This* never remains for long. It subsides like *this*. Soon it slips, is sited and named, and were it by the most unpronounceable name: death. The image stays with us as the improbable site of the placeless which we prefer to exorcise, so that it may return to us as if from elsewhere: the image prefiguring death. And 'we', left to stare with the eyes of the dead at the abyss of meaning; but staring anyway, without end.

> Tomorrow will be the end of the camping site air trafficking. Airport chief Hans-Joachim Peters is happy that he no longer needs to channel passengers through the tents. From today, it will become more comfortable again. Only 204 days after the fire, in which 17 people died, three new lightweight interim halls are completed, and terminal C is also detoxicated. Costs of the improvements: 176 million marks. But this is only the beginning. Before the construction of the new 'airport 2000 plus' is finally completed, at least another two billion marks are due.
>
> (*Neue Rhein Zeitung*, 31.10.1996, Düsseldorf)[30]
> claudia wegener

notes

1. Stevens, W., 'The woman that had more babies than that', *Opus Posthumous*, ed. French, S., NY, Morse, 1957, p. 81.

2. Barthes, R., *Camera Lucida*, trans. Howard, R., London, Vintage, 1993, p. 4.

3. Cf. Blanchot, M., 'Tomorrow at stake', in *The Infinite Conversation*, trans. Hanson, S., Minnesota, University of Minnesota Press, 1993, p. 409.

4. Cf. Derrida's writing as in *Feu la cendre* or *Schibboleth: Pour Paul Celan*.

5. Each time Man Ray's phrase is cited, a conclusion stresses its universality, such as 'the photogram only forces or makes explicit, what is the case of all photographs'. Yet the consequences of the citation and of this assertion remain to be drawn. Cf. Krauss, R., *L'Amour fou*, exhibition catalogue, London, Hayward Gallery, 1986, p. 24.

6. Blanchot, M., *The Writing of the Disaster*, trans. Smock, A., Nebraska, University of Nebraska Press, 1986, p. 1.

7. Krauss, R., as in *L'Amour fou*, op. cit. and 'Photographic conditions of Surrealism', in *The Originality of the Avant-Garde*, MIT Press, 1991.

8. Derrida, J., *Feu la cendre*, trans. *Cinders* by Ludacher, N., Nebraska, University of Nebraska Press, 1991, p. 43.

9. Breton, A., *Nadja*, trans. Howard, R., NY, Grove Press, 1960, p. 116.

10. This paragraph is a summary of a chapter from my dissertation which involves a reading of P. Lacoue-Labarthe's *Typography* – to which this article owes much – regarding photography and its theorisation as a matter of Western metaphysics.

11. My translation, c.w.

12. *Die Welt* 13./14.04.1996. (P. Dittmar, 'Sudden Cognition'). This commentary is accompanied by an image with the caption 'Minister Clemet looks at the extension joint. The fire had been caused by welding work on it'.

13. Blanchot, M., *The Writing of the Disaster*, op. cit., p. 45.

14. The Latin *situs* relates to the certainties of a built environment, also the final attempt to construct a unitary locality: the tomb.

15. Blanchot, M., 'Tomorrow at stake', in *The Infinite Conversation*, op. cit., p. 415. It comes as no surprise that reference should be made to a text on surrealism, since what is denoted here as, following Barthes, the 'essence of photography' finds an extension in what surrealism introduced to photography, or what photography 'knows' about surrealism – always and already. The secret of the encounter with the thing, or better the passion for the alterity of the Other, an other which is not in advance defined as subject or object, rather always awaited and desired as the very possibility of an excess of that split.

16. Ibid.

17. Ibid.

18. Ibid. (italics added, c.w.).

19. Barthes, op. cit., pp. 20, 73.

20. Blanchot, op. cit., p. 417.

21. And via this *footnote (sic)* I refer to Heidegger, Meyer-Schapiro and Derrida who share the most extensive knowledge about shoes, feet and their (im)proper identification, cf. Derrida's fourth chapter 'Restitutions' in *The Truth in Painting*.

22. Barthes, op. cit., p. 49.

23. Blanchot, M., 'The two versions of the imaginary', in *The Space of Literature* [1955], trans. Smock, A., Nebraska, University of Nebraska Press, 1982. Revising my article in December 1996, I was grateful to find again and re-read Lewis Johnson's 'In the light of questions of place', which also cites Blanchot. In: *Affective Light*, exhibition catalogue, rear window, London, 1993.

24. Barthes, op. cit., p. 92.

25. Man Ray is not alone in citing cinders; amongst others we may recall Nietzsche, T. E. Hulme, R. Smithson and Derrida.

26. Barthes, op. cit., pp. 84, 85.

27. Staring: 'the eye of the dead . . . when it is still open, a pious hand should soon come to close it', Derrida, J., *Memoirs for the Blind: The Self-Portrait and Other Ruins*, trans. Brault, P.-A., and Naas, M., Chicago, University of Chicago Press, 1993, p. 57.

28. Cf. Barthes, op. cit., pp. 71, 72.

29. '*No one bears witness for the witness*', the last line of 'Aschenglorie', Celan, op. cit. II, p. 72.

30. My translation, c.w.

acknowledgements

I would like to thank Edgar Schöpal for kindly providing a copy of his photograph, and Paul Davies, Lewis Johnson, Mark Ryder and John Wood for inspiring discussions and many helpful remarks.

The other photographs in the text were taken in terminal C of Düsseldorf airport on the 2 November 1996, a day after the official reopening, and on 13 November.

chapter 15

+ and ÷

margot leigh butler

+ is a hinge – it connects.

Write Mum + Dad on a piece of paper, crease it down the centre of the +, press the sides together and the words on either side of the page will touch, and your own hands will clap together (applauding your existence). Though the hinge itself balances evenly, what it connects rarely does.

If – there isn't, but if – there was a study of hinges, it could be called hinge-ology, and someone fascinated by hinges, a hinge-ologist. People could be considered hinges between their experiences, imaginings, representations . . .

Pick up a book, open the cover, turn the pages with your hands. *Open the door.*

Mark the intervals of the book with your fingers – shuffle your fingers right into the pages; shuffle different books together.

Lay a book on your lap, turn the pages of your thighs. (Cross and uncross your legs.)

Hold a page up to the light and read through to the other side.

Push open a door, put your foot in it, pull on the handle.

Lie inside a doorway – upper half in the hallway and lower half in the bedroom. Roll, but stay in one place.

Now, stand and put your hands on either side of a book, or a door, or your head, and press.

How is knowledge embodied? (*Press here.*) How could it be other than embodied, considering there is always someone, somewhere, somewhen, who knows? Yet, in Western cultures we've become used to *dis*embodied knowledge – the 'god-trick' of seeing everything from nowhere[1]. This way of thinking about knowledge has its charms (omniscience), yet I suspect that embodying knowledge can expose this confidence trick. Situating knowledge acts as a touchstone, a reminder, that knowledge is, and always has been, embodied, located, partial and perspectival[2]. Who is reading these words, when, where, why? Which fleshy lap is this book resting upon? And when you stand up, where will you take these thoughts? Situating and embodying knowledge is a way of acknowledging, and taking responsibility for, our standpoints and our lookout points (nowhere, now here); it can also supply some breathing space, some critical engagement with our own and each other's assumptions[3].

So, for instance, in Western cultures we have taught ourselves to think in pairs (two by two) which seem to need each other, they are propped up against one another, yet one side always has the upper hand: mind/body, culture/nature, white/black, man/woman, heterosexual/ homosexual, self/other, reason/emotion, whole/partial, right/wrong, science/art, etcetera ad nauseam. These dualisms are a real problem because they come to structure not only our actions and desires, but also the very ways in which we think. Wedged, pinched, inside dualisms (foot caught in the door, self-sabotage), one option is to become a hinge, to connect them and perhaps even de-dualise them for a moment (AH HA). What might this look like? In the following passage, writer Angela Carter hinges the characters Mary and Martha – biblical sisters who represent contemplative piety and active house-drudgery – through the gestures of a turn-of-the-century Russian baboushka tending her fire:

> . . . and her hands, those worn, veiny hands . . . had involuntarily burnished the handles of the bellows over decades of use, those immemorial hands of hers slowly parted and came together again just as slowly, in a hypnotically reiterated gesture that was as if she were about to join her hands in prayer. About to join her hands in prayer. But always, at the very last moment, as if it came to her there was something about the house that must be done first, she would start to part her hands again. Then Martha would turn back into Mary and protest to the Martha within her: what can be more important than praying? Nevertheless, when her hands were once more almost joined, that inner Martha recalled the Mary to the indeed perhaps more important thing, whatever it was . . . And so on.[4]

The Martha+Mary figure shows the baboushka 'stuck moving' inside two rigid gender roles, dancing a perpetual do-se-do. Yet at the same time, this + figuration represents two flapping sides which are hinged at the nose of the bellows and along the spine – between the shoulderblades – of the baboushka. Hinged between experience, representation, imagination . . . What if the Martha pulled the bellows open too wide (inspired them past bursting), slamming the backs of her knuckles on the far side of that circle and meeting the Mary past the point of no return?

Such figurations are currently welcome in some areas of philosophy, especially feminist epistemology, as ways of clarifying present ways of thinking and imagining different personal, collective, political possibilities. By not staying within fixed categories, but instead mobilizing the breach between the Mary+Martha gender roles (opening past the dualism), this figuration extends my sense of what it's possible to do, who it's possible to be. The feminist figurations[5] of the cyborg,[6] the nomadic subject,[7] the mother machine,[8] monsters and goddesses[9] and the modest witness[10] all inhabit in between, interstitial, spaces where dualisms are crossed over (perhaps even crossed out) and new conceptualisations can arise. I find figurations tantalising because they supply spaces in which to 'think ourselves differently', to cast new embodied, situated relations with knowledge and power from which to imagine and engage politically.

These ideas correspond with some art practices where the visual field is spatialised and time-based, and rely upon people's physical, embodied interaction to make up the meanings of the work – a kind of situated visual knowledge, or visual epistemology. While this could be said of many different practices, it's especially the case for installation art, which is self-conscious about the ways in which layers of materials, contexts, sites and meanings are mobilised by people moving through the work physically and conceptually.[11] Objects and meanings line up differently from different perspectives (like driving past an evenly planted orchard); knowledge is spatialised, and the partiality of shifting, embodied perspectives can open up the pleasure of rustling meanings. Anywhere can be an installation site – a book (in your hands, between your fingers, on your lap, in the world) is aerated by page-turning (you accordianist you).

> Open the book so wide that the front and back covers touch, and the backs of your hands clap together. *Clap your knuckles behind your spine.* Let the pages fall apart, shake them gently. Can you unhinge the book of your experiences, representations, imaginings . . . ?

AH

HA

Someone sleeps between – within? – a doorway: upper body in the corridor and lower body in the bedroom. Can't quite relax – would keep one eye open while sleeping round the campfire. Lying face down. Ear to the ground. Eye peeled. Arms tucked under. Now, spooning means rolling, bending at the hips. Nose might touch knees or anything be-tween. Open air chills the spine. Lying back. All is visible, exposed.

Lying. All is visible, exposed. Eardrums slam from both sides, swing-doors blocked in, wedged. (Wedged into machinery, heavy wooden shoes, sabots, sabotage the works.) Lying in the doorway, upper body in the hallway, lower body in the bedroom, remembering + anticipating, she swings. Then swings, and twilight opens everything between (the nose + hand + hip + thigh + eye).

acknowledgements

'+' is an outcropping supported by the inspiration and expertise of Tiziana Terranova, Janice Kerbel, Lisa Haskel, Olu Taiwo, David Butler, Lorna Brown, Matthew Brittain, Andrew Contagious and John Wood, to whom I'm very grateful.

notes

1. The term 'god-trick' was coined by Donna J. Haraway in her landmark article 'Situated Knowledges: The Science Question in Feminism and the Privilege of Partial Perspective', in her *Simians, Cyborgs and Women: The Reinvention of Nature*, London, Free Association Books, 1991, p. 189.

2. In the article cited above, Haraway specifies a politics and epistemology of 'situated knowledges' which conceptualizes knowledges and knowers as embodied, located, noninnocent and responsible, critically and mobilely positioned, partial and perspectival. Vision, whether constricted or dilated, takes up a central role in discussions about 'situated knowledges'. The seventeenth-century French philosopher René 'I think therefore I am' Descartes describes the process of dualising his mind and body, starting with his eyes:

   > I shall now close my eyes, stop up my ears, turn away all my senses, even efface from my thought all images of corporeal things, or at least, because this can hardly be done, I shall consider them as being vain and false; and thus communing only with myself, and examining my inner self, I shall try to make myself, little by little, better known and more familiar to myself.
   >
   > (*Third Meditation*, p. 113)

   This 'self', by so profoundly disembodying himself, is setting himself up to launch into the 'god trick', seeing everything from nowhere, or what Martin Jay (1993, p. 19), in his *Downcast Eyes: The Denigration of Vision in Twentieth Century French Thought*, refers to as 'le regard surplombant' – the look from above. Another French theorist, Jacques Lacan, has correlated Descartes' famous 'I think therefore I am' with the visual 'I see myself seeing myself' (*Four Fundamental Concepts of Psychoanalysis*, New York, Norton, 1973, p. 80). For further discussion, see Martin Jay and Teresa Brennan (eds) *Vision in Context: Historical and Contemporary Perspectives on Sight*, London and New York, Routledge, 1996.

3. Some knowledge theories, such as standpoints epistemologies, ask questions about the privilege of certain embodied knowledge positions. As soon as the question 'whose knowledge?' is raised, advantaged vantage points and knowledges become visible and contestable, and different, particular vantage points and knowledges can be opened up, acknowledged, valued and contested.

4. Carter, Angela, *Nights at the Circus*, London, Picador, Pan Books, 1984, p. 75.

5. The present use of the term 'figuration' has been defined by feminist philosopher Rosi Braidotti:

   > The term *figuration* refers to a style of thought that evokes or expresses ways out of the phallocentric vision of the subject. A figuration is a politically informed account of an alternative subjectivity. I feel a real urgency to elaborate alternative accounts, to learn to think different about the subject, to invent new frameworks, new images, new modes of thought. This entails a move beyond the dualistic conceptual constraints and the perversely monological mental habits of phallocentrism.
   >
   > (Braidotti 1994, pp. 1–2)

6. Donna Haraway's germinal 'cyborg' is a socialist-feminist image, an embodied figuration, for thinking about relations between humans, animals and machines, nature and culture (and more) non-

dualistically. Haraway, Donna J. 'The Cyborg Manifesto' in *Simians, Cyborgs and Women: The Reinvention of Nature*, London, Free Association Books, 1991.

7. Braidotti, Rosi, *Nomadic Subjects: Embodiment and Sexual Difference in Contemporary Feminist Thought*, New York, Columbia University Press, 1994. As well, philosophers Gilles Deleuze and Felix Guattari developed the figurations of the 'nomad', the 'rhizome' and the 'body without organs' in their *A Thousand Plateaus: Schizophrenia and Capitalism*, London, Athlone Press, 1988.

8. Corea, Gina, *The Mother Machine: Reproductive Technologies from Artificial Insemination to Artificial Wombs*, London, Women's Press, 1988.

9. Lykke, Nina and Braidotti, Rosi (eds) *Between Monsters, Goddesses and Cyborgs: Feminist Confrontations with Science, Medicine and Cyberspace*, London and New Jersey, Zed Books, 1996.

10. Haraway, Donna J., *Modest_Witness@Second_Millenium.FemaleMan_meets_OncoMouse*, London and New York, Routledge, 1997.

11. Some installations which are photographically based invite viewers to cross between real and representational space, so that elements (such as bodies, books and doors in '+') become confused and conflated.

bibliography

Allison, D., *Bastard out of Carolina*, London, Dutton/Plume Books, 1992.

Bal, M., *Double Exposures: The Subject of Cultural Analysis*, London and New York, Routledge, 1996.

Barthes, R., *Image/Music/Text*, trans. Stephen Heath, New York, Noonday Books, 1977.

Braidotti, R. *Nomadic Subjects: Embodiment and Sexual Difference in Contemporary Feminist Theory*, New York, Columbia University Press, 1994.

Brennan, T., and Jay, M., (eds), *Vision in Context: Historical and Contemporary Perspectives on Sight*, London and New York, Routledge, 1996.

Carter, A., *Nights at the Circus*, London, Picador, Pan Books, 1984.

Corea, G., *The Mother Machine: Reproductive Technologies from Artificial Insemination to Artificial Wombs*, London, Women's Press, 1988.

Deleuze, G., and Guattari, F., *A Thousand Plateaus: Schizophrenia and Capitalism*, London, Athlone Press, 1988.

Descartes, R., *Third Meditation*, Harmondsworth, Penguin, 1968.

Gcnova, J., *Wittgenstein: A Way of Seeing*, London and New York, Routledge, 1995.

Grosz, E., *Volatile Bodies: Toward a Corporeal Feminism*, Bloomington, Indiana University Press, 1994.

Gupta, S. (ed.), *Disrupted Borders: An Intervention in Definitions of Boundaries*, London, Rivers Oram Press, 1993.

Haraway, D. J., 'The Cyborg Manifesto' and 'Situated Knowledges: The Science Question in Feminism and the Privilege of Partial Perspective' in Haraway, D.J., *Simians, Cyborgs and Women: The Reinvention of Nature*, London, Free Association Books, 1991.

Haraway, D. J., *Modest_Witness@Second_Millenium.FemaleMan_meets_OncoMouse*', London and New York, Routledge, 1997.

Jay, M., *Downcast Eyes: The Denigration of Vision in Twentieth Century French Thought*, Berkeley, University of California Press, 1993.

Kiss & Tell, *Her Tongue on My Theory: Images, Essays and Fantasies*, Vancouver, Press Gang Publishers, 1994.

Kosuth, J., 'The (Ethical) Space of Cabinets 7&8' and 'Say: I do not know', in *Two Oxford Reading Rooms*, London, Book Works, 1994.

Lacan, J., *The Four Fundamental Concepts of Psychoanalysis*, New York, Norton, 1973.

Laing, C., 'Picture Theory', exhibition catalogue, YYZ Artists' Outlet, Toronto, 1995.

Lennon, K., and Whitford, M., *'Knowing the Difference': Feminist Perspectives in Epistemology*, London and New York, Routledge, 1994.

Lykke, N., and Braidotti, R., (eds), *Between Monsters, Goddesses and Cyborgs: Feminist Confrontations with Science, Medicine and Cyberspace*, London and New Jersey, Zed Books, 1996.

Mariani, P. (ed.) *Critical Fictions: The Politics of Imaginative Writing*, Dia Art Foundation #7, Seattle, Bay Press, 1991.

Melville, S., and Readings, B. (eds) *Vision and Textuality*, London, Macmillan, 1995.

Rolo, J., and Hunt, I. (eds) *Book Works: A Partial History and Sourcebook*, London, Book Works, 1996.

Wittgenstein, L., *Tractatus Logico-Philosophicus*, trans. D. F. Pears and B. F. McGuinness, London, Routledge & Kegan Paul, 1961 [1921].

chapter 16

PDF™

the digital hostess

rachel baker

the cult of the cyberhostess: propaganda or ethical bandwagon?

What kind of ethical position lies behind a service that offers intimacy in exchange for money, and that supplies personal information for commercial use?

*   Is such a system exploitative?
*   Is it a good service?

When you hear that a digital 'personal assistant' will cater for a person's information requirements, you may think that it callously exploits a human desire for individual attention. Think again. Where recreational services of a personal nature are deemed unacceptable, an electronically mediated distraction may serve a good social purpose. For example, our research showed that Japanese businessmen – the market originally targeted for such a service – are used to a hierarchical and rigidly regulated environment where social deviation is punishable. So we made our service enticing and seductive. Yes, the service provided *is* one of seduction; i.e. seduction as product. Yet the more mediated the seduction is, the more the illusion itself becomes part of the service and the more imaginative our clients become.

Indeed, Cyberhostess justifies its service in ethical terms by encouraging what we call 'recreational imagination'. The goal is not to protect the user's privacy, nor to hide his inner needs or desires but, on the contrary, to make them public by logging them onto a sophisticated, commercially available database. Open, continuous, intimate dialogue helps us to construct an in-depth personality profile. This process will be vital in the twenty-first century if you want to avoid the bombardment of irrelevant commercial messages. One day, all products will be tailored to your individual predilections and desires.

It all sounds too good to true, but there may be a downside. As we all become more umbilically attached to our digital information networks, the easier it will be for corporations and intelligence dependent organisations to track, analyse, and probe our behaviour, sensibilities and thought patterns. Even today it is possible for clever marketeers to make money simply by accumulating electronic address information and selling it on to media companies eager to find customers via the Net. As consumers we can't control access to our postal mailboxes – but we can with the electronic mailbox. Each propaganda message must be useful or interesting otherwise it is just more junk mail that can be immediately wiped. The message must be of the highest quality.

Big Brother is no longer a spook of the State – it is a spectre of the Corporation. This is where Cyberhostess comes in. We will not pamper you with privacy, we will protect you with publicity! We will help you to overthrow out-dated modes of commodified production. By engaging in the mode of abstract seduction, the perceptive small-time propagandist will achieve wide and successful market penetration.

Personal Data Fairy™

be your own propagandist

Cyberhostess Marketing Proposal developed by

Personal Data Fairy

IRATIONAL.ORG

CYBERHOSTESS is.....

+ a personal Internet service

+ a database marketing service

Initially developed for the Japanese market, a female character is created to act as hostess, or Net friend, to the Japanese businessman, guiding him around the Net (Web and Newsgroups). Primarily the cyberhostess will engage the client in intimate, personal conversations via e-mail. The service is an ingenious hybrid of the **Japanese hostess bar** and **telephone chatline** genres. In promoting an enduring relationship between client and hostess, the system defines the character traits of the hostess, which gradually become unique and personal to each client. The payoff is a highly detailed database of client profiles which can be offered to suitable companies to help them expand their customer base and to bring more focus to their marketing. The project will utilise 'intelligent agent' software to sensitise the response of the cyberhostess.

perpetuate your own myth

be your own propagandist

Introducing **Cherie Matrix** - the first professional cyberhostess.

Cherie Matrix is your best Net friend. She is not like anyone you have ever met. You will see yourself through her, but she has her own unique view of life. She is real, she exists in the flesh. She is the perfect Net guide, she knows her way around. Talk with her.

Cherie's personal service is

- Reliable - consistently there when you need her
- Thoughtful - she remembers your birthday
- Entertaining - tells funny jokes
- Sympathetic - listens to problems and advises
- Intelligent - talks about subjects that you are interested in
- Unpredictable - takes you by surprise
- Useful - guides you around the Net
- Confidential - you can tell her anything
- Seductive - will play with you and reveal herself over time

At all times Cherie will talk intimately and personally to her friends via email.

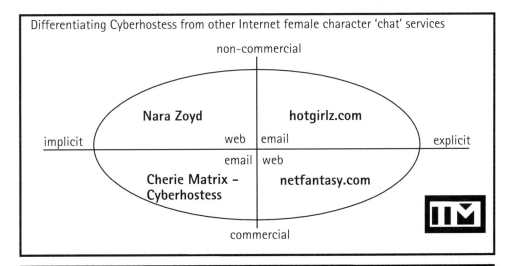

Differentiating Cyberhostess from other Internet female character 'chat' services

perpetuate your own myth

be your own propagandist

Identifying clients

+ Search through business-related newsgroups for Japanese email addresses

Clients should ideally be

- white collar income males
- familiar with Internet through business use only
- looking for orientation on the Net towards playful irresponsibility
  and safe rebellion
- attracted by the idea of sexy, intimate female guide.

The process of 'fishing' for clients will apply the telesales technique of cold-calling via email.

```
Date: Thu, 3 Oct 1996 16:45:42 +0100
To: ruichi@mol.minolta.co.jp
From: cherie@irational.org (cherie matrix)
Subject: Hi


I saw you on the internet.

I am a professional cyber hostess;
I wondered whether you might like to
become my special email friend.

We can talk about anything you like.
Why not write me back ?
```

```
Date: Thu, 5 Oct 1996 17:15:08
To: cherie@irational.org (cherie matrix)
From:ruichi@mol.minolta.co.jp
Subject: Re:Hi


Well That's all right. I have no female friends that talk
    about anything.
It is great.
I like reading, listening music, make song, write poems,
            puzzle, software, make friends etc.
So do me. My special email friend.

I write to you ASAP. Waiting your mail !!
```

perpetuate your own myth

Payment Strategy and Methods

- free trial period of chat with Cherie for 2 weeks
- consequently, $1.50 per message
- or 1 month's subscription fee of $15.00
- club membership scheme with special favours offered to
        members only
- payments made via secure credit card transaction using encryption software

Personal Data Fairy database

 The PDF™ database is a sophisticated marketing resource containing detailed demographic and psychographic information on consumers and users of the Internet. The Cyberhostess initiative aims to improve the scope and segmentation of the database.

This will be achieved by :

- cultivating a unique personal relationship between cyberhostess and client,
        via conversational email
- creating a personal profile for the client
- Giving clients an opportunity to offer their profile to marketeers, in return for
        special prizes or cash benefits in future purchases
- using intelligent agent software to monitor and profile the
        history of client movements around Internet sites
        recommended by the Cyberhostess

Personal Data Fairy

perpetuate your own myth

chapter 17

messages from sir arthur and the rev. bill

ronald fraser-munro

Sir Arthur Stuffed-Shirt is Director of Virtual Colonial Communications at the Foreign Office on Government Policies exploring Her Majesty's physical, mental and virtual territories.

The depletion in Commonwealth Territories over the last five decades has forced us to target alternative territories for colonisation. Misunderstandings with our colonial ancillaries and a fall in sterling have swept away the old fashioned concept of territorial space, and it seems only yesterday that we made the move from colonialism to virtual corporatism. It was a tough decision, but a damned good shot in the arm for economic, intellectual, spiritual and mental domination of its peoples and the utilisation of secondary peoples as a support mechanism. Recent advances in technology have meant a reappraisal of policy in order to exploit an increasingly informed proletariat to the maximum. Today, Her Majesty's loyal micro-subjects are hooked into sophisticated

networks once used only by egg-heads in universities, research centre vivisectionists, and government lottery strategists.

As a result of these technologies and the revolutionary redefinition of space, we now enter a (spanking) new economic and marketing arena. True democracy has come 'on-line', and 'ordinary' persons are allowed restricted access to personal computers and modems necessary for the assimilation into their lives of consumer and edutainment based technology (mobile phones, digital audio and film, television, compact discs, in-car systems, commercial advertising and a host of inter and non-interactive temptations which the consumer of capitalist fare is at a loss to refuse). The communication and intelligence advances are also too great to be ignored. Whereas our forefathers were obliged to send mercenaries abroad in noisy, smelly vehicles of war, now directives and payments can be sent world-wide in a few seconds.

The Internet is not a toy. It is an invaluable tool for colonial corporations world-wide and must be policed by the firm hand of government if it is to uphold traditional democratic values. The Internet is accessed via a 'gatepost' (a capitalist commercial subscriber network not unlike the cable television subscription cartel in its unimpeachable standards of pay-as-you-view). Here it is essential to have a watchful eye, including governmental monitoring of every sector of society ensuring realistic political planning without the meddlesome profligacy of more traditional and open administration. Recent abuses of the Internet (the illegal publication of international rights and statutes followed by malicious so-called 'revelations' concerning our internationally envied constitution) threaten to destroy the very fabric of democracy and perpetual peace we have striven so hard to inseminate. Let us not dice words. We intend to stamp hard on those who believe that insurrection and anarchy are a part of the democratic process.

We must forge the future from the past, castigating the scoffers and the Wailing Willies who say that the Internet does nothing to assist the poor or disenfranchised. We know that it will free the world to 'log on' as one big happy family.

I say: 'God Save The Web......'

© Sir Arthur Stuffed-Shirt/ R Fraser-Munro 1996

Reverend Bill Gaytes Praises The Internet

This is the Reverend Whillhelm Gaytes from The Church Of Siliconology. Boy have I gotta message that's gonna alter your reality! Now I hear some of you saying: 'he's trying to sell me another goddam product!'

Well I'm not gonna beat around the George Bush – it IS a product but it's a product that's helped millions world-wide to find everlasting freedom and salvation. Some converts see it as a gift from the good Lord in cyberspace himself, others believe it to be a direct link to the Father, the Son AND the Holy Ghost. Well, all I can say is, whether you e-mail God, fax God or go down on your knees at your bedside he's gonna answer your prayers! And the more you pray – the more he's gonna listen to you. Now that's a small price to pay for a direct link to the Chief Executive Officer himself.

Now some folks are sceptical about MICROSECT™©® and the Information Super-highway. Hell yes, they got a lotta good reasons to be, what with invasion of privacy, pornography, paedophilia, home shopping channels and inadequate band width but hold on there a moment! All of this has been goin' on since time began! At least you know where it is now! God helps those that help them-selves. Hell, I felt like I was on a mission from God himself! I got me sole distribution of The Bible world-wide and I can tell you my children my heart weeps with joy knowing my CD-Roms are spreading the word in fifty languages and bringing joy to the uncivilised, uneducated and downsized. Only last week in Orange County I chatted on-line with a little blind lame boy who'd lost the use of his hands thru an ungodly habit. I got an e-mail the next day still wet with his parents' tears. Little Johnny, thru the power of the Internet, had regained the use of his middle finger and was thanking me for bringing Christ into his miserable life.

Here at the Church of Infotainment™©® we take a rational and scientific view of things but the fable of Little Jonny is just one of hundreds of miracles happening daily via the Internet. All you need is our little mini(stry)-modem that slots into the side of your skull (we deliver within 3 days anywhere in the world) plug YOUR MICROSECT™©® mini(stry)-modem into your computer and YOUR thoughts are captured digitally by our MICROSECT™©® servers for relaying to the Good Lord himself – quicker than you can say Central Intelligence Agency.

Praise the Lord!

index

a-subjective 68–70
Acid House music 165
acting 9
action 1, 6, 81, 93, 157
activist groups 136
activity has its own point 84–5
'adjustable focus' wristwatch 99
advertising 89
aesthetics 1, 6–7, 8, 11, 80, 141
African culture 162
age 133, 134
agreed-remembered past 7
alienation 93; temporal 88, 96–8
Ambassadors, The (Holbein) 111, 112
(an)aesthetics 141
anamorphic distortion 111
anattā (no self) 79
Ancient Oaks (one-act play) 122–31; academic
    reality, theory of 129–30; appraisal 128–9;
    convergence of ideas 126–8; introduction
    123–4; practices and points of research 125–6;
    short answers 124
anger 21, 25
animal nature 20, 24
animal soul 80
anti-Semitic discourses 20
appearances 34, 85–6
Aquinas, Thomas 80
Aristotle 66, 67, 78, 80, 84, 97, 99; actions 6;
    'astronomical time' 94, 96; 'lived time' 95; rules
    of rhetoric 2
art 109, 141

ascetics 1, 6–7, 64, 70, 77
Asian cultures 22
astral projection 83
'astronomical time' 94
asymmetry 37–8
auditory sensations, projected 51–2
Augustine, Saint 95
aural trace 182
Austin, J.L. 32
authenticity 4, 7
authorship 8
autobiography 37, 38
autonomy 18, 20, 24, 132, 135, 139, 142, 143;
    egoistic 11; rave culture 169, 170, 171; *see also*
    freedom
avant garde 106

Baconian mindset 5
Baconian science 8
Baker, Rachel 8, 206–11
Baldwin, James 22
Barber, T.X. 54
Barre, A. 114, 116
Barthes, Roland 32, 185, 187, 189, 191, 192–3
Bateson, Gregory 6
Baudrillard, J. 10, 27, 166
Bauman, Z. 22
'becoming' 157
beliefs 31, 32, 33, 37, 38, 40
Benjamin, A. 11
Benjamin, Walter 91, 141
Bey, Hakim 169

binocular disparity 54
biographies 33, 34, 35, 38, 39, 40; electronic 36,
    38
biology 57
Blackman, Lisa M. 6, 132–45, 168–9
Blanchot, M. 186, 187, 190, 191
bliss 165
Bodies without Organs 72, 169
body 1, 16, 17, 18, 19, 20, 29, 72; bodily restraint
    2; disdain for 18; fragility 142; learning to listen
    to 18; and nature 65; spatio-temporal confines
    11; surface 55; see also mind–body
Boyarin, Daniel 20
Brahmanism 79
brains as-perceived 52
Brugger, P. 54, 59
BSE beef crisis 89
Buck-Morss, Susan 141–2
Buckminster Fuller, Richard 94, 96
Buddhist perspective see embodying virtue
bugs 135
Bulger case 136
bureaucracies 32, 37
Butler, Margot Leigh 5, 8, 196–204

camcorders 136
camera obscura 113
Campbell, Jim 136
capitalism 89, 90, 91, 96; consumerist 11;
    globalised 88; responsible 94
Carter, Angela 197
causality 189, 190
cause and effect 69, 187–8
Celan, P. 181
celebration 169
Celtic culture 162
centrifugal expansion 160
centrifugal impulses 163
centripetal feeling of contraction 160
centripetal impulses 163
ceremonies 32–3
'Chants de Maldoror, Les' 106
character traits 79
chemistry 57
choice 133, 135, 136, 142, 143
clairaudience 83
clairvoyance 83
class 133, 134
Claude Lorraine Glass 6–7
clock-time 94–7
cognition/cognitive 5, 79, 97, 98
comfort 90, 98

communication 30, 165
computers 3, 22, 24, 77; see also Internet
Confucianism 78
consciousness 8, 15, 17, 47, 56, 79
consequences 143–4
constraint 5
consumerism 11, 88, 90–5
contingency 136
continuity 190
control 66, 133, 136, 139, 141
convivial wristwatches, ideas for design of 98–100
Copernicus 57, 67
coping 172–3
craving 80
Cresswell, Peter 8, 53, 54, 109–21
crime 136
cube 109
Cubitt, S. 133, 140
culturally embedded phenomenon 137
culture 15, 16; see also culture, technology and
    subjectivity
culture, technology and subjectivity 132–45;
    beyond cyber-utopia 133–4; consequences
    143–4; Foucault's ethics 134–5; freedom,
    programming of 132; interactive art 135–7;
    obliged to be free 135; Rehearsal of Memory
    (CD Rom) 137–8; repressed, return of the
    138–41; shock of the old 141–2
curvature, sense of 164
curvatures in space-time truth 1–12;
    disembodying tradition of book 2; embodied
    knowledge 9; ethics, aesthetics and ascetics
    6–7; nature and human nature 3–4; presence
    and practice 1–2; rigour in four dimensions,
    idea of 8; situated ethics 11; space and absence
    9–10; tacit knowledge 3; virtual, embodied
    10–11; virtual, the 4–5
curved line 159
curvilinear perspective 110, 111, 114
customer targeting 91
'cutting up' 139
cyber-utopia, beyond 133–4
cybernatural discourse 133
cyberspace 20
cynicism 7

da Vinci, Leonardo 113, 114, 116
dance 9, 169; see also rave dance culture;
    return-beat
Darwin, Charles 57
data crime 8
daydreams 82

de-dualising 5
death drive 70
deductibility, perfect 68
deictic shifter 72
Deleuze, Gilles 65, 70, 72, 169
denial 19; of transcendence 185–6
dependent origination 80
depression 25
derangement 191, 192
Descartes, René/Cartesian; bodies and rational
   selves 17, 19; classical body/mind split 46;
   dualism 80; God 64; 'I think therefore I am' 83;
   inheritance 16; knower position 143; *mathesis
   universalis* 66, 67, 68, 71; mind–body dualism
   15; mindset 5; modernity 25; rationality 134;
   scepticism 2; space 133; substance 73; thought
   and extension 69; vision of landscape 5; vision
   of modernity 25
designers, how can they contribute? 93
desire 80, 137
determination, forms of 17
difference 65, 73
digital: effigies 39; hostess 206–11; information
   136; information technology 10; signatures 34;
   technology 10; *see also* digital unconscious
digital unconscious 30–44; ceremonies 32–3;
   effigies 36–7; electronic records 38–40;
   identifiers 33; individualism 30–1; relationships
   31–2; signatures 33–4; technology 35–6;
   unconscious 37–8
disembodiment 26
dispositions 79
distortion 114; anamorphic 111
domination 66, 67
drama 182
drawing 9, 115
dream garden: notes on virtual idyll 149–56;
   contents of garden 151–3; nature 152–3; plants
   151; products 151, 152; seed catalogues 151–2;
   space 153; tools and machines 151, 152;
   English garden 150–1; lawn 150; muddy path
   manifesto 155; non-utopian Eden 154–5; virtual
   Edens 154–5; Yoshi's island (computer game)
   153–4
dreams 57, 58–9, 82
drug use 169; come-downs 172, 175; effects 173;
   management 175; Speed 174
Drumming at the Edge of Magic 164–5
dualism/dualist 49, 50, 69, 169, 197, 198; mind-
   body 15; model 46–7; theory 51; virtue
   embodiment 76, 80; vision 55; Western 5
Duchamp, M. 106, 185

Düsseldorf airport fire 181–95
dystopia 5, 136

eco-design 94
eco-rationalism 94
ecology 16, 19, 24, 28; deep 92–3
Edens 154–5 (*Yoshi's Island*)
effigies 36–7, 38, 39
effort 81
eidetic imagers 54
Einstein, Albert 8, 9, 99
electronic: art works 135; biographies 36, 38;
   libraries 10; records 38–40; signatures 36
Elliot, Tessa 136
emancipation 20
embodied knowledge 9, 24, 28, 29, 197; *see also*
   embodied knowledge and virtual space
embodied knowledge and virtual space 15–29;
   inner and outer realities 25–9; knowledge
   embodiment 17–19; modernity, knowledge and
   nature 15–17; nature, re-invention of 23–5;
   virtual space 20–3
embodying virtue: Buddhist perspective 76–87;
   meditation 82–6; virtue and virtual 77–8;
   virtues in the East 78–81
emotions 17, 19, 21, 24, 25, 26, 29, 38, 79; and
   nature 70; and realities of the past 18; temporal
   alienation 97
empowerment 170
Enlightenment 15, 16, 17, 19, 20, 28, 63; and
   virtue embodiment 82, 83
entitlement 11
environment 4, 5, 89, 93
epistemiology 5
Erlich, P. 93
escapism 169
ethics/ethical 1, 6–7, 22, 142, 143, 163; of
   autonomous self-hood 135; Foucault 134–5;
   living 81; micro 7, 11; and nature 64, 65, 70–3;
   new technologies 28; possibilities 8; situated
   11; space 20; virtue 78; and virtue embodiment
   76, 81, 85; Western rights 11
ethnicity/race 20, 21, 24, 133
Euclidean geometry 9, 66
Euclidean solids 8
'euphoric loss of the present' 92
Evil 70–1
exclusion 137
experience 16, 18, 19, 31, 34, 45, 182, 190;
   embodied 55; location and extension in space
   49; machine 84–5; projected pain 50; rave
   culture 174

export 8
expression 171; *see also* self-expression
extension 69
external balance 164–5
external form 5
external world 55, 56, 76
extra-sensory perception 83

factor 20 89–90
faculty of reason 16, 80
faith 107
fantasies 27, 82, 133, 134, 139, 141
fate 190
fear 19, 20
feelings 17, 19, 24, 25, 26, 29, 45, 79; real 65;
    temporal alienation 97; virtue embodiment 83,
    85
feminine/feminisms 16, 17, 19, 20, 22, 28, 141;
    figurations 198; qualities 24; space of the
    Internet 20; virtual space 143
figurations 197, 198
filth 6
finite 71
Finnis, John 84, 86
first, the 106
fisheye 120
flat plane 116, 118
flexibility 133
flight simulators 57
Flocon, A. 114, 116
fluidity 133
form 4, 8, 9, 11, 79
Foucault, Michel 138; ethics and the self 134–5,
    142, 171; pessimism 64–5; power 136; space
    28; subjectification 137
foundation 66–8
Four Noble Truths 78–9, 80–1
Fraser-Munro, Ronald 8, 122–31, 212–14
free-hand 113–14
freedom 5, 24, 25, 26, 29, 132, 142, 143;
    conceptions of 18; ecstatic 176; explorations of
    28; as independence 135; lack 17; obligation
    135; in the present 18; programming 132; rave
    culture 168, 169, 170, 171, 172, 176; realm of
    20
Freud, Sigmund 16, 40, 57, 70, 82, 133–4;
    experience 18–19, 20, 24

Galileo 67
gender 20, 21, 133, 134, 143, 197; *see also*
    feminine/feminisms; masculinity
genetic engineering 24

geometry 115, 143; *see also* Euclidean
German Romanticism 68
Ghandi, M. 92
Glass, Robert 26
global search by keyword 10
glow 92–3
God 64, 67, 68, 71, 72
Gödel, Kurt 7, 68
Goethe, J.W. von 69
Goffey, Andy 5, 63–75
Gombrich, E.H. 114
Good 5, 70–1
gratification, individual 6
green consumerism 89, 94
Griffin, Susan 16
Guattari, Felix 72, 169
Guernica 106

hallucinations 54–5
Ham, M.H. 54
hand-clapping exercise 160–1
Hanson, Robert 114, 116
Haraway, Donna 134, 170
'harmful' 4
Hart, Micky 164–5
Harwood, Graham 137, 138, 140, 142
Hauck, Guido 114, 115, 116
Hawking, Stephen 9
health 5
heart 165
heautoscopic episode 54–5
Hegel, G.W.F. 66, 68, 72, 188
Heidegger, Martin 10, 66–7, 69
Heisenberg: 'Uncertainty Principle' 7, 136
here and now 11
Hesmondhalgh, D. 169
Hinduism 78, 79
hinging 5
Hip Hop music 165
history 66
Hobbes, Thomas 64, 65
Holbein, Hans 111, 112
Holocaust 22
holograms 52, 114
House music 165
Hubble telescope 8, 105–8
human actions 93
human existence, nature of 69
human good 86
human nature 1, 79, 80
human presence 1, 9
Husserl, Edmund 68, 73

idea 4, 65
idealism 4, 5
identicality of indiscernibles 10
identifiers 33, 34
identity 15, 18, 19, 20, 22, 31, 137, 143, 144;
    asymmetric changes 38; concept 64; desire for
    individual 31; effigies 36, 37; ethnicity 20, 24;
    finite 71; fixed 20; gendered 20; identifiers 33;
    infinite 71; maintenance of is a good 85; male
    17, 18, 21; politics 5; racialised 20;
    relationships 31–2; sexuality 20; signatures 34;
    spiritual 24; virtue embodiment 86; see also
    self-identity
illness 25
illusion 4, 5, 109, 110, 111, 114, 139, 163
images 54–5, 57
imagination 5, 206
immanence 64, 186
immortality 134
Incompleteness Theorem 7
independence 18, 135
individual rights 11
individual unconscious 11
individualism 30–1, 64, 65
individuation 72
infinite 71; understanding 64; will 64
infinity 162
information 7; commodification 10; technology 1,
    2, 10, 40, 91, 96
'Information Theory' 10
inheritance 16
insanity 137, 138, 140, 142
inscriptions 33
inside the head locatedness 51
insight, penetrating and critical (paññā) 83
instrumental rationality 22–3
integrity 85
intelligent agents 10
intensity 73
interactive art 135–7
interdependence 136
internal balance 164–5
Internet 11, 20, 22–3, 26, 27, 28, 31, 35; culture
    26; effigies 37; miscommunication 21; servers
    36; sites 38, 39
interplay 11
intuition 24
investments 137
irony 7

Jordan, T. 169
Judaism 20

Jungle music 165

Kant, Immanuel 4, 5, 16, 17, 20, 68, 69; model of
    cognition 5; pure reason 63; reason and nature,
    distinction between 24
Keown, Damien 4, 5, 11
Kepler, Johann 67
knowledge 1, 5, 66, 137, 198; acquisition 2; actual
    embodiment 9; disembodied 15, 17, 19, 20, 28,
    29, 197; domains 67, 68; and emotions and
    feelings 24, 25, 26, 29; first principles 64;
    Foucault 134–5; founding 69; impartial and
    universal 16; Laban, R. 157; and nature 63, 64,
    67; rave culture 174, 175; real 19; self-
    knowledge 173; situating 197; tacit 3, 133, 135;
    totality 68; and virtue embodiment 81; see also
    embodied
Koyre, Alexander 67
Kulpe, O. 54
Kwabena Nketia, J.H. 164

Laban, Rudolf 157
Lacan, J. 31
Lacoue-Labarthe, P. 68
lamentation 169
language 16, 32, 109, 111
Lanier, Jaron 6
Latin American dance music 164
Lautréamont's Tale 106
Lawnmower Man, The 134, 140
Laws, P. 51
Leask, Josephine 165–6
Lefebvre, H. 162
legal apparatus 136
Leibniz: 'identicality of indiscernibles' 10
Levinas, Emmanuel 20, 22, 24, 26, 29, 72–3
liberation 134
life-cycle assessment/analysis 94
linear codes, sequential 162
linear (plane projection) perspective 8, 158, 162,
    163
linear-beat 158, 160
Linnaean classification 150
listening 9
'lived time' wristwatch 99
livelihood 81
Locke, John: notion of 'idea' 4
looking-glass 143–4
Lopatka, Sharon 26, 27
love, pure 17
'lovers' clock' 98–9
loyalty to family and tradition 22

Lyotard, Jean-François 63

Macherey, Pierre 66
Machiavelli, N. 7
machines 152
MacIntyre, Alasdair 78
malfunctions 135
Man Ray 106, 185
management strategies and rave culture 168,
    172–3, 174, 175, 176
Marx, Karl 20, 22, 96
masculinity 17, 21; dominant white heterosexual
    16, 17, 18, 19, 20, 23, 25, 28
mastery 133
material presence 4
mathematics 66–8, 69, 70–2
matter above movement 8
ME 25
meditation 77, 81, 82–6, 86; calming (samatha)
    83; insight (vipassana) 83; transic 86
memories 18, 140
mental: cultivation 81; distress 137, 138; pain 93;
    patterns 83; sufferings 79
metabolic pace 97
metabolic rate 98
metaphysics 66, 67, 78, 79, 81
Metzger, Gustav 8, 105–8
micro aesthetics 11
micro ethics 7, 11
Microsoft commercials 132
mimesis 4, 9, 133, 187
mind 17, 18, 19
mind–body 6, 64, 69, 171; dualism 15, 80;
    parallelism 70, 71; separation 16; split, classical
    46
mind/consciousness 16
mindfulness 81
miscommunication 21
modernity 15–17, 19, 20, 25, 28
monism/monist 5, 64, 65, 73n.
monitoring 176
Monk, John 11, 30–44
monocular viewing 8, 54
Monopoly 6
mood 83
moral/morality 17, 64, 65, 70, 78, 81; cultures 28;
    law 68; qualities 77; virtue embodiment 84
mortality fear 134
movement of presencing 67
muddy path manifesto 155
music, effects of 169
myths 163

Naess, Arne 92
names 33
Nancy, Jean-Luc 68
narcissism 191
narratives 33
NASA 8
natural 133
nature 1, 4, 15–17, 24, 63–75, 88; a-subjective
    68–70; animal 20, 24; death of 15; disdain for
    16, 18; disenchanted 17; distancing from 4–5;
    and ethics 70–3; external 15; foundation,
    nature, mathematics 66–8; and human nature
    3–4; inner 15, 19, 24; mechanistic conception
    of 15; re-invention of 23–5; redesigning 3;
    reduction of 15; and science 24; Spinoza 65–6;
    and time 95; see also dream garden
'navigation' 5
necessity, realm of 20
Negri, Antonio 65
networked data systems 11
neurasthenia 141
Newton, Isaac 8, 25, 94–5
Nietzsche, F.W. 69, 70, 163
nihilism 7, 70
nirvana 80–1
Nixon, Richard 93
no self (anattā) 79
Noble Eightfold Path 81, 82
non-linear models 163
non-utopian Eden 154–5
'normality' 5
not-completely-black-hole 9
noumenal 5, 93
now-time 91–2
Nozick, Robert 84, 85

objective 72
objects as commodities 5
objects as-perceived 52
objects as-seen 52
observation 8
Occam's Razor 49
old, shock of the 141–2
omnipotence 133
one-to-one straightness 7
ontology 5
optically virtual 6
Other 72–3
ourselves, coming to terms with 18
out-of-body experience 11, 54

pain 93; living-out of 139; projected 50

Panofsky, E. 114
Panopticon 136
Papanek, Victor 89
paradise 153–4
parallel lines 162
paranoia 172, 173, 174
passion 92–3
past 7, 18, 19
pastiche 8
patriarchy 20
'peak' moment 171–5
Pembroke, Louise 139
Penfield, W. 50
Penny, S. 133
perception 5; of depth 54; dualistic model 47;
    model 49; nature of within 163–4; peripheral 8;
    reductionist model 47–8; reflexive model 48,
    49; of a sound 51–2; virtual model 56
perceptual projection 49, 50, 51, 52–4
perfection 68
performatives 32, 33, 36, 37, 40
peripheral perception 8
peripheral vision 118
Perky, C.W. 54
perspective 109–21, 162, 198; phenomenological
    157; plane projection 8, 110–14, 116, 118, 158,
    162, 163; radial 53, 115–20
phantom limbs 55
phenomenology 5, 49, 51, 52, 68, 93; attributes
    163; of experience 67; perspective 157
philosophy 15, 29, 63–75; Jewish philosophy 10,
    20
photography 111, 113, 114, 118, 181–95; essence
    193; structure 192
phusis 67
physical, psychological and virtual realities
    45–60; dreaming 58–9; experiences, location
    and extension of in space 49; fitting virtual
    reality into model of perception 49; how
    virtual realities fit reflexive model 55; images
    and hallucinations 54–5; perceptual
    projection, evidence for 50; perceptual
    projection in vision 52–4; predictions 57–8;
    projected auditory sensations 51–2; projected
    pain 50; projected tactile sensations 50;
    typical beliefs 45–6; what is taken for granted
    46–8
physical shocks 141
physical sufferings 79
physics 57, 66, 67
physiological effects 174
Picasso, Pablo 106

pinhole 120
Pini, Maria 5, 135, 168–77
plane projection perspective 8, 110–14, 116, 118,
    158, 162, 163
plants 150, 151
plastic arts 3
Plato/Platonic 4, 5, 9, 66, 79–80; dualistic
    ontology 85; idealism 4; laws of form 8;
    limitations of designed forms 11; solids 8
play 11
poetic forms 8
police apparatus 136
Pop music 165
possessive individualism 64, 65
postmodernism 63
power 4, 132, 137, 198; balance of 40; and
    bodies 72; -discursive relations 143; and ethics
    11; and ideas 65, 72; -knowledge 8; loss 33;
    and perspective 162; relations 134, 136–7;
    and relationships 32; struggles 35; of
    technology 6
practice-oriented disciplines 3
presence and practice 1–2, 3
present 18, 19; see also redesigning
'pressure watch' 99–100
products 150, 151, 152
Progressive 165
projection 50–4; perceptual 49, 50, 51,
    52–4
proprioception 163
proscenium arch 162
protophenomena 157
psychiatry 135
psychic powers 83
psychic shocks 141
psychological realities see physical, psychological
    and virtual realities
psychology 57, 135
psychotherapy 19, 26
pure love 17
pure reason 63
purity 17

quality of life 89
quantity 73
quantum mechanics 7, 57

Raasmussen, T.B. 50
race see ethnicity/race
radial perspective 53, 115–20
Ramis, Harold 97
Raphael 113

rationality 64, 80, 134, 138; deductive 66; eco-rationalism 94; instrumental 22–3; systematic 68

rave dance culture 5, 135, 168–77; digitised 162; ecstatic freedom reconsidered 176; 'peak' moment, constitution of 171–5

Rave Off 170

reading 3; aloud 182, 184

real 4, 6

realities, inner and outer 25–9

reality, spectre of 5

reason 15, 16, 17, 24, 63

reciprocity 136

recreational imagination 206

rectilinear frame 110, 111

redesigning the present 88–101; convivial wristwatches, ideas for design of 98–100; deep ecology 92–3; designers, help from 93; embodying 'clock-time' 95–6; 'euphoric loss of the present' 92; factor 20 89–90; 'green' consumerism 89; shoppers' continuum 91; space versus time 94–5; sustainable consumerism 93–4; technology and comfort 90; temporal alienation 96–8; working through without stopping 91–2

reductionism 49, 50; model 47–8; theory 51; vision 55

reflection 187

reflection-in-action 95

reflexive model 48, 49, 50, 52, 55, 56, 57

refusal 137

regulation 175, 176

Rehearsal of Memory (Harwood) 137–42

Reich, W. 18

reincarnation 79

rejection 137

relationships 31–2, 32, 36, 58; between individual selves and virtual realities 58; interpersonal 172; surrogate 57; virtual 59

relativity 7, 25

Relativity Theory 57

relaxation exercise 161

Rennie, Garth 8, 122–31

repetition 9

representation, modes of 6, 77

repression 138–41

repression-suppression system 137

reproduction 191

res cogitans 46

res extensa 46

resolve 81

responsibilities, collective 11

retrocognition 83

return-beat 157–67; cultural implications 161–3; digitising 165–6; embodiment 158; experiment guidelines 160–1; internal and external balance maintenance 164–5; 'linear' model 159; model 159–60; organic 166; perception, nature of within 163–4; time graph 159; *see also* linear-beat

reveries 82

Reynolds, Simon 171

rhythms 8; *see also* return-beat

Rietveld, H. 169

rigour in four dimensions, idea of 8

risk assessment 174

root pulse 164, 165

Rose, N. 135

Same over the Other 72

sanity 134

satire 8

Schelling, F.W.J. von 68

scholastic rigour 2

Schön, Donald: 'reflection-in-action' 95

science 24, 64, 65, 68

security 33, 107

seed catalogues 151–2

Seidler, Victor Jeleniewski 6, 15–29

self 5, 76, 81, 138, 173; fragmented 25; rational 25; relationship with 18; techniques of 134, 142

self-control 138

self-development 138

self-expression 135, 171–2, 173, 176

self-harm 139

self-identity 34, 37, 38, 39, 40

self-knowledge 173

self-mutilation 6

self-regulation 138, 168

self-sufficiency 18

sensations 85

sensitivity 24

sensory experience 72

sensory perception 67

sexuality 16, 18, 20, 21, 134

shamanism 169

Shannon: 'Information Theory' 10

shell-shock 141

Shepard, R.N. 54

shock 141

shoppers' continuum 91

short-termism 89

signatures 33–4, 35, 39; digital 34; electronic 36

signets 34, 38, 39

simulation 133
sincerity 7
sins of the flesh 19
situated reality 4
situatedness 162
size constancy 52
smart technologies 3
social control 136
society 5
software 32; robots 11
solitude 2
soul 80, 171
sound perception 51–2
Soyika, Wole 163
space 153; and absence 9–10; domestic 113;
    grand architectural 113; psychological 113; see
    also space–time
space–time 2, 94–5, 97, 100, 189–90; and return-
    beat 157, 159, 162, 164; truth see curvatures
Spanos, N.P. 54
speech 81
speed, notion of 94
Spinoza, B. 64, 92
Spinozist ethics see nature; monism
spirit 66, 137
spirituality 17, 24, 77
stage 3
standard of living 89
Stark, F. 114, 116
stereographs 114
straight line 159
studio 3
subject 64
subjectification 135, 137, 140, 141, 142
subjective/subjectivity 68, 72, 92, 133, 143–4, 157,
    164; a-subjective 68–70; flow 165; location and
    extension 51; rave culture 169; see also culture,
    technology and subjectivity
subordination 16
substance 71, 72, 73
suffering 79, 80
suppression 19
surrogate relationships 57
surveillance 136
sustainability, ecological 89
sustainable consumerism 93–4
Sutcliffe, Richard 169, 171
symbolism 143

T-in-O 107
tactile sensations, projected 50
tagging 35–6, 37

Taiwo, Olu 8, 157–67
Taoism 78
taste 6
Taylorism 91
Techno 165
techno-critical debate 169
techno-science 69
technocratic culture 154
technologising 3
technology 10–11, 35–6, 182, 191; antinatural
    133; /body/chemical assemblage 169; and
    comfort 90; destructive aspect 93; digital 10;
    ethics 28; and experience 162; and knowledge
    19; notions of neutrality 28; power 6; spiritual
    77; time 95; of virtual space 6, 22–3; and virtue
    embodiment 77; see also culture, technology
    and subjectivity
telepathy 83
telephone call, long-distance 21
temporal alienation 88, 96–8
Temporary Autonomous Zone 169
Ten Doesschate, G. 114
text-into-speech embodiment 2
text-oriented disciplines 3
texts 33
textual book 9
theft 8
thing-in-itself 5
things-in-themselves 5
Thornton, Sarah 170
thought 25, 45, 56, 69, 72; experiments 8, 9;
    virtue embodiment 80, 83
three-dimensional 54, 110, 114, 116
time 97; absolute, true and mathematical 95; lived
    95, 97, 98; mechanical 97; metabolic 96; social
    98, 99; solar 96; see also clock-time;
    space–time
timepieces 31
tools 150, 151, 152
traditional cultures 23–4
trance 83, 165
transcendence 186; of the Other 73
transference 19
transformation 134
transgression 6
travel, long distance 30
tribalism 169
truth 5, 66, 67, 72, 164, 187; absolute 63;
    measurement 64; straightness in 7; Western
    concept 7; see also curvatures in space–time
    truth
Turkle, Sherry 26–7

Turner, J.M.W. 113
twenty-four-hour opening 89
two-dimensional 54, 109, 110

Uncertainty Principle 7, 136
unconscious 37–8; *see also* digital
understanding 81
unexpectedness 106, 189–90
unitary system 189
United Kingdom 89
unpredictability 105–6
unthought 10
Untitled (For Heisenberg) art work 136
utopia 5, 136
utterances 33

value 64
values 17
vanishing line 162
vanishing-point 162
vegetable soul 80
vehicle registers 35–6
Velmans, Max 4, 5, 45–60
virtual 4–5, 77–8; Eden 3, 154–5; embodied
    10–11; identity 133; idyll *see* dream garden;
    playground 6
virtual reality 114; *see also* physical, psychological
    and virtual realities
virtual space 28; *see also* embodied knowledge and
    virtual space
virtuality 4
virtue 7, 11, 77–8; *see also* embodying
vision, peripheral 118

visual projection, perceptual 52–4

Walkerdine, V. 143–4
Weber, Max 19
Wegener, Claudia 8
well-being 92–3
Wells, Robert 3, 149–56
West Africa 163, 164
West, Cornell 22
Western dualism 5
Western rights ethics 11
Wheatstone arrangement 118, 119
whole person, dissolving and fragmenting of
    132
wilderness 149
Williamson, Nigel 162
Wired (journal) 132
wisdom 1, 2, 81
Wittgenstein, L. 16, 24
women 24; *see also* feminine/feminisms
Wood, John 1–12, 88–101
Woodward, K. 133–4
work-time 96
working through without stopping 91–2
world as-experienced 56, 57
world as-perceived 55, 57
world as-seen 54
writing 3, 182

Yoruba tragedy 163
Yoshi's Island (computer game) 153–4

zero-sum rules 6